High Performance JavaScript

High Performance JavaScript

Nicholas C. Zakas

O'REILLY®

Beijing · Cambridge · Farnham · Köln · Sebastopol · Taipei · Tokyo

High Performance JavaScript
by Nicholas C. Zakas

Published by O'Reilly Media, Inc., 1005 Gravenstein Highway North, Sebastopol, CA 95472.

O'Reilly books may be purchased for educational, business, or sales promotional use. Online editions are also available for most titles (*http://my.safaribooksonline.com*). For more information, contact our corporate/institutional sales department: (800) 998-9938 or *corporate@oreilly.com*.

Editor: Mary E. Treseler	**Indexer:** Fred Brown
Production Editor: Adam Zaremba	**Cover Designer:** Karen Montgomery
Copyeditor: Genevieve d'Entremont	**Interior Designer:** David Futato
Proofreader: Adam Zaremba	**Illustrator:** Robert Romano

Printing History:

March 2010:   First Edition.

RepKover™
This book uses RepKover™, a durable and flexible lay-flat binding.

ISBN: 978-0-596-80279-0

[M]

1268244124

This book is dedicated to my family, Mom, Dad, and Greg, whose love and support have kept me going through the years.

Table of Contents

Preface

When JavaScript was first introduced as part of Netscape Navigator in 1996, performance wasn't that important. The Internet was in its infancy and it was, in all ways, slow. From dial-up connections to underpowered home computers, surfing the Web was more often a lesson in patience than anything else. Users expected to wait for web pages to load, and when the page successfully loaded, it was a cause for celebration.

JavaScript's original goal was to improve the user experience of web pages. Instead of going back to the server for simple tasks such as form validation, JavaScript allowed embedding of this functionality directly in the page. Doing so saved a rather long trip back to the server. Imagine the frustration of filling out a long form, submitting it, and then waiting 30–60 seconds just to get a message back indicating that you had filled in a single field incorrectly. JavaScript can rightfully be credited with saving early Internet users a lot of time.

The Internet Evolves

Over the decade that followed, computers and the Internet continued to evolve. To start, both got much faster. The rapid speed-up of microprocessors, the availability of cheap memory, and the appearance of fiber optic connections pushed the Internet into a new age. With high-speed connections more available than ever, web pages started becoming heavier, embedding more information and multimedia. The Web had changed from a fairly bland landscape of interlinked documents into one filled with different designs and interfaces. Everything changed, that is, except JavaScript.

What previously was used to save server roundtrips started to become more ubiquitous. Where there were once dozens of lines of JavaScript code were now hundreds, and eventually thousands. The introduction of Internet Explorer 4 and dynamic HTML (the ability to change aspects of the page without a reload) ensured that the amount of JavaScript on pages would only increase over time.

The last major step in the evolution of browsers was the introduction of the Document Object Model (DOM), a unified approach to dynamic HTML that was adopted by Internet Explorer 5, Netscape 6, and Opera. This was closely followed by the standardization of JavaScript into ECMA-262, third edition. With all browsers supporting the DOM and (more or less) the same version of JavaScript, a web application platform was born. Despite this huge leap forward, with a common API against which to write JavaScript, the JavaScript engines in charge of executing that code remained mostly unchanged.

Why Optimization Is Necessary

The JavaScript engines that supported web pages with a few dozen lines of JavaScript in 1996 are the same ones running web applications with thousands of lines of JavaScript today. In many ways, the browsers fell behind in their management of the language and in doing the groundwork so that JavaScript could succeed at a large scale. This became evident with Internet Explorer 6, which was heralded for its stability and speed when it was first released but later reviled as a horrible web application platform because of its bugs and slowness.

In reality, IE 6 hadn't gotten any slower; it was just being asked to do more than it had previously. The types of early web applications being created when IE 6 was introduced in 2001 were much lighter and used much less JavaScript than those created in 2005. The difference in the amount of JavaScript code became clear as the IE 6 JavaScript engine struggled to keep up due to its static garbage-collection routine. The engine looked for a fixed number of objects in memory to determine when to collect garbage. Earlier web application developers had run into this threshold infrequently, but with more JavaScript code comes more objects, and complex web applications began to hit this threshold quite often. The problem became clear: JavaScript developers and web applications had evolved while the JavaScript engines had not.

Although other browsers had more logical garbage collection routines, and somewhat better runtime performance, most still used a JavaScript interpreter to execute code. Code interpretation is inherently slower than compilation since there's a translation process between the code and the computer instructions that must be run. No matter how smart and optimized interpreters get, they always incur a performance penalty.

Compilers are filled with all kinds of optimizations that allow developers to write code in whatever way they want without worrying whether it's optimal. The compiler can determine, based on lexical analysis, what the code is attempting to do and then optimize it by producing the fastest-running machine code to complete the task. Interpreters have few such optimizations, which frequently means that code is executed exactly as it is written.

In effect, JavaScript forces the developer to perform the optimizations that a compiler would normally handle in other languages.

Next-Generation JavaScript Engines

In 2008, JavaScript engines got their first big performance boost. Google introduced their brand-new browser called Chrome. Chrome was the first browser released with an optimizing JavaScript engine, codenamed V8. The V8 JavaScript engine is a just-in-time (JIT) compilation engine for JavaScript, which produces machine code from JavaScript code and then executes it. The resulting experience is blazingly fast JavaScript execution.

Other browsers soon followed suit with their own optimizing JavaScript engines. Safari 4 features the Squirrel Fish Extreme (also called Nitro) JIT JavaScript engine, and Firefox 3.5 includes the TraceMonkey engine, which optimizes frequently executed code paths.

With these newer JavaScript engines, optimizations are being done at the compiler-level, where they should be done. Someday, developers may be completely free of worry about performance optimizations in their code. That day, however, is still not here.

Performance Is Still a Concern

Despite advancements in core JavaScript execution time, there are still aspects of JavaScript that these new engines don't handle. Delays caused by network latency and operations affecting the appearance of the page are areas that have yet to be adequately optimized by browsers. While simple optimizations such as function inlining, code folding, and string concatenation algorithms are easily optimized in compilers, the dynamic and multifaceted structure of web applications means that these optimizations solve only part of the performance problem.

Though newer JavaScript engines have given us a glimpse into the future of a much faster Internet, the performance lessons of today will continue to be relevant and important for the foreseeable future.

The techniques and approaches taught in this book address many different aspects of JavaScript, covering execution time, downloading, interaction with the DOM, page life cycle, and more. Of these topics only a small subset, those related to core (ECMAScript) performance, could be rendered irrelevant by advances in JavaScript engines, but that has yet to happen.

The other topics cover ground where faster JavaScript engines won't help: DOM interaction, network latency, blocking and concurrent downloading of JavaScript, and more. These topics will not only continue to be relevant, but will become areas of further focus and research as low-level JavaScript execution time continues to improve.

How This Book Is Organized

The chapters in this book are organized based on a normal JavaScript development life cycle. This begins, in Chapter 1, with the most optimal ways to load JavaScript onto the page. Chapter 2 through Chapter 8 focus on specific programming techniques to help your JavaScript code run as quickly as possible. Chapter 9 discusses the best ways to build and deploy your JavaScript files to a production environment, and Chapter 10 covers performance tools that can help you identify further issues once the code is deployed. Five of the chapters were written by contributing authors:

- Chapter 3, *DOM Scripting*, by Stoyan Stefanov
- Chapter 5, *Strings and Regular Expressions*, by Steven Levithan
- Chapter 7, *Ajax*, by Ross Harmes
- Chapter 9, *Building and Deploying High-Performance JavaScript Applications*, by Julien Lecomte
- Chapter 10, *Tools*, by Matt Sweeney

Each of these authors is an accomplished web developer who has made important contributions to the web development community as a whole. Their names appear on the opening page of their respective chapters to more easily identify their work.

JavaScript Loading

Chapter 1, *Loading and Execution*, starts with the basics of JavaScript: getting code onto the page. JavaScript performance really begins with getting the code onto a page in the most efficient way possible. This chapter focuses on the performance problems associated with loading JavaScript code and presents several ways to mitigate the effects.

Coding Technique

A large source of performance problems in JavaScript is poorly written code that uses inefficient algorithms or utilities. The following seven chapters focus on identifying problem code and presenting faster alternatives that accomplish the same task.

Chapter 2, *Data Access*, focuses on how JavaScript stores and accesses data within a script. Where you store data is just as important as what you store, and this chapter explains how concepts such as the scope chain and prototype chain can affect your overall script performance.

Stoyan Stefanov, who is well versed in the internal workings of a web browser, wrote Chapter 3, *DOM Scripting*. Stoyan explains that DOM interaction is slower than other parts of JavaScript because of the way it is implemented. He covers all aspects of the DOM, including a description of how repaint and reflow can slow down your code.

Chapter 4, *Algorithms and Flow Control*, explains how common programming paradigms such as loops and recursion can work against you when it comes to runtime performance. Optimization techniques such as memoization are discussed, as are browser JavaScript runtime limitations.

Many web applications perform complex string operations in JavaScript, which is why string expert Steven Levithan covers the topic in Chapter 5, *Strings and Regular Expressions*. Web developers have been fighting poor string-handling performance in browsers for years, and Steven explains why some operations are slow and how to work around them.

Chapter 6, *Responsive Interfaces*, puts the spotlight firmly on the user experience. JavaScript can cause the browser to freeze as it executes, leaving users extremely frustrated. This chapter discusses several techniques to ensure that the user interface remains responsive at all times.

In Chapter 7, *Ajax*, Ross Harmes discusses the best ways to achieve fast client-server communication in JavaScript. Ross covers how different data formats can affect Ajax performance and why `XMLHttpRequest` isn't always the best choice.

Chapter 8, *Programming Practices*, is a collection of best practices that are unique to JavaScript programming.

Deployment

Once JavaScript code is written and tested, it's time to make the changes available to everyone. However, you shouldn't just push out your raw source files for use in production. Julien Lecomte shows how to improve the performance of your JavaScript during deployment in Chapter 9, *Building and Deploying High-Performance JavaScript Applications*. Julien discusses using a build system to automatically minify files and using HTTP compression to deliver them to the browser.

Testing

When all of your JavaScript code is deployed, the next step is to begin performance testing. Matt Sweeney covers testing methodology and tools in Chapter 10, *Tools*. He discusses how to use JavaScript to measure performance and also describes common tools both for evaluating JavaScript runtime performance and for uncovering performance problems through HTTP sniffing.

Who This Book Is For

This book is aimed at web developers with an intermediate-to-advanced understanding of JavaScript who are looking to improve the performance of web application interfaces.

Conventions Used in This Book

The following typographical conventions are used in this book:

Italic

> Indicates new terms, URLs, email addresses, filenames, and file extensions.

`Constant width`

> Used for program listings, as well as within paragraphs to refer to program elements such as variable or function names, databases, data types, environment variables, statements, and keywords.

`Constant width bold`

> Shows commands or other text that should be typed literally by the user.

`Constant width italic`

> Shows text that should be replaced with user-supplied values or by values determined by context.

 This icon signifies a tip, suggestion, or general note.

 This icon indicates a warning or caution.

Using Code Examples

This book is here to help you get your job done. In general, you may use the code in this book in your programs and documentation. You do not need to contact us for permission unless you're reproducing a significant portion of the code. For example, writing a program that uses several chunks of code from this book does not require permission. Selling or distributing a CD-ROM of examples from O'Reilly books does require permission. Answering a question by citing this book and quoting example code does not require permission. Incorporating a significant amount of example code from this book into your product's documentation does require permission.

We appreciate, but do not require, attribution. An attribution usually includes the title, author, publisher, and ISBN. For example: "*High Performance JavaScript*, by Nicholas C. Zakas. Copyright 2010 Yahoo!, Inc., 978-0-596-80279-0."

If you feel your use of code examples falls outside fair use or the permission given here, feel free to contact us at *permissions@oreilly.com*.

Safari® Books Online

Safari Books Online is an on-demand digital library that lets you easily search over 7,500 technology and creative reference books and videos to find the answers you need quickly.

With a subscription, you can read any page and watch any video from our library online. Read books on your cell phone and mobile devices. Access new titles before they are available for print, and get exclusive access to manuscripts in development and post feedback for the authors. Copy and paste code samples, organize your favorites, download chapters, bookmark key sections, create notes, print out pages, and benefit from tons of other time-saving features.

O'Reilly Media has uploaded this book to the Safari Books Online service. To have full digital access to this book and others on similar topics from O'Reilly and other publishers, sign up for free at *http://my.safaribooksonline.com*.

How to Contact Us

Please address comments and questions concerning this book to the publisher:

O'Reilly Media, Inc.
1005 Gravenstein Highway North
Sebastopol, CA 95472
800-998-9938 (in the United States or Canada)
707-829-0515 (international or local)
707-829-0104 (fax)

We have a web page for this book, where we list errata, examples, and any additional information. You can access this page at:

http://www.oreilly.com/catalog/9780596802790

To comment or ask technical questions about this book, send email to:

bookquestions@oreilly.com

For more information about our books, conferences, Resource Centers, and the O'Reilly Network, see our website at:

http://www.oreilly.com

Acknowledgments

First and foremost, I'd like to thank all of the contributing authors: Matt Sweeney, Stoyan Stefanov, Stephen Levithan, Ross Harmes, and Julien Lecomte. Having their combined expertise and knowledge as part of this book made the process more exciting and the end result more compelling.

Thanks to all of the performance gurus of the world that I've had the opportunity to meet and interact with, especially Steve Souders, Tenni Theurer, and Nicole Sullivan. You three helped expand my horizons when it comes to web performance, and I'm incredibly grateful for that.

A big thanks to everyone who reviewed the book prior to publication, including Ryan Grove, Oliver Hunt, Matthew Russell, Ted Roden, Remy Sharp, and Venkateswaran Udayasankar. Their early feedback was invaluable in preparing the book for production.

And a huge thanks to everyone at O'Reilly and Yahoo! that made this book possible. I've wanted to write a book for Yahoo! ever since I joined the company in 2006, and Yahoo! Press was a great way to make this happen.

CHAPTER 1

Loading and Execution

JavaScript performance in the browser is arguably the most important usability issue facing developers. The problem is complex because of the blocking nature of JavaScript, which is to say that nothing else can happen while JavaScript code is being executed. In fact, most browsers use a single process for both user interface (UI) updates and JavaScript execution, so only one can happen at any given moment in time. The longer JavaScript takes to execute, the longer it takes before the browser is free to respond to user input.

On a basic level, this means that the very presence of a `<script>` tag is enough to make the page wait for the script to be parsed and executed. Whether the actual JavaScript code is inline with the tag or included in an external file is irrelevant; the page download and rendering must stop and wait for the script to complete before proceeding. This is a necessary part of the page's life cycle because the script may cause changes to the page while executing. The typical example is using `document.write()` in the middle of a page (as often used by advertisements). For example:

```
<html>
<head>
    <title>Script Example</title>
</head>
<body>
  <p>
  <script type="text/javascript">
    document.write("The date is " + (new Date()).toDateString());
  </script>
  </p>
</body>
</html>
```

When the browser encounters a `<script>` tag, as in this HTML page, there is no way of knowing whether the JavaScript will insert content into the `<p>`, introduce additional elements, or perhaps even close the tag. Therefore, the browser stops processing the page as it comes in, executes the JavaScript code, then continues parsing and rendering the page. The same takes place for JavaScript loaded using the `src` attribute; the browser must first download the code from the external file, which takes time, and then parse and execute the code. Page rendering and user interaction are completely blocked during this time.

 The two leading sources of information on JavaScript affecting page download performance are the Yahoo! Exceptional Performance team (*http://developer.yahoo.com/performance/*) and Steve Souders, author of *High Performance Web Sites* (*http://oreilly.com/catalog/9780596529307/*) (O'Reilly) and *Even Faster Web Sites* (*http://oreilly.com/catalog/9780596522315/*) (O'Reilly). This chapter is heavily influenced by their combined research.

Script Positioning

The HTML 4 specification indicates that a `<script>` tag may be placed inside of a `<head>` or `<body>` tag in an HTML document and may appear any number of times within each. Traditionally, `<script>` tags that are used to load external JavaScript files have appeared in the `<head>`, along with `<link>` tags to load external CSS files and other metainformation about the page. The theory was that it's best to keep as many style and behavior dependencies together, loading them first so that the page will come in looking and behaving correctly. For example:

```
<html>
<head>
    <title>Script Example</title>
    <-- Example of inefficient script positioning -->
    <script type="text/javascript" src="file1.js"></script>
    <script type="text/javascript" src="file2.js"></script>
    <script type="text/javascript" src="file3.js"></script>
    <link rel="stylesheet" type="text/css" href="styles.css">
</head>
<body>
    <p>Hello world!</p>
</body>
</html>
```

Though this code seems innocuous, it actually has a severe performance issue: there are three JavaScript files being loaded in the `<head>`. Since each `<script>` tag blocks the page from continuing to render until it has fully downloaded and executed the Java-Script code, the perceived performance of this page will suffer. Keep in mind that browsers don't start rendering anything on the page until the opening `<body>` tag is encountered. Putting scripts at the top of the page in this way typically leads to a noticeable delay, often in the form of a blank white page, before the user can even begin reading or otherwise interacting with the page. To get a good understanding of how this occurs, it's useful to look at a waterfall diagram showing when each resource is downloaded. Figure 1-1 shows when each script and the stylesheet file get downloaded as the page is loading.

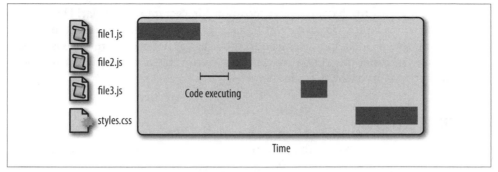

Figure 1-1. JavaScript code execution blocks other file downloads

Figure 1-1 shows an interesting pattern. The first JavaScript file begins to download and blocks any of the other files from downloading in the meantime. Further, there is a delay between the time at which *file1.js* is completely downloaded and the time at which *file2.js* begins to download. That space is the time it takes for the code contained in *file1.js* to fully execute. Each file must wait until the previous one has been down-loaded and executed before the next download can begin. In the meantime, the user is met with a blank screen as the files are being downloaded one at a time. This is the behavior of most major browsers today.

Internet Explorer 8, Firefox 3.5, Safari 4, and Chrome 2 all allow parallel downloads of JavaScript files. This is good news because the `<script>` tags don't necessarily block other `<script>` tags from downloading external resources. Unfortunately, JavaScript downloads still block downloading of other resources, such as images. And even though downloading a script doesn't block other scripts from downloading, the page must still wait for the JavaScript code to be downloaded and executed before continuing. So while the latest browsers have improved performance by allowing parallel downloads, the problem hasn't been completely solved. Script blocking still remains a problem.

Because scripts block downloading of all resource types on the page, it's recommended to place all `<script>` tags as close to the bottom of the `<body>` tag as possible so as not to affect the download of the entire page. For example:

```
<html>
<head>
    <title>Script Example</title>
    <link rel="stylesheet" type="text/css" href="styles.css">
</head>
<body>
  <p>Hello world!</p>

    <-- Example of recommended script positioning -->
    <script type="text/javascript" src="file1.js"></script>
    <script type="text/javascript" src="file2.js"></script>
    <script type="text/javascript" src="file3.js"></script>
</body>
</html>
```

This code represents the recommended position for `<script>` tags in an HTML file. Even though the script downloads will block one another, the rest of the page has already been downloaded and displayed to the user so that the entire page isn't perceived as slow. This is the Yahoo! Exceptional Performance team's first rule about JavaScript: put scripts at the bottom.

Grouping Scripts

Since each `<script>` tag blocks the page from rendering during initial download, it's helpful to limit the total number of `<script>` tags contained in the page. This applies to both inline scripts as well as those in external files. Every time a `<script>` tag is encountered during the parsing of an HTML page, there is going to be a delay while the code is executed; minimizing these delays improves the overall performance of the page.

 Steve Souders has also found that an inline script placed after a `<link>` tag referencing an external stylesheet caused the browser to block while waiting for the stylesheet to download. This is done to ensure that the inline script will have the most correct style information with which to work. Souders recommends never putting an inline script after a `<link>` tag for this reason.

The problem is slightly different when dealing with external JavaScript files. Each HTTP request brings with it additional performance overhead, so downloading one single 100 KB file will be faster than downloading four 25 KB files. To that end, it's helpful to limit the number of external script files that your page references.

Typically, a large website or web application will have several required JavaScript files. You can minimize the performance impact by concatenating these files together into a single file and then calling that single file with a single `<script>` tag. The concatenation can happen offline using a build tool (discussed in Chapter 9) or in real-time using a tool such as the Yahoo! combo handler.

Yahoo! created the combo handler for use in distributing the Yahoo! User Interface (YUI) library files through their Content Delivery Network (CDN). Any website can pull in any number of YUI files by using a combo-handled URL and specifying the files to include. For example, this URL includes two files: *http://yui.yahooapis.com/combo ?2.7.0/build/yahoo/yahoo-min.js&2.7.0/build/event/event-min.js*.

This URL loads the 2.7.0 versions of the *yahoo-min.js* and *event-min.js* files. These files exist separately on the server but are combined when this URL is requested. Instead of using two `<script>` tags (one to load each file), a single `<script>` tag can be used to load both:

```
<html>
<head>
   <title>Script Example</title>
   <link rel="stylesheet" type="text/css" href="styles.css">
</head>
<body>
  <p>Hello world!</p>

   <-- Example of recommended script positioning -->
   <script type="text/javascript" src="
http://yui.yahooapis.com/combo?2.7.0/build/yahoo/yahoo-min.js&
2.7.0/build/event/event-min.js "></script>
</body>
</html>
```

This code has a single `<script>` tag at the bottom of the page that loads multiple Java-Script files, showing the best practice for including external JavaScript on an HTML page.

Nonblocking Scripts

JavaScript's tendency to block browser processes, both HTTP requests and UI updates, is the most notable performance issue facing developers. Keeping JavaScript files small and limiting the number of HTTP requests are only the first steps in creating a responsive web application. The richer the functionality an application requires, the more JavaScript code is required, and so keeping source code small isn't always an option. Limiting yourself to downloading a single large JavaScript file will only result in locking the browser out for a long period of time, despite it being just one HTTP request. To get around this situation, you need to incrementally add more JavaScript to the page in a way that doesn't block the browser.

The secret to nonblocking scripts is to load the JavaScript source code after the page has finished loading. In technical terms, this means downloading the code after the `window`'s `load` event has been fired. There are a few techniques for achieving this result.

Deferred Scripts

HTML 4 defines an additional attribute for the `<script>` tag called `defer`. The `defer` attribute indicates that the script contained within the element is not going to modify the DOM and therefore execution can be safely deferred until a later point in time. The `defer` attribute is supported only in Internet Explorer 4+ and Firefox 3.5+, making it less than ideal for a generic cross-browser solution. In other browsers, the `defer` attribute is simply ignored and so the `<script>` tag is treated in the default (blocking) manner. Still, this solution is useful if your target browsers support it. The following is an example usage:

```
<script type="text/javascript" src="file1.js" defer></script>
```

A `<script>` tag with `defer` may be placed anywhere in the document. The JavaScript file will begin downloading at the point that the `<script>` tag is parsed, but the code will not be executed until the DOM has been completely loaded (before the `onload` event handler is called). When a deferred JavaScript file is downloaded, it doesn't block the browser's other processes, and so these files can be downloaded in parallel with others on the page.

Any `<script>` element marked with `defer` will not execute until after the DOM has been completely loaded; this holds true for inline scripts as well as for external script files. The following simple page demonstrates how the `defer` attribute alters the behavior of scripts:

```
<html>
<head>
    <title>Script Defer Example</title>
</head>
<body>
    <script defer>
        alert("defer");
    </script>
    <script>
        alert("script");
    </script>
    <script>
        window.onload = function(){
            alert("load");
        };
    </script>
</body>
</html>
```

This code displays three alerts as the page is being processed. In browsers that don't support `defer`, the order of the alerts is *"defer"*, *"script"*, and *"load"*. In browsers that support `defer`, the order of the alerts is *"script"*, *"defer"*, and *"load"*. Note that the deferred `<script>` element isn't executed until after the second but is executed before the `onload` event handler is called.

If your target browsers include only Internet Explorer and Firefox 3.5, then deferring scripts in this manner can be helpful. If you have a larger cross-section of browsers to support, there are other solutions that work in a more consistent manner.

Dynamic Script Elements

The Document Object Model (DOM) allows you to dynamically create almost any part of an HTML document using JavaScript. At its root, the `<script>` element isn't any different than any other element on a page: references can be retrieved through the DOM, and they can be moved, removed from the document, and even created. A new `<script>` element can be created very easily using standard DOM methods:

```
var script = document.createElement("script");
script.type = "text/javascript";
script.src = "file1.js";
document.getElementsByTagName("head")[0].appendChild(script);
```

This new <script> element loads the source file *file1.js*. The file begins downloading as soon as the element is added to the page. The important thing about this technique is that the file is downloaded and executed without blocking other page processes, regardless of where the download is initiated. You can even place this code in the <head> of a document without affecting the rest of the page (aside from the one HTTP connection that is used to download the file).

 It's generally safer to add new <script> nodes to the <head> element instead of the <body>, especially if this code is executing during page load. Internet Explorer may experience an "operation aborted" error if all of the <body> contents have not yet been loaded.*

When a file is downloaded using a dynamic script node, the retrieved code is typically executed immediately (except in Firefox and Opera, which will wait until any previous dynamic script nodes have executed). This works well when the script is self-executing but can be problematic if the code contains only interfaces to be used by other scripts on the page. In that case, you need to track when the code has been fully downloaded and is ready for use. This is accomplished using events that are fired by the dynamic <script> node.

Firefox, Opera, Chrome, and Safari 3+ all fire a load event when the src of a <script> element has been retrieved. You can therefore be notified when the script is ready by listening for this event:

```
var script = document.createElement("script")
script.type = "text/javascript";

//Firefox, Opera, Chrome, Safari 3+
script.onload = function(){
    alert("Script loaded!");
};

script.src = "file1.js";
document.getElementsByTagName("head")[0].appendChild(script);
```

Internet Explorer supports an alternate implementation that fires a readystatechange event. There is a readyState property on the <script> element that is changed at various times during the download of an external file. There are five possible values for ready State:

---

* See "The dreaded operation aborted error" at *http://www.nczonline.net/blog/2008/03/17/the -dreaded-operation-aborted-error/* for a more in-depth discussion of this issue.

`"uninitialized"`
> The default state

`"loading"`
> Download has begun

`"loaded"`
> Download has completed

`"interactive"`
> Data is completely downloaded but isn't fully available

`"complete"`
> All data is ready to be used

Microsoft's documentation for `readyState` and each of the possible values seems to indicate that not all states will be used during the lifetime of the `<script>` element, but there is no indication as to which will always be used. In practice, the two states of most interest are `"loaded"` and `"complete"`. Internet Explorer is inconsistent with which of these two `readyState` values indicates the final state, as sometimes the `<script>` element will reach the `"loaded"` state but never reach `"complete"` whereas other times `"complete"` will be reached without `"loaded"` ever having been used. The safest way to use the `readystatechange` event is to check for both of these states and remove the event handler when either one occurs (to ensure the event isn't handled twice):

```
var script = document.createElement("script")
script.type = "text/javascript";

//Internet Explorer
script.onreadystatechange = function(){
    if (script.readyState == "loaded" || script.readyState == "complete"){
        script.onreadystatechange = null;
        alert("Script loaded.");
    }
};

script.src = "file1.js";
document.getElementsByTagName("head")[0].appendChild(script);
```

In most cases, you'll want to use a single approach to dynamically load JavaScript files. The following function encapsulates both the standard and IE-specific functionality:

```
function loadScript(url, callback){

    var script = document.createElement("script")
    script.type = "text/javascript";

    if (script.readyState){  //IE
        script.onreadystatechange = function(){
            if (script.readyState == "loaded" || script.readyState == "complete"){
                script.onreadystatechange = null;
                callback();
            }
        };
```

```
    } else {  //Others
        script.onload = function(){
            callback();
        };
    }

    script.src = url;
    document.getElementsByTagName("head")[0].appendChild(script);
}
```

This function accepts two arguments: the URL of the JavaScript file to retrieve and a callback function to execute when the JavaScript has been fully loaded. Feature detection is used to determine which event handler should monitor the script's progress. The last step is to assign the src property and add the <script> element to the page. The loadScript() function is used as follows:

```
loadScript("file1.js", function(){
    alert("File is loaded!");
});
```

You can dynamically load as many JavaScript files as necessary on a page, but make sure you consider the order in which files must be loaded. Of all the major browsers, only Firefox and Opera guarantee that the order of script execution will remain the same as you specify. Other browsers will download and execute the various code files in the order in which they are returned from the server. You can guarantee the order by chaining the downloads together, such as:

```
loadScript("file1.js", function(){
    loadScript("file2.js", function(){
        loadScript("file3.js", function(){
            alert("All files are loaded!");
        });
    });
});
```

This code waits to begin loading *file2.js* until *file1.js* is available and also waits to download *file3.js* until *file2.js* is available. Though possible, this approach can get a little bit difficult to manage if there are multiple files to download and execute.

If the order of multiple files is important, the preferred approach is to concatenate the files into a single file where each part is in the correct order. That single file can then be downloaded to retrieve all of the code at once (since this is happening asynchronously, there's no penalty for having a larger file).

Dynamic script loading is the most frequently used pattern for nonblocking JavaScript downloads due to its cross-browser compatibility and ease of use.

XMLHttpRequest Script Injection

Another approach to nonblocking scripts is to retrieve the JavaScript code using an XMLHttpRequest (XHR) object and then inject the script into the page. This technique involves creating an XHR object, downloading the JavaScript file, then injecting the JavaScript code into the page using a dynamic `<script>` element. Here's a simple example:

```
var xhr = new XMLHttpRequest();
xhr.open("get", "file1.js", true);
xhr.onreadystatechange = function(){
    if (xhr.readyState == 4){
        if (xhr.status >= 200 && xhr.status < 300 || xhr.status == 304){
            var script = document.createElement("script");
            script.type = "text/javascript";
            script.text = xhr.responseText;
            document.body.appendChild(script);
        }

    }
};
xhr.send(null);
```

This code sends a GET request for the file *file1.js*. The onreadystatechange event handler checks for a **readyState** of 4 and then verifies that the HTTP status code is valid (anything in the 200 range means a valid response, and 304 means a cached response). If a valid response has been received, then a new `<script>` element is created and its **text** property is assigned to the **responseText** received from the server. Doing so essentially creates a `<script>` element with inline code. Once the new `<script>` element is added to the document, the code is executed and is ready to use.

The primary advantage of this approach is that you can download the JavaScript code without executing it immediately. Since the code is being returned outside of a `<script>` tag, it won't automatically be executed upon download, allowing you to defer its execution until you're ready. Another advantage is that the same code works in all modern browsers without exception cases.

The primary limitation of this approach is that the JavaScript file must be located on the same domain as the page requesting it, which makes downloading from CDNs impossible. For this reason, XHR script injection typically isn't used on large-scale web applications.

Recommended Nonblocking Pattern

The recommend approach to loading a significant amount of JavaScript onto a page is a two-step process: first, include the code necessary to dynamically load JavaScript, and then load the rest of the JavaScript code needed for page initialization. Since the first part of the code is as small as possible, potentially containing just the load Script() function, it downloads and executes quickly, and so shouldn't cause much interference with the page. Once the initial code is in place, use it to load the remaining JavaScript. For example:

```
<script type="text/javascript" src="loader.js"></script>
<script type="text/javascript">
    loadScript("the-rest.js", function(){
        Application.init();
    });
</script>
```

Place this loading code just before the closing `</body>` tag. Doing so has several benefits. First, as discussed earlier, this ensures that JavaScript execution won't prevent the rest of the page from being displayed. Second, when the second JavaScript file has finished downloading, all of the DOM necessary for the application has been created and is ready to be interacted with, avoiding the need to check for another event (such as `window.onload`) to know when the page is ready for initialization.

Another option is to embed the `loadScript()` function directly into the page, thus avoiding another HTTP request. For example:

```
<script type="text/javascript">
    function loadScript(url, callback){

        var script = document.createElement("script")
        script.type = "text/javascript";

        if (script.readyState){  //IE
            script.onreadystatechange = function(){
                if (script.readyState == "loaded" ||
                        script.readyState == "complete"){
                    script.onreadystatechange = null;
                    callback();
                }
            };
        } else {  //Others
            script.onload = function(){
                callback();
            };
        }

        script.src = url;
        document.getElementsByTagName("head")[0].appendChild(script);
    }

    loadScript("the-rest.js", function(){
        Application.init();
    });
</script>
```

If you decide to take the latter approach, it's recommended to minify the initial script using a tool such as YUI Compressor (see Chapter 9) for the smallest byte-size impact on your page.

Once the code for page initialization has been completely downloaded, you are free to continue using `loadScript()` to load additional functionality onto the page as needed.

The YUI 3 approach

The concept of a small initial amount of code on the page followed by downloading additional functionality is at the core of the YUI 3 design. To use YUI 3 on your page, begin by including the YUI seed file:

```
<script type="text/javascript"
src="http://yui.yahooapis.com/combo?3.0.0/build/yui/yui-min.js"></script>
```

The seed file is around 10 KB (6 KB gzipped) and includes enough functionality to download any other YUI components from the Yahoo! CDN. For example, if you'd like to use the DOM utility, you specify its name ("dom") with the YUI use() method and then provide a callback that will be executed when the code is ready:

```
YUI().use("dom", function(Y){
    Y.DOM.addClass(docment.body, "loaded");
});
```

This example creates a new instance of the YUI object and then calls the use() method. The seed file has all of the information about filenames and dependencies, so specifying "dom" actually builds up a combo-handler URL with all of the correct dependency files and creates a dynamic script element to download and execute those files. When all of the code is available, the callback method is called and the YUI instance is passed in as the argument, allowing you to immediately start using the newly downloaded functionality.

The LazyLoad library

For a more general-purpose tool, Ryan Grove of Yahoo! Search created the LazyLoad library (available at *http://github.com/rgrove/lazyload/*). LazyLoad is a more powerful version of the loadScript() function. When minified, the LazyLoad file is around 1.5 KB (minified, not gzipped). Example usage:

```
<script type="text/javascript" src="lazyload-min.js"></script>
<script type="text/javascript">
    LazyLoad.js("the-rest.js", function(){
        Application.init();
    });
</script>
```

LazyLoad is also capable of downloading multiple JavaScript files and ensuring that they are executed in the correct order in all browsers. To load multiple JavaScript files, just pass an array of URLs to the LazyLoad.js() method:

```
<script type="text/javascript" src="lazyload-min.js"></script>
<script type="text/javascript">
    LazyLoad.js(["first-file.js", "the-rest.js"], function(){
        Application.init();
    });
</script>
```

Even though the files are downloaded in a nonblocking fashion using dynamic script loading, it's recommended to have as few files as possible. Each download is still a separate HTTP request, and the callback function won't execute until all of the files have been downloaded and executed.

 LazyLoad is also capable of loading CSS files dynamically. This is typically less of an issue because CSS file downloads are always done in parallel and don't block other page activities.

The LABjs library

Another take on nonblocking JavaScript loading is LABjs (*http://labjs.com/*), an open source library written by Kyle Simpson with input from Steve Souders. This library provides more fine-grained control over the loading process and tries to download as much code in parallel as possible. LABjs is also quite small, 4.5 KB (minified, not gzipped), and so has a minimal page footprint. Example usage:

```
<script type="text/javascript" src="lab.js"></script>
<script type="text/javascript">
    $LAB.script("the-rest.js")
        .wait(function(){
            Application.init();
        });
</script>
```

The `$LAB.script()` method is used to define a JavaScript file to download, whereas `$LAB.wait()` is used to indicate that execution should wait until the file is downloaded and executed before running the given function. LABjs encourages chaining, so every method returns a reference to the `$LAB` object. To download multiple JavaScript files, just chain another `$LAB.script()` call:

```
<script type="text/javascript" src="lab.js"></script>
<script type="text/javascript">
    $LAB.script("first-file.js")
        .script("the-rest.js")
        .wait(function(){
            Application.init();
        });
</script>
```

What sets LABjs apart is its ability to manage dependencies. Normal inclusion with `<script>` tags means that each file is downloaded (either sequentially or in parallel, as mentioned previously) and then executed sequentially. In some cases this is truly necessary, but in others it is not.

LABjs allows you to specify which files should wait for others by using `wait()`. In the previous example, the code in *first-file.js* is not guaranteed to execute before the code in *the-rest.js*. To guarantee this, you must add a `wait()` call after the first `script()`:

```
<script type="text/javascript" src="lab.js"></script>
<script type="text/javascript">
    $LAB.script("first-file.js").wait()
        .script("the-rest.js")
        .wait(function(){
            Application.init();
        });
</script>
```

Now the code in *first-file.js* is guaranteed to execute before the code in *the-rest.js*, although the contents of the files are downloaded in parallel.

Summary

Managing JavaScript in the browser is tricky because code execution blocks other browser processes such as UI painting. Every time a `<script>` tag is encountered, the page must stop and wait for the code to download (if external) and execute before continuing to process the rest of the page. There are, however, several ways to minimize the performance impact of JavaScript:

- Put all `<script>` tags at the bottom of the page, just inside of the closing `</body>` tag. This ensures that the page can be almost completely rendered before script execution begins.

- Group scripts together. The fewer `<script>` tags on the page, the faster the page can be loaded and become interactive. This holds true both for `<script>` tags loading external JavaScript files and those with inline code.

- There are several ways to download JavaScript in a nonblocking fashion:
  - Use the `defer` attribute of the `<script>` tag (Internet Explorer and Firefox 3.5+ only)
  - Dynamically create `<script>` elements to download and execute the code
  - Download the JavaScript code using an XHR object, and then inject the code into the page

By using these strategies, you can greatly improve the perceived performance of a web application that requires a large amount of JavaScript code.

CHAPTER 2

Data Access

One of the classic computer science problems is determining where data should be stored for optimal reading and writing. Where data is stored is related to how quickly it can be retrieved during code execution. This problem in JavaScript is somewhat simplified because of the small number of options for data storage. Similar to other languages, though, where data is stored can greatly affect how quickly it can be accessed later. There are four basic places from which data can be accessed in JavaScript:

Literal values
> Any value that represents just itself and isn't stored in a particular location. Java-Script can represent strings, numbers, Booleans, objects, arrays, functions, regular expressions, and the special values `null` and `undefined` as literals.

Variables
> Any developer-defined location for storing data created by using the `var` keyword.

Array items
> A numerically indexed location within a JavaScript `Array` object.

Object members
> A string-indexed location within a JavaScript object.

Each of these data storage locations has a particular cost associated with reading and writing operations involving the data. In most cases, the performance difference between accessing information from a literal value versus a local variable is trivial. Accessing information from array items and object members is more expensive, though exactly which is more expensive depends heavily on the browser. Figure 2-1 shows the relative speed of accessing 200,000 values from each of these four locations in various browsers.

Older browsers using more traditional JavaScript engines, such as Firefox 3, Internet Explorer, and Safari 3.2, show a much larger amount of time taken to access values versus browsers that use optimizing JavaScript engines. The general trends, however, remain the same across all browsers: literal value and local variable access tend to be faster than array item and object member access. The one exception, Firefox 3,

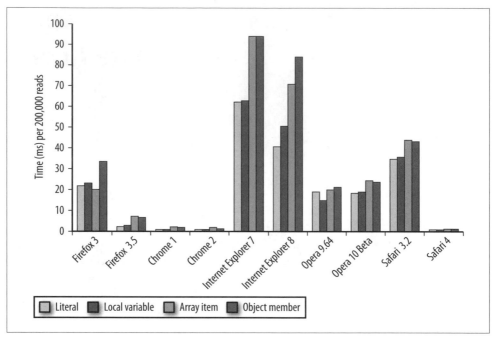

Figure 2-1. Time per 200,000 reads from various data locations

optimized array item access to be much faster. Even so, the general advice is to use literal values and local variables whenever possible and limit use of array items and object members where speed of execution is a concern. To that end, there are several patterns to look for, avoid, and optimize in your code.

Managing Scope

The concept of scope is key to understanding JavaScript not just from a performance perspective, but also from a functional perspective. Scope has many effects in Java-Script, from determining what variables a function can access to assigning the value of this. There are also performance considerations when dealing with JavaScript scopes, but to understand how speed relates to scope, it's necessary to understand exactly how scope works.

Scope Chains and Identifier Resolution

Every function in JavaScript is represented as an object—more specifically, as an instance of Function. Function objects have properties just like any other object, and these include both the properties that you can access programmatically and a series of internal properties that are used by the JavaScript engine but are not accessible through code.

One of these properties is [[Scope]], as defined by ECMA-262, Third Edition (*http://www.ecma-international.org/publications/standards/Ecma-262.htm*).

The internal [[Scope]] property contains a collection of objects representing the scope in which the function was created. This collection is called the function's *scope chain* and it determines the data that a function can access. Each object in the function's scope chain is called a *variable object*, and each of these contains entries for variables in the form of key-value pairs. When a function is created, its scope chain is populated with objects representing the data that is accessible in the scope in which the function was created. For example, consider the following global function:

```
function add(num1, num2){
    var sum = num1 + num2;
    return sum;
}
```

When the add() function is created, its scope chain is populated with a single variable object: the global object representing all of the variables that are globally defined. This global object contains entries for window, navigator, and document, to name a few. Figure 2-2 shows this relationship (note the global object in this figure shows only a few of the global variables as an example; there are many others).

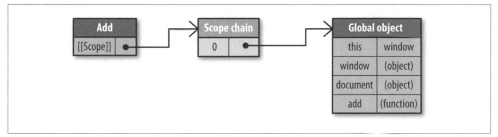

Figure 2-2. Scope chain for the add() function

The add function's scope chain is later used when the function is executed. Suppose that the following code is executed:

```
var total = add(5, 10);
```

Executing the add function triggers the creation of an internal object called an *execution context*. An execution context defines the environment in which a function is being executed. Each execution context is unique to one particular execution of the function, and so multiple calls to the same function result in multiple execution contexts being created. The execution context is destroyed once the function has been completely executed.

An execution context has its own scope chain that is used for identifier resolution. When the execution context is created, its scope chain is initialized with the objects contained in the executing function's [[Scope]] property. These values are copied over into the execution context scope chain in the order in which they appear in the function. Once this is complete, a new object called the *activation object* is created for the execution context. The activation object acts as the variable object for this execution and contains entries for all local variables, named arguments, the arguments collection, and this. This object is then pushed to the front of the scope chain. When the execution context is destroyed, so is the activation object. Figure 2-3 shows the execution context and its scope chain for the previous example code.

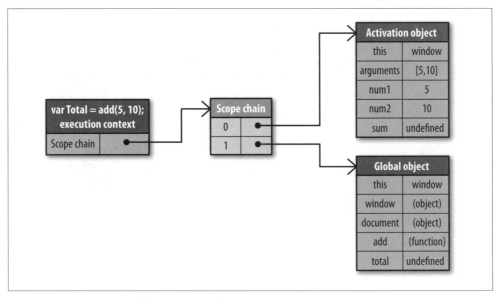

Figure 2-3. Scope chain while executing add()

Each time a variable is encountered during the function's execution, the process of identifier resolution takes place to determine where to retrieve or store the data. During this process, the execution context's scope chain is searched for an identifier with the same name. The search begins at the front of the scope chain, in the execution function's activation object. If found, the variable with the specified identifier is used; if not, the search continues on to the next object in the scope chain. This process continues until either the identifier is found or there are no more variable objects to search, in which case the identifier is deemed to be undefined. The same approach is taken for each identifier found during the function execution, so in the previous example, this would happen for sum, num1, and num2. It is this search process that affects performance.

Note that two variables with the same name may exist in different parts of the scope chain. In that case, the identifier is bound to the variable that is found first in the scope chain traversal, and the first variable is said to *shadow* the second.

Identifier Resolution Performance

Identifier resolution isn't free, as in fact no computer operation really is without some sort of performance overhead. The deeper into the execution context's scope chain an identifier exists, the slower it is to access for both reads and writes. Consequently, local variables are always the fastest to access inside of a function, whereas global variables will generally be the slowest (optimizing JavaScript engines are capable of tuning this in certain situations). Keep in mind that global variables always exist in the last variable object of the execution context's scope chain, so they are always the furthest away to resolve. Figures 2-4 and 2-5 show the speed of identifier resolution based on their depth in the scope chain. A depth of 1 indicates a local variable.

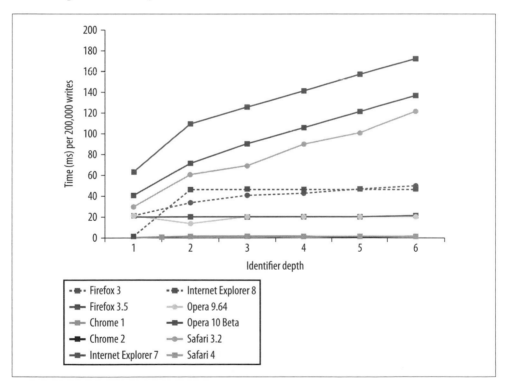

Figure 2-4. Identifier resolution for write operations

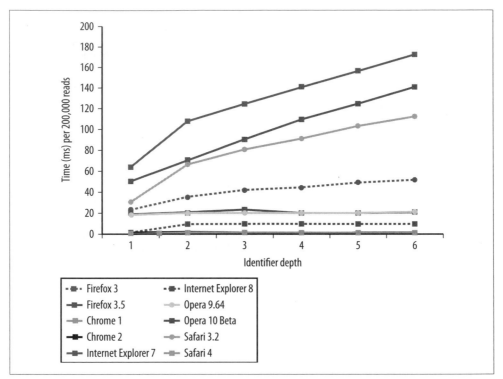

Figure 2-5. Identifier resolution for read operations

The general trend across all browsers is that the deeper into the scope chain an identifier exists, the slower it will be read from or written to. Browsers with optimizing JavaScript engines, such as Chrome and Safari 4, don't have this sort of performance penalty for accessing out-of-scope identifiers, whereas Internet Explorer, Safari 3.2, and others show a more drastic effect. It's worth noting that earlier browsers, such as Internet Explorer 6 and Firefox 2, had incredibly steep slopes and would not even appear within the bounds of this graph at the high point if their data had been included.

Given this information, it's advisable to use local variables whenever possible to improve performance in browsers without optimizing JavaScript engines. A good rule of thumb is to always store out-of-scope values in local variables if they are used more than once within a function. Consider the following example:

```
function initUI(){
    var bd = document.body,
        links = document.getElementsByTagName("a"),
        i= 0,
        len = links.length;

    while(i < len){
        update(links[i++]);
    }
```

```
        document.getElementById("go-btn").onclick = function(){
            start();
        };

        bd.className = "active";
    }
```

This function contains three references to document, which is a global object. The search for this variable must go all the way through the scope chain before finally being resolved in the global variable object. You can mitigate the performance impact of repeated global variable access by first storing the reference in a local variable and then using the local variable instead of the global. For example, the previous code can be rewritten as follows:

```
    function initUI(){
        var doc = document,
            bd = doc.body,
            links = doc.getElementsByTagName("a"),
            i= 0,
            len = links.length;

        while(i < len){
            update(links[i++]);
        }

        doc.getElementById("go-btn").onclick = function(){
            start();
        };

        bd.className = "active";
    }
```

The updated version of initUI() first stores a reference to document in the local doc variable. Instead of accessing a global variables three times, that number is cut down to one. Accessing doc instead of document is faster because it's a local variable. Of course, this simplistic function won't show a huge performance improvement, because it's not doing that much, but imagine larger functions with dozens of global variables being accessed repeatedly; that is where the more impressive performance improvements will be found.

Scope Chain Augmentation

Generally speaking, an execution context's scope chain doesn't change. There are, however, two statements that temporarily augment the execution context's scope chain while it is being executed. The first of these is with.

The with statement is used to create variables for all of an object's properties. This mimics other languages with similar features and is usually seen as a convenience to avoid writing the same code repeatedly. The initUI() function can be written as the following:

```
function initUI(){
    with (document){      //avoid!
        var bd = body,
            links = getElementsByTagName("a"),
            i= 0,
            len = links.length;

        while(i < len){
            update(links[i++]);
        }

        getElementById("go-btn").onclick = function(){
            start();
        };

        bd.className = "active";
    }
}
```

This rewritten version of initUI() uses a with statement to avoid writing document else-where. Though this may seem more efficient, it actually creates a performance problem.

When code execution flows into a with statement, the execution context's scope chain is temporarily augmented. A new variable object is created containing all of the properties of the specified object. That object is then pushed to the front of the scope chain, meaning that all of the function's local variables are now in the second scope chain object and are therefore more expensive to access (see Figure 2-6).

By passing the document object into the with statement, a new variable object containing all of the document object's properties is pushed to the front of the scope chain. This makes it very fast to access document properties but slower to access the local variables such as bd. For this reason, it's best to avoid using the with statement. As shown previously, it's just as easy to store document in a local variable and get the performance improvement that way.

The with statement isn't the only part of JavaScript that artificially augments the execution context's scope chain; the catch clause of the try-catch statement has the same effect. When an error occurs in the try block, execution automatically flows to the catch and the exception object is pushed into a variable object that is then placed at the front of the scope chain. Inside of the catch block, all variables local to the function are now in the second scope chain object. For example:

```
try {
    methodThatMightCauseAnError();
} catch (ex){
    alert(ex.message);   //scope chain is augmented here
}
```

Note that as soon as the catch clause is finished executing, the scope chain returns to its previous state.

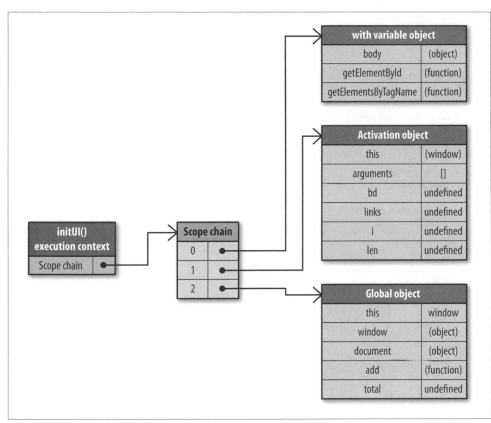

Figure 2-6. Augmented scope chain in a with statement

The `try-catch` statement is very useful when applied appropriately, and so it doesn't make sense to suggest complete avoidance. If you do plan on using a `try-catch`, make sure that you understand the likelihood of error. A `try-catch` should never be used as the solution to a JavaScript error. If you know an error will occur frequently, then that indicates a problem with the code itself that should be fixed.

You can minimize the performance impact of the `catch` clause by executing as little code as necessary within it. A good pattern is to have a method for handling errors that the `catch` clause can delegate to, as in this example:

```
try {
    methodThatMightCauseAnError();
} catch (ex){
    handleError(ex);  //delegate to handler method
}
```

Here a `handleError()` method is the only code that is executed in the `catch` clause. This method is free to handle the error in an appropriate way and is passed the exception object generated from the error. Since there is just one statement executed and no local variables accessed, the temporary scope chain augmentation does not affect the performance of the code.

Dynamic Scopes

Both the `with` statement and the `catch` clause of a `try-catch` statement, as well as a function containing `eval()`, are all considered to be *dynamic scopes*. A dynamic scope is one that exists only through execution of code and therefore cannot be determined simply by static analysis (looking at the code structure). For example:

```
function execute(code) {
  eval(code);

  function subroutine(){
    return window;
  }

  var w = subroutine();

  //what value is w?
};
```

The `execute()` function represents a dynamic scope due to the use of `eval()`. The value of `w` can change based on the value of `code`. In most cases, `w` will be equal to the global `window` object, but consider the following:

```
execute("var window = {};")
```

In this case, `eval()` creates a local `window` variable in `execute()`, so `w` ends up equal to the local `window` instead of the global. There is no way to know if this is the case until the code is executed, which means the value of the `window` identifier cannot be predetermined.

Optimizing JavaScript engines such as Safari's Nitro try to speed up identifier resolution by analyzing the code to determine which variables should be accessible at any given time. These engines try to avoid the traditional scope chain lookup by indexing identifiers for faster resolution. When a dynamic scope is involved, however, this optimization is no longer valid. The engines need to switch back to a slower hash-based approach for identifier resolution that more closely mirrors traditional scope chain lookup.

For this reason, it's recommended to use dynamic scopes only when absolutely necessary.

Closures, Scope, and Memory

Closures are one of the most powerful aspects of JavaScript, allowing a function to access data that is outside of its local scope. The use of closures has been popularized through the writings of Douglas Crockford and is now ubiquitous in most complex web applications. There is, however, a performance impact associated with using closures.

To understand the performance issues with closures, consider the following:

```
function assignEvents(){

    var id = "xdi9592";

    document.getElementById("save-btn").onclick = function(event){
        saveDocument(id);
    };
}
```

The `assignEvents()` function assigns an event handler to a single DOM element. This event handler is a closure, as it is created when the `assignEvents()` is executed and can access the `id` variable from the containing scope. In order for this closure to access `id`, a specific scope chain must be created.

When `assignEvents()` is executed, an activation object is created that contains, among other things, the `id` variable. This becomes the first object in the execution context's scope chain, with the global object coming second. When the closure is created, its `[[Scope]]` property is initialized with both of these objects (see Figure 2-7).

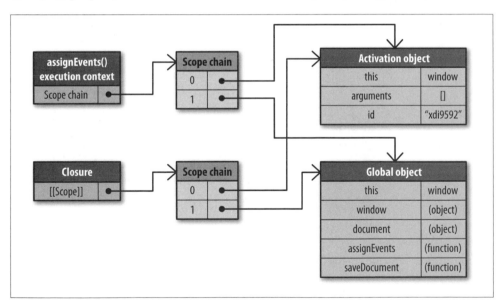

Figure 2-7. Scope chains of the assignEvents() execution context and closure

Since the closure's `[[Scope]]` property contains references to the same objects as the execution context's scope chain, there is a side effect. Typically, a function's activation object is destroyed when the execution context is destroyed. When there's a closure involved, though, the activation object isn't destroyed, because a reference still exists in the closure's `[[Scope]]` property. This means that closures require more memory overhead in a script than a nonclosure function. In large web applications, this might become a problem, especially where Internet Explorer is concerned. IE implements DOM objects as nonnative JavaScript objects, and as such, closures can cause memory leaks (see Chapter 3 for more information).

When the closure is executed, an execution context is created whose scope chain is initialized with the same two scope chain objects referenced in `[[Scope]]`, and then a new activation object is created for the closure itself (see Figure 2-8).

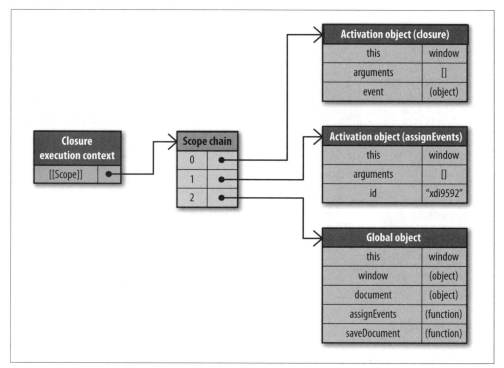

Figure 2-8. Executing the closure

Note that both identifiers used in the closure, `id` and `saveDocument`, exist past the first object in the scope chain. This is the primary performance concern with closures: you're often accessing a lot of out-of-scope identifiers and therefore are incurring a performance penalty with each access.

It's best to exercise caution when using closures in your scripts, as they have both memory and execution speed concerns. However, you can mitigate the execution speed impact by following the advice from earlier in this chapter regarding out-of-scope variables: store any frequently used out-of-scope variables in local variables, and then access the local variables directly.

Object Members

Most JavaScript is written in an object-oriented manner, either through the creation of custom objects or the use of built-in objects such as those in the Document Object Model (DOM) and Browser Object Model (BOM). As such, there tends to be a lot of object member access.

Object members are both properties and methods, and there is little difference between the two in JavaScript. A named member of an object may contain any data type. Since functions are represented as objects, a member may contain a function in addition to the more traditional data types. When a named member references a function, it's considered a method, whereas a member referencing a nonfunction data type is considered a property.

As discussed earlier in this chapter, object member access tends to be slower than accessing data in literals or variables, and in some browsers slower than accessing array items. To understand why this is the case, it's necessary to understand the nature of objects in JavaScript.

Prototypes

Objects in JavaScript are based on *prototypes*. A prototype is an object that serves as the base of another object, defining and implementing members that a new object must have. This is a completely different concept than the traditional object-oriented programming concept of classes, which define the process for creating a new object. Prototype objects are shared amongst all instances of a given object type, and so all instances also share the prototype object's members.

An object is tied to its prototype by an internal property. Firefox, Safari, and Chrome expose this property to developers as __proto__; other browsers do not allow script access to this property. Any time you create a new instance of a built-in type, such as Object or Array, these instances automatically have an instance of Object as their prototype.

Consequently, objects can have two types of members: instance members (also called "own" members) and prototype members. Instance members exist directly on the object instance itself, whereas prototype members are inherited from the object prototype. Consider the following example:

```
var book = {
    title: "High Performance JavaScript",
    publisher: "Yahoo! Press"
};

alert(book.toString());   //"[object Object]"
```

In this code, the book object has two instance members: title and publisher. Note that there is no definition for the method toString() but that the method is called and behaves appropriately without throwing an error. The toString() method is a prototype member that the book object is inheriting. Figure 2-9 shows this relationship.

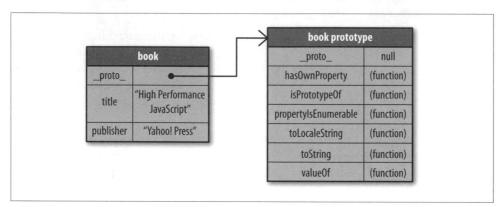

Figure 2-9. Relationship between an instance and prototype

The process of resolving an object member is very similar to resolving a variable. When book.toString() is called, the search for a member named "toString" begins on the object instance. Since book doesn't have a member named toString, the search then flows to the prototype object, where the toString() method is found and executed. In this way, book has access to every property or method on its prototype.

You can determine whether an object has an instance member with a given name by using the hasOwnProperty() method and passing in the name of the member. To determine whether an object has access to a property with a given name, you can use the in operator. For example:

```
var book = {
    title: "High Performance JavaScript",
    publisher: "Yahoo! Press"
};

alert(book.hasOwnProperty("title"));      //true
alert(book.hasOwnProperty("toString"));   //false

alert("title" in book);      //true
alert("toString" in book);   //true
```

In this code, hasOwnProperty() returns true when "title" is passed in because title is an object instance; the method returns false when "toString" is passed in because it doesn't exist on the instance. When each property name is used with the in operator, the result is true both times because it searches the instance and prototype.

Prototype Chains

The prototype of an object determines the type or types of which it is an instance. By default, all objects are instances of Object and inherit all of the basic methods, such as toString(). You can create a prototype of another type by defining and using a constructor. For example:

```
function Book(title, publisher){
    this.title = title;
    this.publisher = publisher;
}

Book.prototype.sayTitle = function(){
    alert(this.title);
};

var book1 = new Book("High Performance JavaScript", "Yahoo! Press");
var book2 = new Book("JavaScript: The Good Parts", "Yahoo! Press");

alert(book1 instanceof Book);    //true
alert(book1 instanceof Object);  //true

book1.sayTitle();           //"High Performance JavaScript"
alert(book1.toString());    //"[object Object]"
```

The Book constructor is used to create a new instance of Book. The book1 instance's prototype (__proto__) is Book.prototype, and Book.prototype's prototype is Object. This creates a prototype chain from which both book1 and book2 inherit their members. Figure 2-10 shows this relationship.

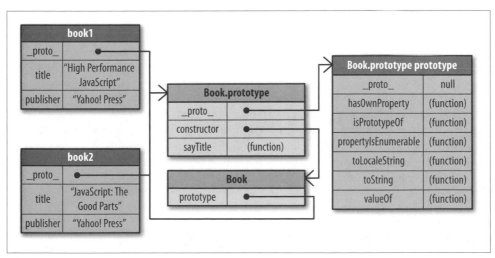

Figure 2-10. Prototype chains

Note that both instances of Book share the same prototype chain. Each instance has its own title and publisher properties, but everything else is inherited through prototypes.

Now when `book1.toString()` is called, the search must go deeper into the prototype chain to resolve the object member "toString". As you might suspect, the deeper into the prototype chain that a member exists, the slower it is to retrieve. Figure 2-11 shows the relationship between member depth in the prototype and time to access the member.

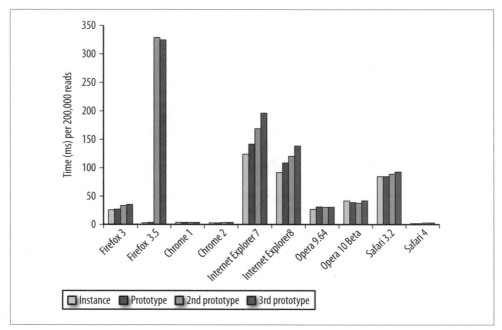

Figure 2-11. Data access going deeper into the prototype chain

Although newer browsers with optimizing JavaScript engines perform this task well, older browsers—especially Internet Explorer and Firefox 3.5—incur a performance penalty with each additional step into the prototype chain. Keep in mind that the process of looking up an instance member is still more expensive than accessing data from a literal or a local variable, so adding more overhead to traverse the prototype chain just amplifies this effect.

Nested Members

Since object members may contain other members, it's not uncommon to see patterns such as `window.location.href` in JavaScript code. These nested members cause the JavaScript engine to go through the object member resolution process each time a dot is encountered. Figure 2-12 shows the relationship between object member depth and time to access.

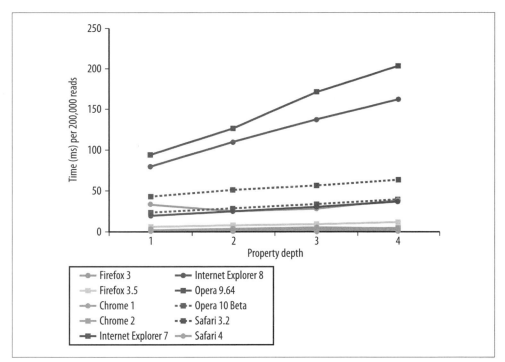

Figure 2-12. Access time related to property depth

It should come as no surprise, then, that the deeper the nested member, the slower the data is accessed. Evaluating `location.href` is always faster than `window.location.href`, which is faster than `window.location.href.toString()`. If these properties aren't on the object instances, then member resolution will take longer as the prototype chain is searched at each point.

> In most browsers, there is no discernible difference between accessing an object member using dot notation (`object.name`) versus bracket notation (`object["name"]`). Safari is the only browser in which dot notation is consistently faster, but not by enough to suggest not using bracket notation.

Caching Object Member Values

With all of the performance issues related to object members, it's easy to believe that they should be avoided whenever possible. To be more accurate, you should be careful to use object member only when necessary. For instance, there's no reason to read the value of an object member more than once in a single function:

```
function hasEitherClass(element, className1, className2){
    return element.className == className1 || element.className == className2;
}
```

In this code, `element.className` is accessed twice. Clearly this value isn't going to change during the course of the function, yet there are still two object member lookups performed. You can eliminate one property lookup by storing the value in a local variable and using that instead:

```
function hasEitherClass(element, className1, className2){
    var currentClassName = element.className;
    return currentClassName == className1 || currentClassName == className2;
}
```

This rewritten version of the function limits the number of member lookups to one. Since both member lookups were reading the property's value, it makes sense to read the value once and store it in a local variable. That local variable then is much faster to access.

Generally speaking, if you're going to read an object property more than one time in a function, it's best to store that property value in a local variable. The local variable can then be used in place of the property to avoid the performance overhead of another property lookup. This is especially important when dealing with nested object members that have a more dramatic effect on execution speed.

JavaScript namespacing, such as the technique used in YUI, is a source of frequently accessed nested properties. For example:

```
function toggle(element){
    if (YAHOO.util.Dom.hasClass(element, "selected")){
        YAHOO.util.Dom.removeClass(element, "selected");
        return false;
    } else {
        YAHOO.util.Dom.addClass(element, "selected");
        return true;
    }
}
```

This code repeats `YAHOO.util.Dom` three times to access three different methods. For each method there are three member lookups, for a total of nine, making this code quite inefficient. A better approach is to store `YAHOO.util.Dom` in a local variable and then access that local variable:

```
function toggle(element){
    var Dom = YAHOO.util.Dom;
    if (Dom.hasClass(element, "selected")){
        Dom.removeClass(element, "selected");
        return false;
    } else {
        Dom.addClass(element, "selected");
        return true;
    }
}
```

The total number of member lookups in this code has been reduced from nine to five. You should never look up an object member more than once within a single function, unless the value may have changed.

 One word of caution: it is not recommended to use this technique for object methods. Many object methods use `this` to determine the context in which they are being called, and storing a method in a local variable causes `this` to be bound to `window`. Changing the value of `this` leads to programmatic errors, as the JavaScript engine won't be able to resolve the appropriate object members it may depend on.

Summary

Where you store and access data in JavaScript can have a measurable impact on the overall performance of your code. There are four places to access data from: literal values, variables, array items, and object members. These locations all have different performance considerations.

- Literal values and local variables can be accessed very quickly, whereas array items and object members take longer.

- Local variables are faster to access than out-of-scope variables because they exist in the first variable object of the scope chain. The further into the scope chain a variable is, the longer it takes to access. Global variables are always the slowest to access because they are always last in the scope chain.

- Avoid the `with` statement because it augments the execution context scope chain. Also, be careful with the `catch` clause of a `try-catch` statement because it has the same effect.

- Nested object members incur significant performance impact and should be minimized.

- The deeper into the prototype chain that a property or method exists, the slower it is to access.

- Generally speaking, you can improve the performance of JavaScript code by storing frequently used object members, array items, and out-of-scope variables in local variables. You can then access the local variables faster than the originals.

By using these strategies, you can greatly improve the perceived performance of a web application that requires a large amount of JavaScript code.

CHAPTER 3

DOM Scripting

Stoyan Stefanov

DOM scripting is expensive, and it's a common performance bottleneck in rich web applications. This chapter discusses the areas of DOM scripting that can have a negative effect on an application's responsiveness and gives recommendations on how to improve response time. The three categories of problems discussed in the chapter include:

- Accessing and modifying DOM elements
- Modifying the styles of DOM elements and causing repaints and reflows
- Handling user interaction through DOM events

But first—what is DOM and why is it slow?

DOM in the Browser World

The Document Object Model (DOM) is a language-independent application interface (API) for working with XML and HTML documents. In the browser, you mostly work with HTML documents, although it's not uncommon for web applications to retrieve XML documents and use the DOM APIs to access data from those documents.

Even though the DOM is a language-independent API, in the browser the interface is implemented in JavaScript. Since most of the work in client-side scripting has to do with the underlying document, DOM is an important part of everyday JavaScript coding.

It's common across browsers to keep DOM and JavaScript implementations independent of each other. In Internet Explorer, for example, the JavaScript implementation is called JScript and lives in a library file called *jscript.dll*, while the DOM implementation lives in another library, *mshtml.dll* (internally called Trident). This separation allows other technologies and languages, such as VBScript, to benefit from the DOM and the rendering functionality Trident has to offer. Safari uses WebKit's WebCore for DOM and rendering and has a separate JavaScriptCore engine (dubbed SquirrelFish in its latest version). Google Chrome also uses WebCore libraries from WebKit for rendering pages but implements its own JavaScript engine called V8. In Firefox, Spider-Monkey (the latest version is called TraceMonkey) is the JavaScript implementation, a separate part of the Gecko rendering engine.

Inherently Slow

What does that mean for performance? Simply having two separate pieces of functionality interfacing with each other will always come at a cost. An excellent analogy is to think of DOM as a piece of land and JavaScript (meaning ECMAScript) as another piece of land, both connected with a toll bridge (see John Hrvatin, Microsoft, MIX09, *http://videos.visitmix.com/MIX09/T53F*). Every time your ECMAScript needs access to the DOM, you have to cross this bridge and pay the performance toll fee. The more you work with the DOM, the more you pay. So the general recommendation is to cross that bridge as few times as possible and strive to stay in ECMAScript land. The rest of the chapter focuses on what this means exactly and where to look in order to make user interactions faster.

DOM Access and Modification

Simply accessing a DOM element comes at a price—the "toll fee" discussed earlier. Modifying elements is even more expensive because it often causes the browser to recalculate changes in the page geometry.

Naturally, the worst case of accessing or modifying elements is when you do it in loops, and especially in loops over HTML collections.

Just to give you an idea of the scale of the problems with DOM scripting, consider this simple example:

```
function innerHTMLLoop() {
    for (var count = 0; count < 15000; count++) {
        document.getElementById('here').innerHTML += 'a';
    }
}
```

This is a function that updates the contents of a page element in a loop. The problem with this code is that for every loop iteration, the element is accessed twice: once to read the value of the `innerHTML` property and once to write it.

A more efficient version of this function would use a local variable to store the updated contents and then write the value only once at the end of the loop:

```
function innerHTMLLoop2() {
    var content = '';
    for (var count = 0; count < 15000; count++) {
        content += 'a';
    }
    document.getElementById('here').innerHTML += content;
}
```

This new version of the function will run much faster across all browsers. Figure 3-1 shows the results of measuring the time improvement in different browsers. The y-axis in the figure (as with all the figures in this chapter) shows execution time improvement, i.e., how much faster it is to use one approach versus another. In this case, for example, using `innerHTMLLoop2()` is 155 times faster than `innerHTMLLoop()` in IE6.

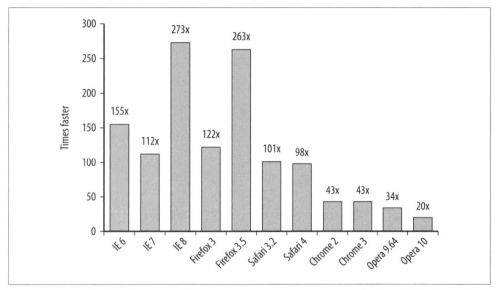

Figure 3-1. One benefit of staying within ECMAScript: innerHTMLLoop2() is hundreds of times faster than innerHTMLLoop()

As these results clearly show, the more you access the DOM, the slower your code executes. Therefore, the general rule of thumb is this: touch the DOM lightly, and stay within ECMAScript as much as possible.

innerHTML Versus DOM methods

Over the years, there have been many discussions in the web development community over this question: is it better to use the nonstandard but well-supported `innerHTML` property to update a section of a page, or is it best to use only the pure DOM methods, such as `document.createElement()`? Leaving the web standards discussion aside, does it matter for performance? The answer is: it matters increasingly less, but still, `innerHTML` is faster in all browsers except the latest WebKit-based ones (Chrome and Safari).

Let's examine a sample task of creating a table of 1000 rows in two ways:

- By concatenating an HTML string and updating the DOM with `innerHTML`
- By using only standard DOM methods such as `document.createElement()` and `document.createTextNode()`

Our example table has content similar to content that would have come from a Content Management System (CMS). The end result is shown in Figure 3-2.

id	yes?	name	url	action
1	And the answer is... yes	my name is #1	http://example.org/1.html	• edit • delete
2	And the answer is... no	my name is #2	http://example.org/2.html	• edit • delete

Figure 3-2. End result of generating an HTML table with 1,000 rows and 5 columns

The code to generate the table with `innerHTML` is as follows:

```
function tableInnerHTML() {
    var i, h = ['<table border="1" width="100%">'];

    h.push('<thead>');

    h.push('<tr><th>id<\/th><th>yes?<\/th><th>name<\/th><th>url<\/th><th>action<\/th>
<\/tr>');
    h.push('<\/thead>');
    h.push('<tbody>');
    for (i = 1; i <= 1000; i++) {
        h.push('<tr><td>');
        h.push(i);
        h.push('<\/td><td>');
        h.push('And the answer is... ' + (i % 2 ? 'yes' : 'no'));
        h.push('<\/td><td>');
        h.push('my name is #' + i);
        h.push('<\/td><td>');
        h.push('<a href="http://example.org/' + i + '.html">http://example.org/'
+ i + '.html<\/a>');
        h.push('<\/td><td>');
        h.push('<ul>');
        h.push(' <li><a href="edit.php?id=' + i + '">edit<\/a><\/li>');
        h.push(' <li><a href="delete.php?id="' + i + '-id001">delete<\/a><\/li>');
        h.push('<\/ul>');
        h.push('<\/td>');
        h.push('<\/tr>');
```

```
    }

    h.push('<\/tbody>');
    h.push('<\/table>');

    document.getElementById('here').innerHTML = h.join('');
};
```

In order to generate the same table with DOM methods alone, the code is a little more
verbose:

```
function tableDOM() {

    var i, table, thead, tbody, tr, th, td, a, ul, li;

    tbody = document.createElement('tbody');

    for (i = 1; i <= 1000; i++) {

        tr = document.createElement('tr');
        td = document.createElement('td');
        td.appendChild(document.createTextNode((i % 2) ? 'yes' : 'no'));
        tr.appendChild(td);
        td = document.createElement('td');
        td.appendChild(document.createTextNode(i));
        tr.appendChild(td);
        td = document.createElement('td');
        td.appendChild(document.createTextNode('my name is #' + i));
        tr.appendChild(td);

        a = document.createElement('a');
        a.setAttribute('href', 'http://example.org/' + i + '.html');
        a.appendChild(document.createTextNode('http://example.org/' + i +
'.html'));
        td = document.createElement('td');
        td.appendChild(a);
        tr.appendChild(td);

        ul = document.createElement('ul');
        a = document.createElement('a');
        a.setAttribute('href', 'edit.php?id=' + i);
        a.appendChild(document.createTextNode('edit'));
        li = document.createElement('li');
        li.appendChild(a);
        ul.appendChild(li);
        a = document.createElement('a');
        a.setAttribute('href', 'delete.php?id=' + i);
        a.appendChild(document.createTextNode('delete'));
        li = document.createElement('li');
        li.appendChild(a);
        ul.appendChild(li);
        td = document.createElement('td');
        td.appendChild(ul);
        tr.appendChild(td);

        tbody.appendChild(tr);
```

```
    }

    tr = document.createElement('tr');
    th = document.createElement('th');
    th.appendChild(document.createTextNode('yes?'));
    tr.appendChild(th);
    th = document.createElement('th');
    th.appendChild(document.createTextNode('id'));
    tr.appendChild(th);
    th = document.createElement('th');
    th.appendChild(document.createTextNode('name'));
    tr.appendChild(th);
    th = document.createElement('th');
    th.appendChild(document.createTextNode('url'));
    tr.appendChild(th);
    th = document.createElement('th');
    th.appendChild(document.createTextNode('action'));
    tr.appendChild(th);

    thead = document.createElement('thead');
    thead.appendChild(tr);
    table = document.createElement('table');
    table.setAttribute('border', 1);
    table.setAttribute('width', '100%');
    table.appendChild(thead);
    table.appendChild(tbody);

    document.getElementById('here').appendChild(table);
};
```

The results of generating the HTML table using innerHTML as compared to using pure DOM methods are shown in Figure 3-3. The benefits of innerHTML are more obvious in older browser versions (innerHTML is 3.6 times faster in IE6), but the benefits are less pronounced in newer versions. And in newer WebKit-based browsers it's the opposite: using DOM methods is slightly faster. So the decision about which approach to take will depend on the browsers your users are commonly using, as well as your coding preferences.

 As a side note, keep in mind that this example used string concatenation, which is not optimal in older IE versions (see Chapter 5). Using an array to concatenate large strings will make innerHTML even faster in those browsers.

Using innerHTML will give you faster execution in most browsers in performance-critical operations that require updating a large part of the HTML page. But for most everyday cases there isn't a big difference, and so you should consider readability, maintenance, team preferences, and coding conventions when deciding on your approach.

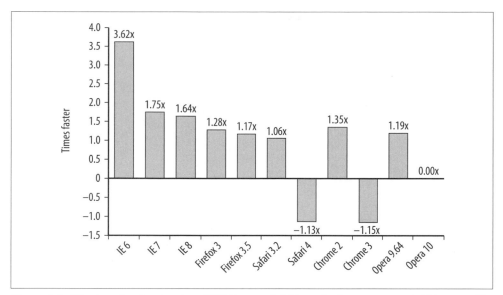

Figure 3-3. The benefit of using innerHTML over DOM methods to create a 1,000-row table; innerHTML is more than three times faster in IE6 and slightly slower in the latest WebKit browsers

Cloning Nodes

Another way of updating page contents using DOM methods is to clone existing DOM elements instead of creating new ones—in other words, using `element.cloneNode()` (where `element` is an existing node) instead of `document.createElement()`.

Cloning nodes is more efficient in most browsers, but not by a big margin. Regenerating the table from the previous example by creating the repeating elements only once and then copying them results in slightly faster execution times:

- 2% in IE8, but no change in IE6 and IE7
- Up to 5.5% in Firefox 3.5 and Safari 4
- 6% in Opera (but no savings in Opera 10)
- 10% in Chrome 2 and 3% in Chrome 3

As an illustration, here's a partial code listing for generating the table using `element.cloneNode()`:

```
function tableClonedDOM() {

    var i, table, thead, tbody, tr, th, td, a, ul, li,
        oth = document.createElement('th'),
        otd = document.createElement('td'),
        otr = document.createElement('tr'),
        oa  = document.createElement('a'),
        oli = document.createElement('li'),
```

```
        oul = document.createElement('ul');

    tbody = document.createElement('tbody');

    for (i = 1; i <= 1000; i++) {

        tr = otr.cloneNode(false);
        td = otd.cloneNode(false);
        td.appendChild(document.createTextNode((i % 2) ? 'yes' : 'no'));
        tr.appendChild(td);
        td = otd.cloneNode(false);
        td.appendChild(document.createTextNode(i));
        tr.appendChild(td);
        td = otd.cloneNode(false);
        td.appendChild(document.createTextNode('my name is #' + i));
        tr.appendChild(td);

        // ... the rest of the loop ...

    }

    // ... the rest of the table generation ...
}
```

HTML Collections

HTML collections are array-like objects containing DOM node references. Examples of collections are the values returned by the following methods:

- document.getElementsByName()
- document.getElementsByClassName()
- document.getElementsByTagName()

The following properties also return HTML collections:

document.images
    All img elements on the page

document.links
    All a elements

document.forms
    All forms

document.forms[0].elements
    All fields in the first form on the page

These methods and properties return HTMLCollection objects, which are array-like lists. They are not arrays (because they don't have methods such as push() or slice()), but provide a length property just like arrays and allow indexed access to the elements in the list. For example, document.images[1] returns the second element in the collection. As defined in the DOM standard, HTML collections are "assumed to be *live*, meaning that they are automatically updated when the underlying document is updated" (see *http://www.w3.org/TR/DOM-Level-2-HTML/html.html#ID-75708506*).

The HTML collections are in fact queries against the document, and these queries are being reexecuted every time you need up-to-date information, such as the number of elements in the collection (i.e., the collection's `length`). This could be a source of inefficiencies.

Expensive collections

To demonstrate that the collections are live, consider the following snippet:

```
// an accidentally infinite loop
var alldivs = document.getElementsByTagName('div');
for (var i = 0; i < alldivs.length; i++) {
    document.body.appendChild(document.createElement('div'))
}
```

This code looks like it simply doubles the number of `div` elements on the page. It loops through the existing `divs` and creates a new `div` every time, appending it to the `body`. But this is in fact an infinite loop because the loop's exit condition, `alldivs.length`, increases by one with every iteration, reflecting the current state of the underlying document.

Looping through HTML collections like this may lead to logic mistakes, but it's also slower, due to the fact that the query needs to run on every iteration (see Figure 3-4).

As discussed in Chapter 4, accessing an array's `length` property in loop control conditions is not recommended. Accessing a collection's `length` is even slower than accessing a regular array's `length` because it means rerunning the query every time. This is demonstrated by the following example, which takes a collection `coll`, copies it into an array `arr`, and then compares how much time it takes to iterate through each.

Consider a function that copies an HTML collection into a regular array:

```
function toArray(coll) {
    for (var i = 0, a = [], len = coll.length; i < len; i++) {
        a[i] = coll[i];
    }
    return a;
}
```

And setting up a collection and a copy of it into an array:

```
var coll = document.getElementsByTagName('div');
var ar   = toArray(coll);
```

The two functions to compare would be:

```
//slower
function loopCollection() {
    for (var count = 0; count < coll.length; count++) {
        /* do nothing */
    }
```

```
    }

    // faster
    function loopCopiedArray() {
        for (var count = 0; count < arr.length; count++) {
            /* do nothing */
        }
    }
```

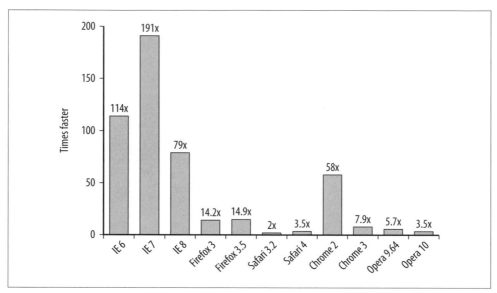

Figure 3-4. Looping over an array is significantly faster than looping through an HTML collection of the same size and content

When the `length` of the collection is accessed on every iteration, it causes the collection to be updated and has a significant performance penalty across all browsers. The way to optimize this is to simply cache the length of the collection into a variable and use this variable to compare in the loop's exit condition:

```
    function loopCacheLengthCollection() {
        var coll = document.getElementsByTagName('div'),
            len = coll.length;
        for (var count = 0; count < len; count++) {
            /* do nothing */
        }
    }
```

This function will run about as fast as `loopCopiedArray()`.

For many use cases that require a single loop over a relatively small collection, just caching the `length` of the collection is good enough. But looping over an array is faster that looping over a collection, so if the elements of the collection are copied into an array first, accessing their properties is faster. Keep in mind that this comes at the price of an extra step and another loop over the collection, so it's important to profile and decide whether using an array copy will be beneficial in your specific case.

Consult the function `toArray()` shown earlier for an example of a generic collection-to-array function.

Local variables when accessing collection elements

The previous example used just an empty loop, but what happens when the elements of the collection are accessed within the loop?

In general, for any type of DOM access it's best to use a local variable when the same DOM property or method is accessed more than once. When looping over a collection, the first optimization is to store the collection in a local variable and cache the `length` outside the loop, and then use a local variable inside the loop for elements that are accessed more than once.

In the next example, three properties of each element are accessed within the loop. The slowest version accesses the global `document` every time, an optimized version caches a reference to the collection, and the fastest version also stores the current element of the collection into a variable. All three versions cache the length of the collection.

```
// slow
function collectionGlobal() {

    var coll = document.getElementsByTagName('div'),
        len = coll.length,
        name = '';
    for (var count = 0; count < len; count++) {
        name = document.getElementsByTagName('div')[count].nodeName;
        name = document.getElementsByTagName('div')[count].nodeType;
        name = document.getElementsByTagName('div')[count].tagName;
    }
    return name;

};

// faster
function collectionLocal() {

    var coll = document.getElementsByTagName('div'),
        len = coll.length,
        name = '';
    for (var count = 0; count < len; count++) {
        name = coll[count].nodeName;
        name = coll[count].nodeType;
        name = coll[count].tagName;
    }
    return name;

};

// fastest
```

```
function collectionNodesLocal() {

    var coll = document.getElementsByTagName('div'),
        len = coll.length,
        name = '',
        el = null;
    for (var count = 0; count < len; count++) {
        el = coll[count];
        name = el.nodeName;
        name = el.nodeType;
        name = el.tagName;
    }
    return name;

};
```

Figure 3-5 shows the benefits of optimizing collection loops. The first bar plots how many times faster it is to access the collection through a local reference, and the second bar shows that there's additional benefit to caching collection items when they are accessed multiple times.

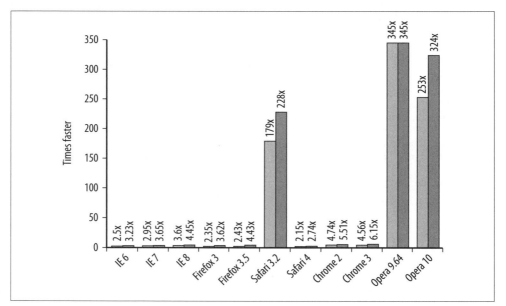

Figure 3-5. Benefit of using local variables to store references to a collection and its elements during loops

Walking the DOM

The DOM API provides multiple avenues to access specific parts of the overall document structure. In cases when you can choose between approaches, it's beneficial to use the most efficient API for a specific job.

Crawling the DOM

Often you need to start from a DOM element and work with the surrounding elements, maybe recursively iterating over all children. You can do so by using the `childNodes` collection or by getting each element's sibling using `nextSibling`.

Consider these two equivalent approaches to a nonrecursive visit of an element's children:

```
function testNextSibling() {
    var el = document.getElementById('mydiv'),
        ch = el.firstChild,
        name = '';
    do {
        name = ch.nodeName;
    } while (ch = ch.nextSibling);
    return name;
};

function testChildNodes() {
    var el = document.getElementById('mydiv'),
        ch = el.childNodes,
        len = ch.length,
        name = '';
    for (var count = 0; count < len; count++) {
        name = ch[count].nodeName;
    }
    return name;
};
```

Bear in mind that `childNodes` is a collection and should be approached carefully, caching the `length` in loops so it's not updated on every iteration.

The two approaches are mostly equal in terms of execution time across browsers. But in IE, `nextSibling` performs much better than `childNodes`. In IE6, `nextSibling` is 16 times faster, and in IE7 it's 105 times faster. Given these results, using `nextSibling` is the preferred method of crawling the DOM in older IE versions in performance-critical cases. In all other cases, it's mostly a question of personal and team preference.

Element nodes

DOM properties such as `childNodes`, `firstChild`, and `nextSibling` don't distinguish between element nodes and other node types, such as comments and text nodes (which are often just spaces between two tags). In many cases, only the element nodes need to be accessed, so in a loop it's likely that the code needs to check the type of node returned and filter out nonelement nodes. This type checking and filtering is unnecessary DOM work.

Many modern browsers offer APIs that only return element nodes. It's better to use those when available, because they'll be faster than if you do the filtering yourself in JavaScript. Table 3-1 lists those convenient DOM properties.

Table 3-1. DOM properties that distinguish element nodes (HTML tags) versus all nodes

Property	Use as a replacement for
children	childNodes
childElementCount	childNodes.length
firstElementChild	firstChild
lastElementChild	lastChild
nextElementSibling	nextSibling
previousElementSibling	previousSibling

All of the properties listed in Table 3-1 are supported as of Firefox 3.5, Safari 4, Chrome 2, and Opera 9.62. Of these properties, IE versions 6, 7, and 8 only support `children`.

Looping over `children` instead of `childNodes` is faster because there are usually less items to loop over. Whitespaces in the HTML source code are actually text nodes, and they are not included in the `children` collection. `children` is faster than `childNodes` across all browsers, although usually not by a big margin—1.5 to 3 times faster. One notable exception is IE, where iterating over the `children` collection is significantly faster than iterating over `childNodes`—24 times faster in IE6 and 124 times faster in IE7.

The Selectors API

When identifying the elements in the DOM to work with, developers often need finer control than methods such as `getElementById()` and `getElementsByTagName()` can provide. Sometimes you combine these calls and iterate over the returned nodes in order to get to the list of elements you need, but this refinement process can become inefficient.

On the other hand, using CSS selectors is a convenient way to identify nodes because developers are already familiar with CSS. Many JavaScript libraries have provided APIs for that purpose, and now recent browser versions provide a method called `querySelectorAll()` as a native browser DOM method. Naturally this approach is faster than using JavaScript and DOM to iterate and narrow down a list of elements.

Consider the following:

```
var elements = document.querySelectorAll('#menu a');
```

The value of `elements` will contain a list of references to all `a` elements found inside an element with `id="menu"`. The method `querySelectorAll()` takes a CSS selector string as an argument and returns a `NodeList`—an array-like object containing matching nodes. The method doesn't return an HTML collection, so the returned nodes do not represent the live structure of the document. This avoids the performance (and potentially logic) issues with HTML collection discussed previously in this chapter.

To achieve the same goal as the preceding code without using `querySelectorAll()`, you will need the more verbose:

```
var elements = document.getElementById('menu').getElementsByTagName('a');
```

In this case `elements` will be an HTML collection, so you'll also need to copy it into an array if you want the exact same type of static list as returned by `querySelectorAll()`.

Using `querySelectorAll()` is even more convenient when you need to work with a union of several queries. For example, if the page has some `div` elements with a class name of "warning" and some with a class of "notice", to get a list of all of them you can use `querySelectorAll()`:

```
var errs = document.querySelectorAll('div.warning, div.notice');
```

Getting the same list without `querySelectorAll()` is considerably more work. One way is to select all `div` elements and iterate through them to filter out the ones you don't need.

```
var errs = [],
    divs = document.getElementsByTagName('div'),
    classname = '';
for (var i = 0, len = divs.length; i < len; i++) {
    classname = divs[i].className;
    if (classname === 'notice' || classname === 'warning') {
        errs.push(divs[i]);
    }
}
```

Comparing the two pieces of code shows that using the Selectors API is 2 to 6 times faster across browsers (Figure 3-6).

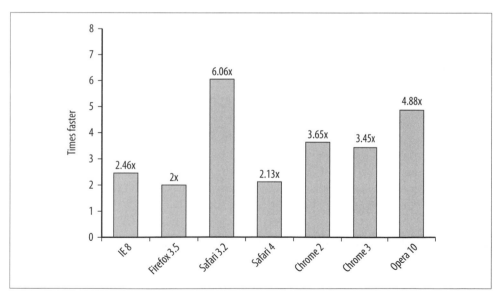

Figure 3-6. The benefit of using the Selectors API over iterating instead of the results of getElementsbyTagName()

The Selectors API is supported natively in browsers as of these versions: Internet Explorer 8, Firefox 3.5, Safari 3.1, Chrome 1, and Opera 10.

As the results in the figure show, it's a good idea to check for support for `document.querySelectorAll()` and use it when available. Also, if you're using a selector API provided by a JavaScript library, make sure the library uses the native API under the hood. If not, you probably just need to upgrade the library version.

You can also take advantage of another method called `querySelector()`, a convenient method that returns only the first node matched by the query.

These two methods are properties of the DOM nodes, so you can use `document.querySelector('.myclass')` to query nodes in the whole document, or you can query a subtree using `elref.querySelector('.myclass')`, where `elref` is a reference to a DOM element.

Repaints and Reflows

Once the browser has downloaded all the components of a page—HTML markup, JavaScript, CSS, images—it parses through the files and creates two internal data structures:

A DOM tree
    A representation of the page structure

A render tree
    A representation of how the DOM nodes will be displayed

The render tree has at least one node for every node of the DOM tree that needs to be displayed (hidden DOM elements don't have a corresponding node in the render tree). Nodes in the render tree are called *frames* or *boxes* in accordance with the CSS model that treats page elements as boxes with padding, margins, borders, and position. Once the DOM and the render trees are constructed, the browser can display ("paint") the elements on the page.

When a DOM change affects the geometry of an element (width and height)—such as a change in the thickness of the border or adding more text to a paragraph, resulting in an additional line—the browser needs to recalculate the geometry of the element as well as the geometry and position of other elements that could have been affected by the change. The browser invalidates the part of the render tree that was affected by the change and reconstructs the render tree. This process is known as a *reflow*. Once the reflow is complete, the browser redraws the affected parts of the screen in a process called *repaint*.

Not all DOM changes affect the geometry. For example, changing the background color of an element won't change its width or height. In this case, there is a repaint only (no reflow), because the layout of the element hasn't changed.

Repaints and reflows are expensive operations and can make the UI of a web application less responsive. As such, it's important to reduce their occurrences whenever possible.

When Does a Reflow Happen?

As mentioned earlier, a reflow is needed whenever layout and geometry change. This happens when:

- Visible DOM elements are added or removed
- Elements change position
- Elements change size (because of a change in margin, padding, border thickness, width, height, etc.)
- Content is changed, e.g., text changes or an image is replaced with one of a different size
- Page renders initially
- Browser window is resized

Depending on the nature of the change, a smaller or bigger part of the render tree needs to be recalculated. Some changes may cause a reflow of the whole page: for example, when a scroll bar appears.

Queuing and Flushing Render Tree Changes

Because of the computation costs associated with each reflow, most browsers optimize the reflow process by queuing changes and performing them in batches. However, you may (often involuntarily) force the queue to be flushed and require that all scheduled changes be applied right away. Flushing the queue happens when you want to retrieve layout information, which means using any of the following:

- `offsetTop`, `offsetLeft`, `offsetWidth`, `offsetHeight`
- `scrollTop`, `scrollLeft`, `scrollWidth`, `scrollHeight`
- `clientTop`, `clientLeft`, `clientWidth`, `clientHeight`
- `getComputedStyle()` (`currentStyle` in IE)

The layout information returned by these properties and methods needs to be up to date, and so the browser has to execute the pending changes in the rendering queue and reflow in order to return the correct values.

During the process of changing styles, it's best not to use any of the properties shown in the preceding list. All of these will flush the render queue, even in cases where you're retrieving layout information that wasn't recently changed or isn't even relevant to the latest changes.

Consider the following example of changing the same style property three times (this is probably not something you'll see in real code, but is an isolated illustration of an important topic):

```
// setting and retrieving styles in succession
var computed,
    tmp = '',
    bodystyle = document.body.style;

if (document.body.currentStyle) { // IE, Opera
    computed = document.body.currentStyle;
} else { // W3C
    computed = document.defaultView.getComputedStyle(document.body, '');
}

// inefficient way of modifying the same property
// and retrieving style information right after
bodystyle.color = 'red';
tmp = computed.backgroundColor;
bodystyle.color = 'white';
tmp = computed.backgroundImage;
bodystyle.color = 'green';
tmp = computed.backgroundAttachment;
```

In this example, the foreground color of the body element is being changed three times, and after every change, a computed style property is retrieved. The retrieved properties—backgroundColor, backgroundImage, and backgroundAttachment—are unrelated to the color being changed. Yet the browser needs to flush the render queue and reflow due to the fact that a computed style property was requested.

A better approach than this inefficient example is to never request layout information while it's being changed. If the computed style retrieval is moved to the end, the code looks like this:

```
bodystyle.color = 'red';
bodystyle.color = 'white';
bodystyle.color = 'green';
tmp = computed.backgroundColor;
tmp = computed.backgroundImage;
tmp = computed.backgroundAttachment;
```

The second example will be faster across all browsers, as seen in Figure 3-7.

Minimizing Repaints and Reflows

Reflows and repaints can be expensive, and therefore a good strategy for responsive applications is to reduce their number. In order to minimize this number, you should combine multiple DOM and style changes into a batch and apply them once.

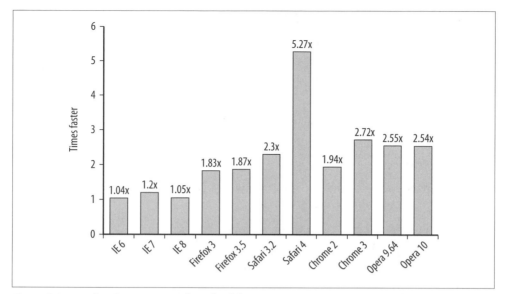

Figure 3-7. Benefit of preventing reflows by delaying access to layout information

Style changes

Consider this example:

```
var el = document.getElementById('mydiv');
el.style.borderLeft = '1px';
el.style.borderRight = '2px';
el.style.padding = '5px';
```

Here there are three style properties being changed, each of them affecting the geometry of the element. In the worst case, this will cause the browser to reflow three times. Most modern browsers optimize for such cases and reflow only once, but it can still be inefficient in older browsers or if there's a separate asynchronous process happening at the same time (i.e., using a timer). If other code is requesting layout information while this code is running, it could cause up to three reflows. Also, the code is touching the DOM four times and can be optimized.

A more efficient way to achieve the same result is to combine all the changes and apply them at once, modifying the DOM only once. This can be done using the `cssText` property:

```
var el = document.getElementById('mydiv');
el.style.cssText = 'border-left: 1px; border-right: 2px; padding: 5px;';
```

Modifying the `cssText` property as shown in the example overwrites existing style information, so if you want to keep the existing styles, you can append this to the `cssText` string:

```
el.style.cssText += '; border-left: 1px;';
```

Another way to apply style changes only once is to change the CSS class name instead of changing the inline styles. This approach is applicable in cases when the styles do not depend on runtime logic and calculations. Changing the CSS class name is cleaner and more maintainable; it helps keep your scripts free of presentation code, although it might come with a slight performance hit because the cascade needs to be checked when changing classes.

```
var el = document.getElementById('mydiv');
el.className = 'active';
```

Batching DOM changes

When you have a number of changes to apply to a DOM element, you can reduce the number of repaints and reflows by following these steps:

1. Take the element off of the document flow.
2. Apply multiple changes.
3. Bring the element back to the document.

This process causes two reflows—one at step 1 and one at step 3. If you omit those steps, every change you make in step 2 could cause its own reflows.

There are three basic ways to modify the DOM off the document:

- Hide the element, apply changes, and show it again.
- Use a document fragment to build a subtree outside of the live DOM and then copy it to the document.
- Copy the original element into an off-document node, modify the copy, and then replace the original element once you're done.

To illustrate the off-document manipulations, consider a list of links that must be updated with more information:

```
<ul id="mylist">
    <li><a href="http://phpied.com">Stoyan</a></li>
    <li><a href="http://julienlecomte.com">Julien</a></li>
</ul>
```

Suppose additional data, already contained in an object, needs to be inserted into this list. The data is defined as:

```
var data = [
  {
    "name": "Nicholas",
    "url": "http://nczonline.net"
  },
  {
    "name": "Ross",
    "url": "http://techfoolery.com"
  }
];
```

The following is a generic function to update a given node with new data:

```
function appendDataToElement(appendToElement, data) {
    var a, li;
    for (var i = 0, max = data.length; i < max; i++) {
        a = document.createElement('a');
        a.href = data[i].url;
        a.appendChild(document.createTextNode(data[i].name));
        li = document.createElement('li');
        li.appendChild(a);
        appendToElement.appendChild(li);
    }
};
```

The most obvious way to update the list with the data without worrying about reflows would be the following:

```
var ul = document.getElementById('mylist');
appendDataToElement(ul, data);
```

Using this approach, however, every new entry from the data array will be appended to the live DOM tree and cause a reflow. As discussed previously, one way to reduce reflows is to temporarily remove the <ul> element from the document flow by changing the display property and then revert it:

```
var ul = document.getElementById('mylist');
ul.style.display = 'none';
appendDataToElement(ul, data);
ul.style.display = 'block';
```

Another way to minimize the number of reflows is to create and update a document fragment, completely off the document, and then append it to the original list. A document fragment is a lightweight version of the document object, and it's designed to help with exactly this type of task—updating and moving nodes around. One syntactically convenient feature of the document fragments is that when you append a fragment to a node, the fragment's children actually get appended, not the fragment itself. The following solution takes one less line of code, causes only one reflow, and touches the live DOM only once:

```
var fragment = document.createDocumentFragment();
appendDataToElement(fragment, data);
document.getElementById('mylist').appendChild(fragment);
```

A third solution would be to create a copy of the node you want to update, work on the copy, and then, once you're done, replace the old node with the newly updated copy:

```
var old = document.getElementById('mylist');
var clone = old.cloneNode(true);
appendDataToElement(clone, data);
old.parentNode.replaceChild(clone, old);
```

The recommendation is to use document fragments (the second solution) whenever possible because they involve the least amount of DOM manipulations and reflows.

The only potential drawback is that the practice of using document fragments is currently underused and some team members may not be familiar with the technique.

Caching Layout Information

As already mentioned, browsers try to minimize the number of reflows by queuing changes and executing them in batches. But when you request layout information such as offsets, scroll values, or computed style values, the browser flushes the queue and applies all the changes in order to return the updated value. It is best to minimize the number of requests for layout information, and when you do request it, assign it to local variables and work with the local values.

Consider an example of moving an element `myElement` diagonally, one pixel at a time, starting from position 100 × 100px and ending at 500 × 500px. In the body of a timeout loop you could use:

```
// inefficient
myElement.style.left = 1 + myElement.offsetLeft + 'px';
myElement.style.top = 1 + myElement.offsetTop + 'px';
if (myElement.offsetLeft >= 500) {
    stopAnimation();
}
```

This is not efficient, though, because every time the element moves, the code requests the offset values, causing the browser to flush the rendering queue and not benefit from its optimizations. A better way to do the same thing is to take the start value position once and assign it to a variable such as `var current = myElement.offsetLeft;`. Then, inside of the animation loop, work with the `current` variable and don't request offsets:

```
current++
myElement.style.left = current + 'px';
myElement.style.top = current + 'px';
if (current >= 500) {
    stopAnimation();
}
```

Take Elements Out of the Flow for Animations

Showing and hiding parts of a page in an expand/collapse manner is a common interaction pattern. It often includes geometry animation of the area being expanded, which pushes down the rest of the content on the page.

Reflows sometimes affect only a small part of the render tree, but they can affect a larger portion, or even the whole tree. The less the browser needs to reflow, the more responsive your application will be. So when an animation at the top of the page pushes down almost the whole page, this will cause a big reflow and can be expensive, appearing choppy to the user. The more nodes in the render tree that need recalculation, the worse it becomes.

A technique to avoid a reflow of a big part of the page is to use the following steps:

1. Use absolute positioning for the element you want to animate on the page, taking it out of the layout flow of the page.
2. Animate the element. When it expands, it will temporarily cover part of the page. This is a repaint, but only of a small part of the page instead of a reflow and repaint of a big page chunk.
3. When the animation is done, restore the positioning, thereby pushing down the rest of the document only once.

IE and :hover

Since version 7, IE can apply the `:hover` CSS pseudo-selector on any element (in strict mode). However, if you have a significant number of elements with a `:hover`, the responsiveness degrades. The problem is even more visible in IE 8.

For example, if you create a table with 500–1000 rows and 5 columns and use `tr:hover` to change the background color and highlight the row the user is on, the performance degrades as the user moves over the table. The highlight is slow to apply, and the CPU usage increases to 80%–90%. So avoid this effect when you work with a large number of elements, such as big tables or long item lists.

Event Delegation

When there are a large number of elements on a page and each of them has one or more event handlers attached (such as `onclick`), this may affect performance. Attaching every handler comes at a price—either in the form of heavier pages (more markup or JavaScript code) or in the form of runtime execution time. The more DOM nodes you need to touch and modify, the slower your application, especially because the event attaching phase usually happens at the `onload` (or `DOMContentReady`) event, which is a busy time for every interaction-rich web page. Attaching events takes processing time, and, in addition, the browser needs to keep track of each handler, which takes up memory. And at the end of it, a great number of these event handlers might never be needed (because the user clicked one button or link, not all 100 of them, for example), so a lot of the work might not be necessary.

A simple and elegant technique for handling DOM events is event delegation. It's based on the fact that events bubble up and can be handled by a parent element. With event delegation, you attach only one handler on a wrapper element to handle all events that happen to the children descendant of that parent wrapper.

According to the DOM standard, each event has three phases:

- Capturing
- At target

- Bubbling

Capturing is not supported by IE, but bubbling is good enough for the purposes of delegation. Consider a page with the structure shown in Figure 3-8.

Figure 3-8. An example DOM tree

When the user clicks the "menu #1" link, the click event is first received by the `<a>` element. Then it bubbles up the DOM tree and is received by the `<li>` element, then the `<ul>`, then the `<div>`, and so on, all the way to the top of the document and even the `window`. This allows you to attach only one event handler to a parent element and receive notifications for all events that happen to the children.

Suppose that you want to provide a progressively enhanced Ajax experience for the document shown in the figure. If the user has JavaScript turned off, then the links in the menu work normally and reload the page. But if JavaScript is on and the user agent is capable enough, you want to intercept all clicks, prevent the default behavior (which is to follow the link), send an Ajax request to get the content, and update a portion of the page without a refresh. To do this using event delegation, you can attach a click listener to the UL "menu" element that wraps all links and inspect all clicks to see whether they come from a link.

```
document.getElementById('menu').onclick = function(e) {

    // x-browser target
    e = e || window.event;
    var target = e.target || e.srcElement;

    var pageid, hrefparts;

    // only interesed in hrefs
    // exit the function on non-link clicks
    if (target.nodeName !== 'A') {
        return;
    }

    // figure out page ID from the link
    hrefparts = target.href.split('/');
    pageid = hrefparts[hrefparts.length - 1];
```

```
    pageid = pageid.replace('.html', '');

    // update the page
    ajaxRequest('xhr.php?page=' + id, updatePageContents);

    // x-browser prevent default action and cancel bubbling
    if (typeof e.preventDefault === 'function') {
        e.preventDefault();
        e.stopPropagation();
    } else {
        e.returnValue = false;
        e.cancelBubble = true;
    }

};
```

As you can see, the event delegation technique is not complicated; you only need to inspect events to see whether they come from elements you're interested in. There's a little bit of verbose cross-browser code, but if you move this part to a reusable library, the code becomes pretty clean. The cross-browser parts are:

- Access to the event object and identifying the source (target) of the event
- Cancel the bubbling up the document tree (optional)
- Prevent the default action (optional, but needed in this case because the task was to trap the links and not follow them)

Summary

DOM access and manipulation are an important part of modern web applications. But every time you cross the bridge from ECMAScript to DOM-land, it comes at a cost. To reduce the performance costs related to DOM scripting, keep the following in mind:

- Minimize DOM access, and try to work as much as possible in JavaScript.
- Use local variables to store DOM references you'll access repeatedly.
- Be careful when dealing with HTML collections because they represent the live, underlying document. Cache the collection `length` into a variable and use it when iterating, and make a copy of the collection into an array for heavy work on collections.
- Use faster APIs when available, such as `querySelectorAll()` and `firstElementChild`.
- Be mindful of repaints and reflows; batch style changes, manipulate the DOM tree "offline," and cache and minimize access to layout information.
- Position absolutely during animations, and use drag and drop proxies.
- Use event delegation to minimize the number of event handlers.

Algorithms and Flow Control

The overall structure of your code is one of the main determinants as to how fast it will execute. Having a very small amount of code doesn't necessarily mean that it will run quickly, and having a large amount of code doesn't necessarily mean that it will run slowly. A lot of the performance impact is directly related to how the code has been organized and how you're attempting to solve a given problem.

The techniques in this chapter aren't necessarily unique to JavaScript and are often taught as performance optimizations for other languages. There are some deviations from advice given for other languages, though, as there are many more JavaScript engines to deal with and their quirks need to be considered, but all of the techniques are based on prevailing computer science knowledge.

Loops

In most programming languages, the majority of code execution time is spent within loops. Looping over a series of values is one of the most frequently used patterns in programming and as such is also one of the areas where efforts to improve performance must be focused. Understanding the performance impact of loops in JavaScript is especially important, as infinite or long-running loops severely impact the overall user experience.

Types of Loops

ECMA-262, 3rd Edition, the specification that defines JavaScript's basic syntax and behavior, defines four types of loops. The first is the standard for loop, which shares its syntax with other C-like languages:

```
for (var i=0; i < 10; i++){
    //loop body
}
```

The for loop tends to be the most commonly used JavaScript looping construct. There are four parts to the for loop: initialization, pretest condition, post-execute, and the loop body. When a for loop is encountered, the initialization code is executed first, followed by the pretest condition. If the pretest condition evaluates to true, then the body of the loop is executed. After the body is executed, the post-execute code is run. The perceived encapsulation of the for loop makes it a favorite of developers.

 Note that placing a var statement in the initialization part of a for loop creates a function-level variable, not a loop-level one. JavaScript has only function-level scope, and so defining a new variable inside of a for loop is the same as defining a new function outside of the loop.

The second type of loop is the while loop. A while loop is a simple pretest loop comprised of a pretest condition and a loop body:

```
var i = 0;
while(i < 10){
    //loop body
    i++;
}
```

Before the loop body is executed, the pretest condition is evaluated. If the condition evaluates to true, then the loop body is executed; otherwise, the loop body is skipped. Any for loop can also be written as a while loop and vice versa.

The third type of loop is the do-while loop. A do-while loop is the only post-test loop available in JavaScript and is made up of two parts, the loop body and the post-test condition:

```
var i = 0;
do {
    //loop body
} while (i++ < 10);
```

In a do-while loop, the loop body is always executed at least once, and the post-test condition determines whether the loop should be executed again.

The fourth and last loop is the for-in loop. This loop has a very special purpose: it enumerates the named properties of any object. The basic format is as follows:

```
for (var prop in object){
    //loop body
}
```

Each time the loop is executed, the prop variable is filled with the name of another property (a string) that exists on the object until all properties have been returned. The returned properties are both those that exist on the object instance and those inherited through its prototype chain.

Loop Performance

A constant source of debate regarding loop performance is which loop to use. Of the four loop types provided by JavaScript, only one of them is significantly slower than the others: the `for-in` loop.

Since each iteration through the loop results in a property lookup either on the instance or on a prototype, the `for-in` loop has considerably more overhead per iteration and is therefore slower than the other loops. For the same number of loop iterations, a `for-in` loop can end up as much as seven times slower than the other loop types. For this reason, it's recommended to avoid the `for-in` loop unless your intent is to iterate over an unknown number of object properties. If you have a finite, known list of properties to iterate over, it is faster to use one of the other loop types and use a pattern such as this:

```
var props = ["prop1", "prop2"],
    i = 0;

while (i < props.length){
    process(object[props[i]]);
}
```

This code creates an array whose members are property names. The `while` loop is used to iterate over this small number of properties and process the appropriate member on `object`. Rather than looking up each and every property on `object`, the code focuses on only the properties of interest, saving loop overhead and time.

 You should never use `for-in` to iterate over members of an array.

Aside from the `for-in` loop, all other loop types have equivalent performance characteristics such that it's not useful to try to determine which is fastest. The choice of loop type should be based on your requirements rather than performance concerns.

If loop type doesn't contribute to loop performance, then what does? There are actually just two factors:

- Work done per iteration
- Number of iterations

By decreasing either or both of these, you can positively impact the overall performance of the loop.

Decreasing the work per iteration

It stands to reason that if a single pass through a loop takes a long time to execute, then multiple passes through the loop will take even longer. Limiting the number of expensive operations done in the loop body is a good way to speed up the entire loop.

A typical array-processing loop can be created using any of the three faster loop types. The code is most frequently written as follows:

```
//original loops
for (var i=0; i < items.length; i++){
    process(items[i]);
}

var j=0;
while (j < items.length){
    process(items[j++]]);
}

var k=0;
do {
    process(items[k++]);
} while (k < items.length);
```

In each of these loops, there are several operations happening each time the loop body is executed:

1. One property lookup (`items.length`) in the control condition
2. One comparison (`i < items.length`) in the control condition
3. One comparison to see whether the control condition evaluates to `true` (`i < items.length == true`)
4. One increment operation (`i++`)
5. One array lookup (`items[i]`)
6. One function call (`process(items[i])`)

There's a lot going on per iteration of these simple loops, even though there's not much code. The speed at which the code will execute is largely determined by what `process()` does to each item, but even so, reducing the total number of operations per iteration can greatly improve the overall loop performance.

The first step in optimizing the amount of work in a loop is to minimize the number of object member and array item lookups. As discussed in Chapter 2, these take significantly longer to access in most browsers versus local variables or literal values. The previous examples do a property lookup for `items.length` each and every time through the loop. Doing so is wasteful, as this value won't change during the execution of the loop and is therefore an unnecessary performance hit. You can improve the loop performance easily by doing the property lookup once, storing the value in a local variable, and then using that variable in the control condition:

```
//minimizing property lookups
for (var i=0, len=items.length; i < len; i++){
    process(items[i]);
}

var j=0,
    count = items.length;
```

```
while (j < count){
    process(items[j++]]);
}

var k=0,
    num = items.length;
do {
    process(items[k++]);
} while (k < num);
```

Each of these rewritten loops makes a single property lookup for the array length prior to the loop executing. This allows the control condition to be comprised solely of local variables and therefore run much faster. Depending on the length of the array, you can save around 25% off the total loop execution time in most browsers (and up to 50% in Internet Explorer).

You can also increase the performance of loops by reversing their order. Frequently, the order in which array items are processed is irrelevant to the task, and so starting at the last item and processing toward the first item is an acceptable alternative. Reversing loop order is a common performance optimization in programming languages but generally isn't very well understood. In JavaScript, reversing a loop does result in a small performance improvement for loops, provided that you eliminate extra operations as a result:

```
//minimizing property lookups and reversing
for (var i=items.length; i--; ){
    process(items[i]);
}

var j = items.length;
while (j--){
    process(items[j]]);
}

var k = items.length-1;
do {
    process(items[k]);
} while (k--);
```

The loops in this example are reversed and combine the control condition with the decrement operation. Each control condition is now simply a comparison against zero. Control conditions are compared against the value true, and any nonzero number is automatically coerced to true, making zero the equivalent of false. Effectively, the control condition has been changed from two comparisons (is the iterator less than the total and is that equal to true?) to just a single comparison (is the value true?). Cutting down from two comparisons per iteration to one speeds up the loops even further. By reversing loops and minimizing property lookups, you can see execution times that are up to 50%–60% faster than the original.

As a comparison to the originals, here are the operations being performed per iteration for these loops:

1. One comparison (`i == true`) in the control condition

2. One decrement operation (`i--`)

3. One array lookup (`items[i]`)

4. One function call (`process(items[i])`)

The new loop code has two fewer operations per iteration, which can lead to increasing performance gains as the number of iterations increases.

 Decreasing the work done per iteration is most effective when the loop has a complexity of *O(n)*. When the loop is more complex than *O(n)*, it is advisable to focus your attention on decreasing the number of iterations.

Decreasing the number of iterations

Even the fastest code in a loop body will add up when iterated thousands of times. Additionally, there is a small amount of performance overhead associated with executing a loop body, which just adds to the overall execution time. Decreasing the number of iterations throughout the loop can therefore lead to greater performance gains. The most well known approach to limiting loop iterations is a pattern called *Duff's Device*.

Duff's Device is a technique of unrolling loop bodies so that each iteration actually does the job of many iterations. Jeff Greenberg is credited with the first published port of Duff's Device to JavaScript from its original implementation in C. A typical implementation looks like this:

```
//credit: Jeff Greenberg
var iterations = Math.floor(items.length / 8),
    startAt    = items.length % 8,
    i          = 0;

do {
    switch(startAt){
        case 0: process(items[i++]);
        case 7: process(items[i++]);
        case 6: process(items[i++]);
        case 5: process(items[i++]);
        case 4: process(items[i++]);
        case 3: process(items[i++]);
        case 2: process(items[i++]);
        case 1: process(items[i++]);
    }
    startAt = 0;
} while (--iterations);
```

The basic idea behind this Duff's Device implementation is that each trip through the loop is allowed a maximum of eight calls to `process()`. The number of iterations through the loop is determined by dividing the total number of items by eight. Because

---

not all numbers are evenly divisible by eight, the `startAt` variable holds the remainder and indicates how many calls to `process()` will occur in the first trip through the loop. If there were 12 items, then the first trip through the loop would call `process()` 4 times, and then the second trip would call `process()` 8 times, for a total of two trips through the loop instead of 12.

A slightly faster version of this algorithm removes the `switch` statement and separates the remainder processing from the main processing:

```
//credit: Jeff Greenberg
var i = items.length % 8;
while(i){
    process(items[i--]);
}

i = Math.floor(items.length / 8);

while(i){
    process(items[i--]);
    process(items[i--]);
    process(items[i--]);
    process(items[i--]);
    process(items[i--]);
    process(items[i--]);
    process(items[i--]);
    process(items[i--]);
}
```

Even though this implementation is now two loops instead of one, it runs faster than the original by removing the `switch` statement from the loop body.

Whether or not it's worthwhile to use Duff's Device, either the original or the modified version, depends largely on the number of iterations you're already doing. In cases where the loop iterations are less than 1,000, you're likely to see only an insignificant amount of performance improvement over using a regular loop construct. As the number of iterations increases past 1,000, however, the efficacy of Duff's Device increases significantly. At 500,000 iterations, for instance, the execution time is up to 70% less than a regular loop.

Function-Based Iteration

The fourth edition of ECMA-262 introduced a new method on the native `array` object call `forEach()`. This method iterates over the members of an array and runs a function on each. The function to be run on each item is passed into `forEach()` as an argument and will receive three arguments when called, which are the array item value, the index of the array item, and the array itself. The following is an example usage:

```
items.forEach(function(value, index, array){
    process(value);
});
```

The forEach() method is implemented natively in Firefox, Chrome, and Safari. Additionally, most JavaScript libraries have the logical equivalent:

```
//YUI 3
Y.Array.each(items, function(value, index, array){
    process(value);
});

//jQuery
jQuery.each(items, function(index, value){
    process(value);
});

//Dojo
dojo.forEach(items, function(value, index, array){
    process(value);
});

//Prototype
items.each(function(value, index){
    process(value);
});

//MooTools
$each(items, function(value, index){
    process(value);
});
```

Even though function-based iteration represents a more convenient method of iteration, it is also quite a bit slower than loop-based iteration. The slowdown can be accounted for by the overhead associated with an extra method being called on each array item. In all cases, function-based iteration takes up to eight times as long as loop-based iteration and therefore isn't a suitable approach when execution time is a significant concern.

Conditionals

Similar in nature to loops, conditionals determine how execution flows through JavaScript. The traditional argument of whether to use if-else statements or a switch statement applies to JavaScript just as it does to other languages. Since different browsers have implemented different flow control optimizations, it is not always clear which technique to use.

if-else Versus switch

The prevailing theory on using if-else versus switch is based on the number of conditions being tested: the larger the number of conditions, the more inclined you are to use a switch instead of if-else. This typically comes down to which code is easier to read. The argument is that if-else is easier to read when there are fewer conditions and switch is easier to read when the number of conditions is large. Consider the following:

```
if (found){
    //do something
} else {
    //do something else
}

switch(found){
    case true:
        //do something
        break;

    default:
        //do something else
}
```

Though both pieces of code perform the same task, many would argue that the if-else statement is much easier to read than the switch. Increasing the number of conditions, however, usually reverses that opinion:

```
if (color == "red"){
    //do something
} else if (color == "blue"){
    //do something
} else if (color == "brown"){
    //do something
} else if (color == "black"){
    //do something
} else {
    //do something
}

switch (color){
    case "red":
        //do something
        break;

    case "blue":
        //do something
        break;

    case "brown":
        //do something
        break;

    case "black":
        //do something
        break;

    default:
        //do something
}
```

Most would consider the `switch` statement in this code to be more readable than the `if-else` statement.

As it turns out, the `switch` statement is faster in most cases when compared to `if-else`, but significantly faster only when the number of conditions is large. The primary difference in performance between the two is that the incremental cost of an additional condition is larger for `if-else` than it is for `switch`. Therefore, our natural inclination to use `if-else` for a small number of conditions and a `switch` statement for a larger number of conditions is exactly the right advice when considering performance.

Generally speaking, `if-else` is best used when there are two discrete values or a few different ranges of values for which to test. When there are more than two discrete values for which to test, the `switch` statement is the most optimal choice.

Optimizing if-else

When optimizing `if-else`, the goal is always to minimize the number of conditions to evaluate before taking the correct path. The easiest optimization is therefore to ensure that the most common conditions are first. Consider the following:

```
if (value < 5) {
    //do something
} else if (value > 5 && value < 10) {
    //do something
} else {
    //do something
}
```

This code is optimal only if `value` is most frequently less than 5. If `value` is typically greater than or equal to 10, then two conditions must be evaluated each time before the correct path is taken, ultimately increasing the average amount of time spent in this statement. Conditions in an `if-else` should always be ordered from most likely to least likely to ensure the fastest possible execution time.

Another approach to minimizing condition evaluations is to organize the `if-else` into a series of nested `if-else` statements. Using a single, large `if-else` typically leads to slower overall execution time as each additional condition is evaluated. For example:

```
if (value == 0){
    return result0;
} else if (value == 1){
    return result1;
} else if (value == 2){
    return result2;
} else if (value == 3){
    return result3;
} else if (value == 4){
    return result4;
} else if (value == 5){
    return result5;
} else if (value == 6){
```

```
        return result6;
    } else if (value == 7){
        return result7;
    } else if (value == 8){
        return result8;
    } else if (value == 9){
        return result9;
    } else {
        return result10;
    }
```

With this if-else statement, the maximum number of conditions to evaluate is 10. This slows down the average execution time if you assume that the possible values for value are evenly distributed between 0 and 10. To minimize the number of conditions to evaluate, the code can be rewritten into a series of nested if-else statements, such as:

```
if (value < 6){

    if (value < 3){
        if (value == 0){
            return result0;
        } else if (value == 1){
            return result1;
        } else {
            return result2;
        }
    } else {
        if (value == 3){
            return result3;
        } else if (value == 4){
            return result4;
        } else {
            return result5;
        }
    }

} else {

    if (value < 8){
        if (value == 6){
            return result6;
        } else {
            return result7;
        }
    } else {
        if (value == 8){
            return result8;
        } else if (value == 9){
            return result9;
        } else {
            return result10;
        }
    }
}
```

The rewritten `if-else` statement has a maximum number of four condition evaluations each time through. This is achieved by applying a binary-search-like approach, splitting the possible values into a series of ranges to check and then drilling down further in that section. The average amount of time it takes to execute this code is roughly half of the time it takes to execute the previous `if-else` statement when the values are evenly distributed between 0 and 10. This approach is best when there are ranges of values for which to test (as opposed to discrete values, in which case a `switch` statement is typically more appropriate).

Lookup Tables

Sometimes the best approach to conditionals is to avoid using `if-else` and `switch` altogether. When there are a large number of discrete values for which to test, both `if-else` and `switch` are significantly slower than using a lookup table. Lookup tables can be created using arrays or regular objects in JavaScript, and accessing data from a lookup table is much faster than using `if-else` or `switch`, especially when the number of conditions is large (see Figure 4-1).

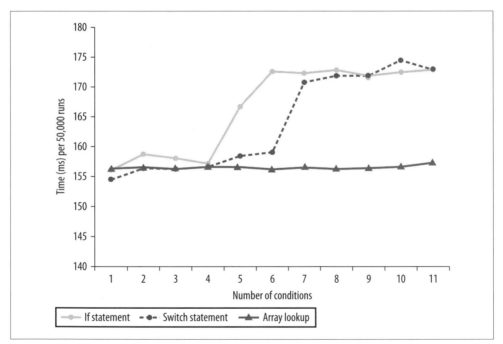

Figure 4-1. Array item lookup versus using if-else or switch in Internet Explorer 7

Lookup tables are not only very fast in comparison to `if-else` and `switch`, but they also help to make code more readable when there are a large number of discrete values for which to test. For example, `switch` statements start to get unwieldy when large, such as:

```
switch(value){
    case 0:
        return result0;
    case 1:
        return result1;
    case 2:
        return result2;
    case 3:
        return result3;
    case 4:
        return result4;
    case 5:
        return result5;
    case 6:
        return result6;
    case 7:
        return result7;
    case 8:
        return result8;
    case 9:
        return result9;
    default:
        return result10;
}
```

The amount of space that this `switch` statement occupies in code is probably not proportional to its importance. The entire structure can be replaced by using an array as a lookup table:

```
//define the array of results
var results = [result0, result1, result2, result3, result4, result5, result6,
               result7, result8, result9, result10]

//return the correct result
return results[value];
```

When using a lookup table, you have completely eliminated all condition evaluations. The operation becomes either an array item lookup or an object member lookup. This is a major advantage for lookup tables: since there are no conditions to evaluate, there is little or no additional overhead as the number of possible values increases.

Lookup tables are most useful when there is logical mapping between a single key and a single value (as in the previous example). A `switch` statement is more appropriate when each key requires a unique action or set of actions to take place.

Recursion

Complex algorithms are typically made easier by using recursion. In fact, there are some traditional algorithms that presume recursion as the implementation, such as a function to return factorials:

```
function factorial(n){
    if (n == 0){
        return 1;
    } else {
        return n * factorial(n-1);
    }
}
```

The problem with recursive functions is that an ill-defined or missing terminal condition can lead to long execution times that freeze the user interface. Further, recursive functions are more likely to run into browser call stack size limits.

Call Stack Limits

The amount of recursion supported by JavaScript engines varies and is directly related to the size of the JavaScript call stack. With the exception of Internet Explorer, for which the call stack is related to available system memory, all other browsers have static call stack limits. The call stack size for the most recent browser versions is relatively high compared to older browsers (Safari 2, for instance, had a call stack size of 100). Figure 4-2 shows call stack sizes over the major browsers.

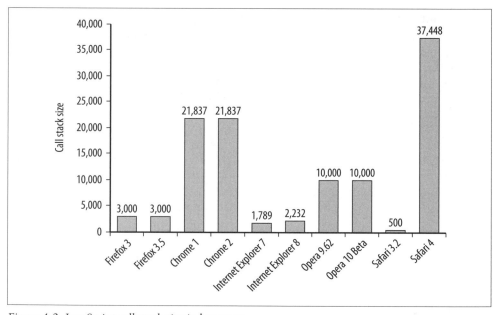

Figure 4-2. JavaScript call stack size in browsers

When you exceed the maximum call stack size by introducing too much recursion, the browser will error out with one of the following messages:

- Internet Explorer: "Stack overflow at line x"

- Firefox: "Too much recursion"
- Safari: "Maximum call stack size exceeded"
- Opera: "Abort (control stack overflow)"

Chrome is the only browser that doesn't display a message to the user when the call stack size has been exceeded.

Perhaps the most interesting part of stack overflow errors is that they are actual Java-Script errors in some browsers, and can therefore be trapped using a `try-catch` statement. The exception type varies based on the browser being used. In Firefox, it's an `InternalError`; in Safari and Chrome, it's a `RangeError`; and Internet Explorer throws a generic `Error` type. (Opera doesn't throw an error; it just stops the JavaScript engine.) This makes it possible to handle such errors right from JavaScript:

```
try {
    recurse();
} catch (ex){
    alert("Too much recursion!");
}
```

If left unhandled, these errors bubble up as any other error would (in Firefox, it ends up in the Firebug and error consoles; in Safari/Chrome it shows up in the JavaScript console), except in Internet Explorer. IE will not only display a JavaScript error, but will also display a dialog box that looks just like an alert with the stack overflow message.

 Even though it is possible to trap these errors in JavaScript, it is not recommended. No script should ever be deployed that has the potential to exceed the maximum call stack size.

Recursion Patterns

When you run into a call stack size limit, your first step should be to identify any instances of recursion in the code. To that end, there are two recursive patterns to be aware of. The first is the straightforward recursive pattern represented in the `factorial()` function shown earlier, when a function calls itself. The general pattern is as follows:

```
function recurse(){
    recurse();
}

recurse();
```

This pattern is typically easy to identify when errors occur. A second, subtler pattern involves two functions:

```
function first(){
    second();
```

```
    }

    function second(){
        first();
    }

    first();
```

In this recursion pattern, two functions each call the other, such that an infinite loop is formed. This is the more troubling pattern and a far more difficult one to identify in large code bases.

Most call stack errors are related to one of these two recursion patterns. A frequent cause of stack overflow is an incorrect terminal condition, so the first step after identifying the pattern is to validate the terminal condition. If the terminal condition is correct, then the algorithm contains too much recursion to safely be run in the browser and should be changed to use iteration, memoization, or both.

Iteration

Any algorithm that can be implemented using recursion can also be implemented using iteration. Iterative algorithms typically consist of several different loops performing different aspects of the process, and thus introduce their own performance issues. However, using optimized loops in place of long-running recursive functions can result in performance improvements due to the lower overhead of loops versus that of executing a function.

As an example, the merge sort algorithm is most frequently implemented using recursion. A simple JavaScript implementation of merge sort is as follows:

```
    function merge(left, right){
        var result = [];

        while (left.length > 0 && right.length > 0){
            if (left[0] < right[0]){
                result.push(left.shift());
            } else {
                result.push(right.shift());
            }
        }

        return result.concat(left).concat(right);
    }

    function mergeSort(items){

        if (items.length == 1) {
            return items;
        }

        var middle = Math.floor(items.length / 2),
            left    = items.slice(0, middle),
```

```
    right   = items.slice(middle);

    return merge(mergeSort(left), mergeSort(right));
}
```

The code for this merge sort is fairly simple and straightforward, but the `mergeSort()` function itself ends up getting called very frequently. An array of n items ends up calling `mergeSort()` $2 * n - 1$ times, meaning that an array with more than 1,500 items would cause a stack overflow error in Firefox.

Running into the stack overflow error doesn't necessarily mean the entire algorithm has to change; it simply means that recursion isn't the best implementation. The merge sort algorithm can also be implemented using iteration, such as:

```
//uses the same mergeSort() function from previous example

function mergeSort(items){

    if (items.length == 1) {
        return items;
    }

    var work = [];
    for (var i=0, len=items.length; i < len; i++){
        work.push([items[i]]);
    }
    work.push([]);   //in case of odd number of items

    for (var lim=len; lim > 1; lim = (lim+1)/2){
        for (var j=0,k=0; k < lim; j++, k+=2){
            work[j] = merge(work[k], work[k+1]);
        }
        work[j] = [];   //in case of odd number of items
    }

    return work[0];
}
```

This implementation of `mergeSort()` does the same work as the previous one without using recursion. Although the iterative version of merge sort may be somewhat slower than the recursive option, it doesn't have the same call stack impact as the recursive version. Switching recursive algorithms to iterative ones is just one of the options for avoiding stack overflow errors.

Memoization

Work avoidance is the best performance optimization technique. The less work your code has to do, the faster it executes. Along those lines, it also makes sense to avoid work repetition. Performing the same task multiple times is a waste of execution time. Memoization is an approach to avoid work repetition by caching previous calculations for later reuse, which makes memoization a useful technique for recursive algorithms.

When recursive functions are called multiple times during code execution, there tends to be a lot of work duplication. The `factorial()` function, introduced earlier in "Recursion" on page 73, is a great example of how work can be repeated multiple times by recursive functions. Consider the following code:

```
var fact6 = factorial(6);
var fact5 = factorial(5);
var fact4 = factorial(4);
```

This code produces three factorials and results in the `factorial()` function being called a total of 18 times. The worst part of this code is that all of the necessary work is completed on the first line. Since the factorial of 6 is equal to 6 multiplied by the factorial 5, the factorial of 5 is being calculated twice. Even worse, the factorial of 4 is being calculated three times. It makes far more sense to save those calculations and reuse them instead of starting over anew with each function call.

You can rewrite the `factorial()` function to make use of memoization in the following way:

```
function memfactorial(n){

    if (!memfactorial.cache){
        memfactorial.cache = {
            "0": 1,
            "1": 1
        };
    }

    if (!memfactorial.cache.hasOwnProperty(n)){
        memfactorial.cache[n] = n * memfactorial (n-1);
    }

    return memfactorial.cache[n];
}
```

The key to this memoized version of the factorial function is the creation of a cache object. This object is stored on the function itself and is prepopulated with the two simplest factorials: 0 and 1. Before calculating a factorial, this cache is checked to see whether the calculation has already been performed. No cache value means the calculation must be done for the first time and the result stored in the cache for later usage. This function is used in the same manner as the original `factorial()` function:

```
var fact6 = memfactorial(6);
var fact5 = memfactorial(5);
var fact4 = memfactorial(4);
```

This code returns three different factorials but makes a total of eight calls to `memfactorial()`. Since all of the necessary calculations are completed on the first line, the next two lines need not perform any recursion because cached values are returned.

The memoization process may be slightly different for each recursive function, but generally the same pattern applies. To make memoizing a function easier, you can define a `memoize()` function that encapsulates the basic functionality. For example:

```
function memoize(fundamental, cache){
    cache = cache || {};

    var shell = function(arg){
        if (!cache.hasOwnProperty(arg)){
            cache[arg] = fundamental(arg);
        }
        return cache[arg];
    };

    return shell;
}
```

This `memoize()` function accepts two arguments: a function to memoize and an optional cache object. The cache object can be passed in if you'd like to prefill some values; otherwise a new cache object is created. A shell function is then created that wraps the original (`fundamental`) and ensures that a new result is calculated only if it has never previously been calculated. This shell function is returned so that you can call it directly, such as:

```
//memoize the factorial function
var memfactorial = memoize(factorial, { "0": 1, "1": 1 });

//call the new function
var fact6 = memfactorial(6);
var fact5 = memfactorial(5);
var fact4 = memfactorial(4);
```

Generic memoization of this type is less optimal that manually updating the algorithm for a given function because the `memoize()` function caches the result of a function call with specific arguments. Recursive calls, therefore, are saved only when the shell function is called multiple times with the same arguments. For this reason, it's better to manually implement memoization in those functions that have significant performance issues rather than apply a generic memoization solution.

Summary

Just as with other programming languages, the way that you factor your code and the algorithm you choose affects the execution time of JavaScript. Unlike other programming languages, JavaScript has a restricted set of resources from which to draw, so optimization techniques are even more important.

- The `for`, `while`, and `do-while` loops all have similar performance characteristics, and so no one loop type is significantly faster or slower than the others.
- Avoid the `for-in` loop unless you need to iterate over a number of unknown object properties.

- The best ways to improve loop performance are to decrease the amount of work done per iteration and decrease the number of loop iterations.

- Generally speaking, `switch` is always faster than `if-else`, but isn't always the best solution.

- Lookup tables are a faster alternative to multiple condition evaluation using `if-else` or `switch`.

- Browser call stack size limits the amount of recursion that JavaScript is allowed to perform; stack overflow errors prevent the rest of the code from executing.

- If you run into a stack overflow error, change the method to an iterative algorithm or make use of memoization to avoid work repetition.

The larger the amount of code being executed, the larger the performance gain realized from using these strategies.

Strings and Regular Expressions

Steven Levithan

Practically all JavaScript programs are intimately tied to strings. For example, many applications use Ajax to fetch strings from a server, convert those strings into more easily usable JavaScript objects, and then generate strings of HTML from the data. A typical program deals with numerous tasks like these that require you to merge, split, rearrange, search, iterate over, and otherwise handle strings; and as web applications become more complex, progressively more of this processing is done in the browser.

In JavaScript, regular expressions are essential for anything more than trivial string processing. A lot of this chapter is therefore dedicated to helping you understand how regular expression engines[*] internally process your strings and teaching you how to write regular expressions that take advantage of this knowledge.

Since the term *regular expression* is a bit unwieldy, *regex* is often used for short, and *regexes* to denote the plural.

Also in this chapter, you'll learn about the fastest cross-browser methods for concatenating and trimming strings, discover how to increase regex performance by reducing backtracking, and pick up plenty of other tips and tricks for efficiently processing strings and regular expressions.

String Concatenation

String concatenation can be surprisingly performance intensive. It's a common task to build a string by continually adding to the end of it in a loop (e.g., when building up

---

[*] The engine is just the software that makes your regular expressions work. Each browser has its own regex engine (or, if you prefer, implementation) with a unique set of performance strengths.

an HTML table or an XML document), but this sort of processing is notorious for its poor performance in some browsers.

So how can you optimize these kinds of tasks? For starters, there is more than one way to merge strings (see Table 5-1).

Table 5-1. String concatenation methods

Method	Example
The + operator	str = "a" + "b" + "c";
The += operator	str = "a";
	str += "b";
	str += "c";
array.join()	str = ["a", "b", "c"].join("");
string.concat()	str = "a";
	str = str.concat("b", "c");

All of these methods are fast when concatenating a few strings here and there, so for casual use, you should go with whatever is the most practical. As the length and number of strings that must be merged increases, however, some methods start to show their strength.

Plus (+) and Plus-Equals (+=) Operators

These operators provide the simplest method for concatenating strings and, in fact, all modern browsers except IE7 and earlier optimize them well enough that you don't really need to look at other options. However, several techniques maximize the efficiency of these operators.

First, an example. Here's a common way to assign a concatenated string:

```
str += "one" + "two";
```

When evaluating this code, four steps are taken:

1. A temporary string is created in memory.
2. The concatenated value **"onetwo"** is assigned to the temporary string.
3. The temporary string is concatenated with the current value of **str**.
4. The result is assigned to **str**.

This is actually an approximation of how browsers implement this task, but it's close.

The following code avoids the temporary string (steps 1 and 2 in the list) by directly appending to **str** using two discrete statements. This ends up running about 10%–40% faster in most browsers:

```
str += "one";
str += "two";
```

In fact, you can get the same performance improvement using one statement, as follows:

```
str = str + "one" + "two";
// equivalent to str = ((str + "one") + "two")
```

This avoids the temporary string because the assignment expression starts with `str` as the base and appends one string to it at a time, with each intermediary concatenation performed from left to right. If the concatenation were performed in a different order (e.g., `str = "one" + str + "two"`), you would lose this optimization. This is because of the way that browsers allocate memory when merging strings. Apart from IE, browsers try to expand the memory allocation for the string on the left of an expression and simply copy the second string to the end of it (see Figure 5-1). If, in a loop, the base string is furthest to the left, you avoid repeatedly copying a progressively larger base string.

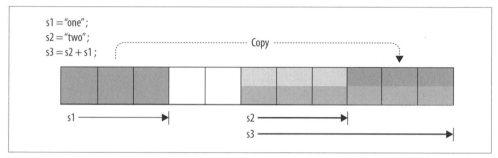

Figure 5-1. Example of memory use when concatenating strings: s1 is copied to the end of s2 to create s3; the base string s2 is not copied

These techniques don't apply to IE. They have little, if any, effect in IE8 and can actually make things slower in IE7 and earlier. That's because of how IE executes concatenation under the hood. In IE8's implementation, concatenating strings merely stores references to the existing string parts that compose the new string. At the last possible moment (when you actually use the concatenated string), the string parts are each copied into a new "real" string, which then replaces the previously stored string references so that this assembly doesn't have to be performed every time the string is used.

> IE8's implementation can throw off synthetic benchmarks—making concatenation appear faster than it really is—unless you force concatenation to occur after you've finished building your test string. For example, this can be done by calling the `toString()` method on your final string, checking its `length` property, or inserting it into the DOM.

IE7 and earlier use an inferior implementation of concatenation in which each pair of concatenated strings must always be copied to a new memory location. You'll see the potentially dramatic impact of this in the upcoming section "Array Joining". With the pre-IE8 implementation, the advice in this section can make things slower since it's faster to concatenate short strings before merging them with a larger base string (thereby avoiding the need to copy the larger string multiple times). For instance, with `largeStr = largeStr + s1 + s2`, IE7 and earlier must copy the large string twice, first to merge it with `s1`, then with `s2`. Conversely, `largeStr += s1 + s2` first merges the two smaller strings and then concatenates the result with the large string. Creating the intermediary string of `s1 + s2` is a much lighter performance hit than copying the large string twice.

Firefox and compile-time folding

When all strings concatenated in an assignment expression are compile-time constants, Firefox automatically merges them at compile time. Here's a way to see this in action:

```
function foldingDemo() {
    var str = "compile" + "time" + "folding";
    str += "this" + "works" + "too";
    str = str + "but" + "not" + "this";
}

alert(foldingDemo.toString());

/* In Firefox, you'll see this:
function foldingDemo() {
    var str = "compiletimefolding";
    str += "thisworkstoo";
    str = str + "but" + "not" + "this";
} */
```

When strings are folded together like this, there are no intermediary strings at runtime and the time and memory that would be spent concatenating them is reduced to zero. This is great when it occurs, but it doesn't help very often because it's much more common to build strings from runtime data than from compile-time constants.

 The YUI Compressor performs this optimization at build time. See "JavaScript Minification" on page 168 for more about this tool.

Array Joining

The `Array.prototype.join` method merges all elements of an array into a string and accepts a separator string to insert between each element. By passing in an empty string as the separator, you can perform a simple concatenation of all elements in an array.

Array joining is slower than other methods of concatenation in most browsers, but this is more than compensated for by the fact that it is the only efficient way to concatenate lots of strings in IE7 and earlier.

The following example code demonstrates the kind of performance problem that array joining solves:

```
var str = "I'm a thirty-five character string.",
    newStr = "",
    appends = 5000;

while (appends--) {
    newStr += str;
}
```

This code concatenates 5,000 35-character strings. Figure 5-2† shows how long it takes to complete this test in IE7, starting with 5,000 concatenations and then gradually increasing that number.

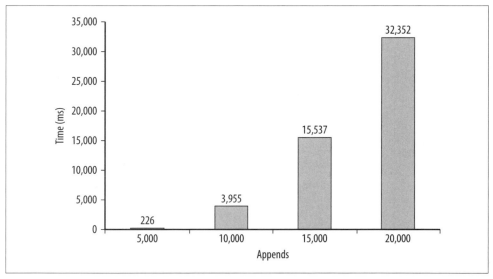

Figure 5-2. Time to concatenate strings using += in IE7

IE7's naive concatenation algorithm requires that the browser repeatedly copy and allocate memory for larger and larger strings each time through the loop. The result is quadratic running time and memory consumption.

The good news is that all other modern browsers (including IE8) perform far better in this test and do not exhibit the quadratic complexity that is the real killer here. However, this demonstrates the impact that seemingly simple string concatenation can have; 226 milliseconds for 5,000 concatenations is already a significant performance hit that would be nice to reduce as much as possible, but locking up a user's browser for more

† The numbers in Figures 5-2 and 5-3 were generated by averaging the result of running each test 10 times in IE7 on a Windows XP virtual machine with modest specs (2 GHz Core 2 Duo CPU and 1 GB of dedicated RAM).

than 32 seconds in order to concatenate 20,000 short strings is unacceptable for nearly any application.

Now consider the following test, which generates the same string via array joining:

```
var str = "I'm a thirty-five character string.",
    strs = [],
    newStr,
    appends = 5000;

while (appends--) {
    strs[strs.length] = str;
}

newStr = strs.join("");
```

Figure 5-3 shows this test's running time in IE7.

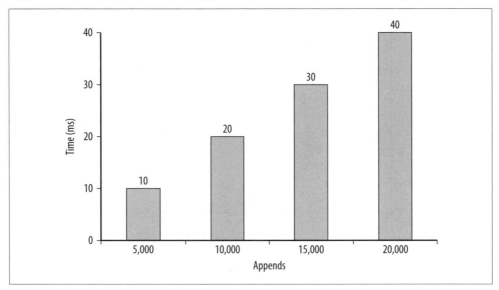

Figure 5-3. Time to concatenate strings using array joining in IE7

This dramatic improvement results from avoiding repeatedly allocating memory for and copying progressively larger and larger strings. When joining an array, the browser allocates enough memory to hold the complete string, and never copies the same part of the final string more than once.

String.prototype.concat

The native string `concat` method accepts any number of arguments and appends each to the string that the method is called on. This is the most flexible way to concatenate strings because you can use it to append just one string, a few strings at a time, or an entire array of strings.

```
// append one string
str = str.concat(s1);

// append three strings
str = str.concat(s1, s2, s3);

// append every string in an array by using the array
// as the list of arguments
str = String.prototype.concat.apply(str, array);
```

Unfortunately, concat is a little slower than simple + and += operators in most cases, and can be substantially slower in IE, Opera, and Chrome. Moreover, although using concat to merge all strings in an array appears similar to the array joining approach discussed previously, it's usually slower (except in Opera), and it suffers from the same potentially catastrophic performance problem as + and += when building large strings in IE7 and earlier.

Regular Expression Optimization

Incautiously crafted regexes can be a major performance bottleneck (the upcoming section, "Runaway Backtracking" on page 91, contains several examples showing how severe this can be), but there is a lot you can do to improve regex efficiency. Just because two regexes match the same text doesn't mean they do so at the same speed.

Many factors affect a regex's efficiency. For starters, the text a regex is applied to makes a big difference because regexes spend more time on partial matches than obvious nonmatches. Each browser's regex engine also has different internal optimizations.[‡]

Regex optimization is a fairly broad and nuanced topic. There's only so much that can be covered in this section, but what's included should put you well on your way to understanding the kinds of issues that affect regex performance and mastering the art of crafting efficient regexes.

Note that this section assumes you already have some experience with regular expressions and are primarily interested in how to make them faster. If you're new to regular expressions or need to brush up on the basics, numerous resources are available on the Web and in print. *Regular Expressions Cookbook (http://oreilly.com/catalog/9780596520694/)* (O'Reilly) by Jan Goyvaerts and Steven Levithan (that's me!) is written for people who like to learn by doing, and covers JavaScript and several other programming languages equally.

[‡] A consequence of this is that seemingly insignificant changes can make a regex faster in one browser and slower in another.

How Regular Expressions Work

In order to use regular expressions efficiently, it's important to understand how they work their magic. The following is a quick rundown of the basic steps a regex goes through:

Step 1: Compilation

> When you create a regex object (using a regex literal or the `RegExp` constructor), the browser checks your pattern for errors and then converts it into a native code routine that is used to actually perform matches. If you assign your regex to a variable, you can avoid performing this step more than once for a given pattern.

Step 2: Setting the starting position

> When a regex is put to use, the first step is to determine the position within the target string where the search should start. This is initially the start of the string or the position specified by the regex's `lastIndex` property,[§] but when returning here from step 4 (due to a failed match attempt), the position is one character after where the last attempt started.

> Optimizations that browser makers build into their regex engines can help avoid a lot of unnecessary work at this stage by deciding early that certain work can be skipped. For instance, if a regex starts with ^, IE and Chrome can usually determine that a match cannot be found after the start of a string and avoid foolishly searching subsequent positions. Another example is that if all possible matches contain x as the third character, a smart implementation may be able to determine this, quickly search for the next x, and set the starting position two characters back from where it's found (e.g., recent versions of Chrome include this optimization).

Step 3: Matching each regex token

> Once the regex knows where to start, it steps through the text and the regex pattern. When a particular token fails to match, the regex tries to backtrack to a prior point in the match attempt and follow other possible paths through the regex.

Step 4: Success or failure

> If a complete match is found at the current position in the string, the regex declares success. If all possible paths through the regex have been attempted but a match was not found, the regex engine goes back to step 2 to try again at the next character in the string. Only after this cycle completes for every character in the string (as well as the position after the last character) and no matches have been found does the regex declare overall failure.

[§] The value of a regex's `lastIndex` property is used as the search start position by the regex `exec` and `test` methods only, and only if the regex was built with the `/g` (global) flag. Nonglobal regexes and any regex passed to the string `match`, `replace`, `search`, and `split` methods always initiate their search at the beginning of the target string.

Keeping this process in mind will help you make informed decisions about the types of issues that affect regex performance. Next up is a deeper look into a key feature of the matching process in step 3: *backtracking*.

Understanding Backtracking

In most modern regex implementations (including those required by JavaScript), backtracking is a fundamental component of the matching process. It's also a big part of what makes regular expressions so expressive and powerful. However, backtracking is computationally expensive and can easily get out of hand if you're not careful. Although backtracking is only part of the overall performance equation, understanding how it works and how to minimize its use is perhaps the most important key to writing efficient regexes. The next few sections therefore cover the topic at some length.

As a regex works its way through a target string, it tests whether a match can be found at each position by stepping through the components in the regex from left to right. For each quantifier and alternation,‖ a decision must be made about how to proceed. With a quantifier (such as *, +?, or {2,}), the regex must decide when to try matching additional characters, and with alternation (via the | operator), it must try one option from those available.

Each time the regex makes such a decision, it remembers the other options to return to later if necessary. If the chosen option is successful, the regex continues through the regex pattern, and if the remainder of the regex is also successful, the match is complete. But if the chosen option can't find a match or anything later in the regex fails, the regex backtracks to the last decision point where untried options remain and chooses one. It continues on like this until a match is found or all possible permutations of the quantifiers and alternation options in the regex have been tried unsuccessfully, at which point it gives up and moves on to start this process all over at the next character in the string.

Alternation and backtracking

Here's an example that demonstrates how this process plays out with alternation.

```
/h(ello|appy) hippo/.test("hello there, happy hippo");
```

This regex matches "hello hippo" or "happy hippo". It starts this test by searching for an h, which it finds immediately as the first character in the target string. Next, the subexpression (ello|appy) provides two ways to proceed. The regex chooses the leftmost option (alternation always works from left to right), and checks whether ello matches the next characters in the string. It does, and the regex is also able to match the following space character. At that point, though, it reaches a dead end because the

---

‖ Although character classes like [a-z] and shorthand character classes like \s or dot allow variation, they are not implemented using backtracking and thus do not encounter the same performance issues.

h in `hippo` cannot match the `t` that comes next in the string. The regex can't give up yet, though, because it hasn't tried all of its options, so it backtracks to the last decision point (just after it matched the leading `h`) and tries to match the second alternation option. That doesn't work, and since there are no more options to try, the regex determines that a match cannot be found starting from the first character in the string and moves on to try again at the second character. It doesn't find an `h` there, so it continues searching until it reaches the 14th character, where it matches the `h` in "happy". It then steps through the alternatives again. This time `ello` doesn't match, but after backtracking and trying the second alternative, it's able to continue until it matches the full string "happy hippo" (see Figure 5-4). Success.

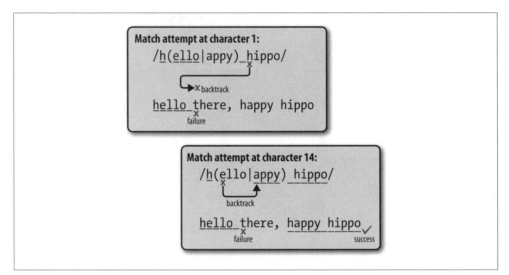

Figure 5-4. Example of backtracking with alternation

Repetition and backtracking

This next example shows how backtracking works with repetition quantifiers.

```
var str = "<p>Para 1.</p>" +
          "<img src='smiley.jpg'>" +
          "<p>Para 2.</p>" +
          "<div>Div.</div>";

/<p>.*<\/p>/i.test(str);
```

Here, the regex starts by matching the three literal characters `<p>` at the start of the string. Next up is `.*`. The dot matches any character except line breaks, and the greedy asterisk quantifier repeats it zero or more times—as many times as possible. Since there are no line breaks in the target string, this gobbles up the rest of the string! There's still more to match in the regex pattern, though, so the regex tries to match `<`. This doesn't work at the end of the string, so the regex backtracks one character at a time, continually trying to match <, until it gets back to the < at the beginning of the </div> tag. It then tries to match \/ (an escaped backslash), which works, followed by p, which doesn't. The regex backtracks again, repeating this process until it eventually matches the </p> at the end of the second paragraph. The match is returned successfully, spanning from the start of the first paragraph until the end of the last one, which is probably not what you wanted.

You can change the regex to match individual paragraphs by replacing the greedy * quantifier with the lazy (aka nongreedy) *?. Backtracking for lazy quantifiers works in the opposite way. When the regex /<p>.*?<\/p>/ comes to the .*?, it first tries to skip this altogether and move on to matching <\/p>. It does so because *? repeats its preceding element zero or more times, as *few* times as possible, and the fewest possible times it can repeat is zero. However, when the following < fails to match at this point in the string, the regex backtracks and tries to match the next fewest number of characters: one. It continues backtracking forward like this until the <\/p> that follows the quantifier is able to fully match at the end of the first paragraph.

You can see that even if there was only one paragraph in the target string and therefore the greedy and lazy versions of this regex were equivalent, they would go about finding their matches differently (see Figure 5-5).

Runaway Backtracking

When a regular expression stalls your browser for seconds, minutes, or longer, the problem is most likely a bad case of runaway backtracking. To demonstrate the problem, consider the following regex, which is designed to match an entire HTML file. The regex is wrapped across multiple lines in order to fit the page. Unlike most other regex flavors, JavaScript does not have an option to make dots match any character, including line breaks, so this example uses [\s\S] to match any character.

```
/<html>[\s\S]*?<head>[\s\S]*?<title>[\s\S]*?<\/title>[\s\S]*?<\/head>
[\s\S]*?<body>[\s\S]*?<\/body>[\s\S]*?<\/html>/
```

This regex works fine when matching a suitable HTML string, but it turns ugly when the string is missing one or more required tags. If the </html> tag is missing, for instance, the last [\s\S]*? expands to the end of the string since there is no </html> tag to be found, and then, instead of giving up, the regex sees that each of the previous [\s\S]*? sequences remembered backtracking positions that allow them to expand further. The regex tries expanding the second-to-last [\s\S]*?—using it to match the </body> tag that was previously matched by the literal <\/body> pattern in the regex—and continues to expand it in search of a second </body> tag until the end of the string is reached again. When all of that fails, the third-to-last [\s\S]*? expands to the end of the string, and so on.

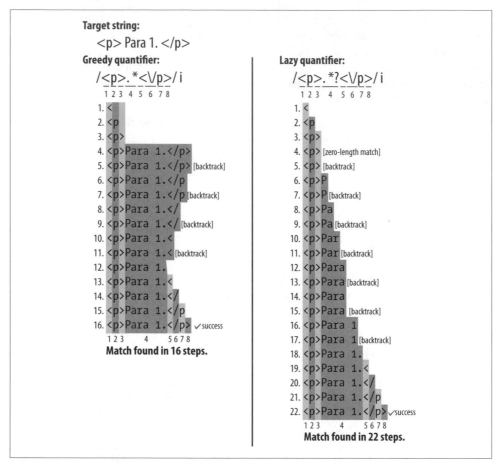

Figure 5-5. Example of backtracking with greedy and lazy quantifiers

The solution: Be specific

The way around a problem like this is to be as specific as possible about what characters can be matched between your required delimiters. Take the pattern ".*?", which is intended to match a string delimited by double-quotes. By replacing the overly permissive .*? with the more specific [^"\r\n]*, you remove the possibility that backtracking will force the dot to match a double-quote and expand beyond what was intended.

With the HTML example, this workaround is not as simple. You can't use a negated character class like [^<] in place of [\s\S] because there may be other tags between those you're searching for. However, you can reproduce the effect by repeating a non-capturing group that contains a negative lookahead (blocking the next required tag) and the [\s\S] (any character) metasequence. This ensures that the tags you're looking for fail at every intermediate position, and, more importantly, that the [\s\S] patterns cannot expand beyond where the tags you are blocking via negative lookahead are found. Here's how the regex ends up looking using this approach:

```
/<html>(?:(?!<head>)[\s\S])*<head>(?:(?!<title>)[\s\S])*<title>
(?:(?!<\/title>)[\s\S])*<\/title>(?:(?!<\/head>)[\s\S])*<\/head>
(?:(?!<body>)[\s\S])*<body>(?:(?!<\/body>)[\s\S])*<\/body>
(?:(?!<\/html>)[\s\S])*<\/html>/
```

Although this removes the potential for runaway backtracking and allows the regex to fail at matching incomplete HTML strings in linear time, it's not going to win any awards for efficiency. Repeating a lookahead for each matched character like this is rather inefficient in its own right and significantly slows down successful matches. This approach works well enough when matching short strings, but since in this case the lookaheads may need to be tested thousands of times in order to match an HTML file, there's another solution that works better. It relies on a little trick, and it's described next.

Emulating atomic groups using lookahead and backreferences

Some regex flavors, including .NET, Java, Oniguruma, PCRE, and Perl, support a feature called *atomic grouping*. Atomic groups—written as (?>...), where the ellipsis represents any regex pattern—are noncapturing groups with a special twist. As soon as a regex exits an atomic group, any backtracking positions within the group are thrown away. This provides a much better solution to the HTML regex's backtracking problem: if you were to place each [\s\S]*? sequence and its following HTML tag together inside an atomic group, then every time one of the required HTML tags was found, the match thus far would essentially be locked in. If a later part of the regex failed to match, no backtracking positions would be remembered for the quantifiers within the atomic groups, and thus the [\s\S]*? sequences could not attempt to expand beyond what they already matched.

That's great, but JavaScript does not support atomic groups or provide any other feature to eliminate needless backtracking. It turns out, though, that you can emulate atomic groups by exploiting a little-known behavior of lookahead: that lookaheads *are* atomic groups.[#] The difference is that lookaheads don't consume any characters as part of the overall match; they merely check whether the pattern they contain can be matched at that position. However, you can get around this by wrapping a lookahead's pattern inside a capturing group and adding a backreference to it just outside the lookahead. Here's what this looks like:

```
(?=(pattern to make atomic))\1
```

This construct is reusable in any pattern where you want to use an atomic group. Just keep in mind that you need to use the appropriate backreference number if your regex contains more than one capturing group.

[#] It's safe to rely on this behavior of lookahead since it is consistent across all major regex flavors and explicitly required by the ECMAScript standards.

Here's how this looks when applied to the HTML regex:

```
/<html>(?=([\s\S]*?<head>))\1(?=([\s\S]*?<title>))\2(?=([\s\S]*?
<\/title>))\3(?=([\s\S]*?<\/head>))\4(?=([\s\S]*?<body>))\5
(?=([\s\S]*?<\/body>))\6[\s\S]*?<\/html>/
```

Now, if there is no trailing `</html>` and the last `[\s\S]*?` expands to the end of the string, the regex immediately fails because there are no backtracking points to return to. Each time the regex finds an intermediate tag and exits a lookahead, it throws away all backtracking positions from within the lookahead. The following backreference simply rematches the literal characters found within the lookahead, making them a part of the actual match.

Nested quantifiers and runaway backtracking

So-called nested quantifiers always warrant extra attention and care in order to ensure that you're not creating the potential for runaway backtracking. A quantifier is nested when it occurs within a grouping that is itself repeated by a quantifier (e.g., `(x+)*`).

Nesting quantifiers is not actually a performance hazard in and of itself. However, if you're not careful, it can easily create a massive number of ways to divide text between the inner and outer quantifiers while attempting to match a string.

As an example, let's say you want to match HTML tags, and you come up with the following regex:

```
/<(?:[^>"']|"[^"]*"|'[^']*')*>/
```

This is perhaps overly simplistic, as it does not handle all cases of valid and invalid markup correctly, but it might work OK if used to process only snippets of valid HTML. Its advantage over even more naive solutions such as `/<[^>]*>/` is that it accounts for `>` characters that occur within attribute values. It does so using the second and third alternatives in the noncapturing group, which match entire double- and single-quoted attribute values in single steps, allowing all characters except their respective quote type to occur within them.

So far, there's no risk of runaway backtracking, despite the nested `*` quantifiers. The second and third alternation options match exactly one quoted string sequence per repetition of the group, so the potential number of backtracking points increases linearly with the length of the target string.

However, look at the first alternative in the noncapturing group: `[^>"']`. This can match only one character at a time, which seems a little inefficient. You might think it would be better to add a `+` quantifier at the end of this character class so that more than one suitable character can be matched during each repetition of the group—and at positions within the target string where the regex finds a match—and you'd be right. By matching more than one character at a time, you'd let the regex skip many unnecessary steps on the way to a successful match.

What might not be as readily apparent is the negative consequence such a change could lead to. If the regex matches an opening < character, but there is no following > that would allow the match attempt to complete successfully, runaway backtracking will kick into high gear because of the huge number of ways the new inner quantifier can be combined with the outer quantifier (following the noncapturing group) to match the text that follows <. The regex must try all of these permutations before giving up on the match attempt. Watch out!

From bad to worse. For an even more extreme example of nested quantifiers resulting in runaway backtracking, apply the regex /(A+A+)+B/ to a string containing only As. Although this regex would be better written as /AA+B/, for the sake of discussion imagine that the two As represent different patterns that are capable of matching some of the same strings.

When applied to a string composed of 10 As ("AAAAAAAAAA"), the regex starts by using the first A+ to match all 10 characters. The regex then backtracks one character, letting the second A+ match the last one. The grouping then tries to repeat, but since there are no more As and the group's + quantifier has already met its requirement of matching at least once, the regex then looks for the B. It doesn't find it, but it can't give up yet, since there are more paths through the regex that haven't been tried. What if the first A+ matched eight characters and the second matched two? Or if the first matched three characters, the second matched two, and the group repeated twice? How about if during the first repetition of the group, the first A+ matched two characters and the second matched three; then on the second repetition the first matched one and the second matched four? Although to you and me it's obviously silly to think that any amount of backtracking will produce the missing B, the regex will dutifully check all of these futile options and a lot more. The worst-case complexity of this regex is an appalling $O(2n)$, or two to the nth power, where n is the length of the string. With the 10 As used here, the regex requires 1,024 backtracking steps for the match to fail, and with 20 As, that number explodes to more than a million. Thirty-five As should be enough to hang Chrome, IE, Firefox, and Opera for at least 10 minutes (if not permanently) while they process the more than 34 billion backtracking steps required to invalidate all permutations of the regex. The exception is recent versions of Safari, which are able to detect that the regex is going in circles and quickly abort the match (Safari also imposes a cap of allowed backtracking steps, and aborts match attempts when this is exceeded).

The key to preventing this kind of problem is to make sure that two parts of a regex cannot match the same part of a string. For this regex, the fix is to rewrite it as /AA+B/, but the issue may be harder to avoid with complex regexes. Adding an emulated atomic group often works well as a last resort, although other solutions, when possible, will most likely keep your regexes easier to understand. Doing so for this regex looks like /((?=(A+A+))\2)+B/, and completely removes the backtracking problem.

A Note on Benchmarking

Because a regex's performance can be wildly different depending on the text it's applied to, there's no straightforward way to benchmark regexes against each other. For the best result, you need to benchmark your regexes on test strings of varying lengths that match, don't match, and nearly match.

That's one reason for this chapter's lengthy backtracking coverage. Without a firm understanding of backtracking, you won't be able to anticipate and identify backtracking-related problems. To help you catch runaway backtracking early, always test your regexes with long strings that contain partial matches. Think about the kinds of strings that your regexes will nearly but not quite match, and include those in your tests.

More Ways to Improve Regular Expression Efficiency

The following are a variety of additional regex efficiency techniques. Several of the points here have already been touched upon during the backtracking discussion.

Focus on failing faster

Slow regex processing is usually caused by slow failure rather than slow matching. This is compounded by the fact that if you're using a regex to match small parts of a large string, the regex will fail at many more positions than it will succeed. A change that makes a regex match faster but fail slower (e.g., by increasing the number of backtracking steps needed to try all regex permutations) is usually a losing trade.

Start regexes with simple, required tokens

Ideally, the leading token in a regex should be fast to test and rule out as many obviously nonmatching positions as possible. Good starting tokens for this purpose are anchors (^ or $), specific characters (e.g., x or \u263A), character classes (e.g., [a-z] or shorthands like \d), and word boundaries (\b). If possible, avoid starting regexes with groupings or optional tokens, and avoid top-level alternation such as /one|two/ since that forces the regex to consider multiple leading tokens. Firefox is sensitive to the use of any quantifier on leading tokens, and is better able to optimize, e.g., \s\s* than \s+ or \s{1,}. Other browsers mostly optimize away such differences.

Make quantified patterns and their following token mutually exclusive

When the characters that adjacent tokens or subexpressions are able to match overlap, the number of ways a regex will try to divide text between them increases. To help avoid this, make your patterns as specific as possible. Don't use ".*?" (which relies on backtracking) when you really mean "[^"\r\n]*".

Reduce the amount and reach of alternation

Alternation using the | vertical bar may require that all alternation options be tested at every position in a string. You can often reduce the need for alternation by using character classes and optional components, or by pushing the alternation further back into the regex (allowing some match attempts to fail before reaching the alternation). The following table shows examples of these techniques.

Instead of	Use
cat|bat	[cb]at
red|read	rea?d
red|raw	r(?:ed|aw)
(.|\r|\n)	[\s\S]

 Character classes that match any character (such as [\s\S], [\d \D], [\w\W], or [\0-\uFFFF]) are actually equivalent to (?:.\|\r\|\n\| \u2028\|\u2029). This includes the four characters that are not matched by the dot (carriage return, line feed, line separator, and paragraph separator).

Character classes are faster than alternation because they are implemented using bit vectors (or other fast implementations) rather than backtracking. When alternation is necessary, put frequently occurring alternatives first if this doesn't affect what the regex matches. Alternation options are attempted from left to right, so the more frequently an option is expected to match, the sooner you want it to be considered.

Note that Chrome and Firefox perform some of these optimizations automatically, and are therefore less affected by techniques for hand-tuning alternation.

Use noncapturing groups

Capturing groups spend time and memory remembering backreferences and keeping them up to date. If you don't need a backreference, avoid this overhead by using a noncapturing group—i.e., (?:…) instead of (…). Some people like to wrap their regexes in a capturing group when they need a backreference to the entire match. This is unnecessary since you can reference full matches via, e.g., element zero in arrays returned by regex.exec() or $& in replacement strings.

Replacing capturing groups with their noncapturing kin has minimal impact in Firefox, but can make a big difference in other browsers when dealing with long strings.

Capture interesting text to reduce postprocessing

As a caveat to the last tip, if you need to reference *parts* of a match, then, by all means, capture those parts and use the backreferences produced. For example, if you're writing code to process the contents of quoted strings matched by a regex, use /"([^"]*)"/ and work with backreference one, rather than using /"[^"]*"/ and manually stripping the quote marks from the result. When used in a loop, this kind of work reduction can save significant time.

Expose required tokens

In order to help regex engines make smart decisions about how to optimize a search routine, try to make it easy to determine which tokens are required. When tokens are used within subexpressions or alternation, it's harder for regex engines to determine whether they are required, and some won't make the effort to do so. For instance, the regex /^(ab|cd)/ exposes its start-of-string anchor. IE and Chrome see this and prevent the regex from trying to find matches after the start of a string, thereby making this search near instantaneous regardless of string length. However, because the equivalent regex /(^ab|^cd)/ doesn't expose its ^ anchor, IE doesn't apply the same optimization and ends up pointlessly searching for matches at every position in the string.

Use appropriate quantifiers

As described in the earlier section "Repetition and backtracking" on page 90, greedy and lazy quantifiers go about finding matches differently, even when they match the same strings. Using the more appropriate quantifier type (based on the anticipated amount of backtracking) in cases where they are equally correct can significantly improve performance, especially with long strings.

Lazy quantifiers are particularly slow in Opera 9.x and earlier, but Opera 10 removes this weakness.

Reuse regexes by assigning them to variables

Assigning regexes to variables lets you avoid repeatedly compiling them. Some people go overboard, using regex caching schemes that aim to avoid ever compiling a given pattern and flag combination more than once. Don't bother; regex compilation is fast, and such schemes likely add more overhead than they evade. The important thing is to avoid repeatedly recompiling regexes within loops. In other words, don't do this:

```
while (/regex1/.test(str1)) {
    /regex2/.exec(str2);
    ...
}
```

Do this instead:

```
var regex1 = /regex1/,
    regex2 = /regex2/;
while (regex1.test(str1)) {
    regex2.exec(str2);
    ...
}
```

Split complex regexes into simpler pieces

Try to avoid doing too much with a single regex. Complicated search problems that require conditional logic are easier to solve and usually more efficient when broken into two or more regexes, with each regex searching within the matches of the last. Regex monstrosities that do everything in one pattern are difficult to maintain, and are prone to backtracking-related problems.

When Not to Use Regular Expressions

When used with care, regexes are very fast. However, they're usually overkill when you are merely searching for literal strings. This is especially true if you know in advance which part of a string you want to test. For instance, if you want to check whether a string ends with a semicolon, you could use something like this:

```
endsWithSemicolon = /;$/.test(str);
```

You might be surprised to learn, though, that none of the big browsers are currently smart enough to realize in advance that this regex can match only at the end of the string. What they end up doing is stepping through the entire string. Each time a semicolon is found, the regex advances to the next token ($), which checks whether the match is at the end of the string. If not, the regex continues searching for a match until it finally makes its way through the entire string. The longer your string (and the more semicolons it contains), the longer this takes.

In this case, a better approach is to skip all the intermediate steps required by a regex and simply check whether the last character is a semicolon:

```
endsWithSemicolon = str.charAt(str.length - 1) == ";";
```

This is just a bit faster than the regex-based test with small target strings, but, more importantly, the string's length no longer affects the time needed to perform the test.

This example used the charAt method to read the character at a specific position. The string methods slice, substr, and substring work well when you want to extract and check the value of more than one character at a specific position. Additionally, the indexOf and lastIndexOf methods are great for finding the position of literal strings or checking for their presence. All of these string methods are fast and can help you avoid invoking the overhead of regular expressions when searching for literal strings that don't rely on fancy regex features.

String Trimming

Removing leading and trailing whitespace from a string is a simple but common task. Although ECMAScript 5 adds a native string trim method (and you should therefore start to see this method in upcoming browsers), JavaScript has not historically included it. For the current browser crop, it's still necessary to implement a trim method yourself or rely on a library that includes it.

Trimming strings is not a common performance bottleneck, but it serves as a decent case study for regex optimization since there are a variety of ways to implement it.

Trimming with Regular Expressions

Regular expressions allow you to implement a trim method with very little code, which is important for JavaScript libraries that focus on file size. Probably the best all-around solution is to use two substitutions—one to remove leading whitespace and another to remove trailing whitespace. This keeps things simple and fast, especially with long strings.

```
if (!String.prototype.trim) {
    String.prototype.trim = function() {
        return this.replace(/^\s+/, "").replace(/\s+$/, "");
    }
}

// test the new method...
// tab (\t) and line feed (\n) characters are
// included in the leading whitespace.

var str = " \t\n  test string  ".trim();
alert(str == "test string"); // alerts "true"
```

The `if` block surrounding this code avoids overriding the `trim` method if it already exists, since native methods are optimized and usually far faster than anything you can implement yourself using a JavaScript function. Subsequent implementations of this example assume that this conditional is in place, though it is not written out each time.

You can give Firefox a performance boost of roughly 35% (less or more depending on the target string's length and content)[*] by replacing /\s+$/ (the second regex) with /\s\s*$/. Although these two regexes are functionally identical, Firefox provides additional optimization for regexes that start with a nonquantified token. In other browsers, the difference is less significant or is optimized differently altogether. However, changing the regex that matches at the beginning of strings to /^\s\s*/ does not produce a measurable difference, because the leading ^ anchor takes care of quickly invalidating nonmatching positions (precluding a slight performance difference from compounding over thousands of match attempts within a long string).

Following are several more regex-based `trim` implementations, which are some of the more common alternatives you might encounter. You can see cross-browser performance numbers for all `trim` implementations described here in Table 5-2 at the end of this section. There are, in fact, many ways beyond those listed here that you can write a regular expression to help you trim strings, but they are invariably slower (or at least less consistently decent cross-browser) than using two simple substitutions when working with long strings.

```
// trim 2
String.prototype.trim = function() {
    return this.replace(/^\s+|\s+$/g, "");
}
```

This is probably the most common solution. It combines the two simple regexes via alternation, and uses the /g (global) flag to replace all matches rather than just the first (it will match twice when its target contains both leading and trailing whitespace). This

---

[*] Tested in Firefox versions 2, 3, and 3.5.

isn't a terrible approach, but it's slower than using two simple substitutions when working with long strings since the two alternation options need to be tested at every character position.

```
// trim 3
String.prototype.trim = function() {
    return this.replace(/^\s*([\s\S]*?)\s*$/, "$1");
}
```

This regex works by matching the entire string and capturing the sequence from the first to the last nonwhitespace characters (if any) to backreference one. By replacing the entire string with backreference one, you're left with a trimmed version of the string.

This approach is conceptually simple, but the lazy quantifier inside the capturing group makes the regex do a lot of extra work (i.e., backtracking), and therefore tends to make this option slow with long target strings. After the regex enters the capturing group, the [\s\S] class's lazy *? quantifier requires that it be repeated as few times as possible. Thus, the regex matches one character at a time, stopping after each character to try to match the remaining \s*$ pattern. If that fails because nonwhitespace characters remain somewhere after the current position in the string, the regex matches one more character, updates the backreference, and then tries the remainder of the pattern again.

Lazy repetition is particularly slow in Opera 9.x and earlier. Consequently, trimming long strings with this method in Opera 9.64 performs about 10 to 100 times slower than in the other big browsers. Opera 10 fixes this longstanding weakness, bringing this method's performance in line with other browsers.

```
// trim 4
String.prototype.trim = function() {
    return this.replace(/^\s*([\s\S]*\S)?\s*$/, "$1");
}
```

This is similar to the last regex, but it replaces the lazy quantifier with a greedy one for performance reasons. To make sure that the capturing group still only matches up to the last nonwhitespace character, a trailing \S is required. However, since the regex must be able to match whitespace-only strings, the entire capturing group is made optional by adding a trailing question mark quantifier.

Here, the greedy asterisk in [\s\S]* repeats its any-character pattern to the end of the string. The regex then backtracks one character at a time until it's able to match the following \S, or until it backtracks to the first character matched within the group (after which it skips the group).

Unless there's more trailing whitespace than other text, this generally ends up being faster than the previous solution that used a lazy quantifier. In fact, it's so much faster that in IE, Safari, Chrome, and Opera 10, it even beats using two substitutions. That's because those browsers contain special optimization for greedy repetition of character classes that match any character. The regex engine jumps to the end of the string without evaluating intermediate characters (although backtracking positions must still be recorded), and then backtracks as appropriate. Unfortunately, this method is considerably slower in Firefox and Opera 9, so at least for now, using two substitutions still holds up better cross-browser.

```
// trim 5
String.prototype.trim = function() {
    return this.replace(/^\s*(\S*(\s+\S+)*)\s*$/, "$1");
}
```

This is a relatively common approach, but there's no good reason to use it since it's consistently one of the slowest of the options shown here, in all browsers. It's similar to the last two regexes in that it matches the entire string and replaces it with the part you want to keep, but because the inner group matches only one word at a time, there are a lot of discrete steps the regex must take. The performance hit may be unnoticeable when trimming short strings, but with long strings that contain many words, this regex can become a performance problem.

Changing the inner group to a noncapturing group—i.e., changing (\s+\S+) to (?:\s+ \S+)—helps a bit, slashing roughly 20%–45% off the time needed in Opera, IE, and Chrome, along with much slighter improvements in Safari and Firefox. Still, a non-capturing group can't redeem this implementation. Note that the outer group cannot be converted to a noncapturing group since it is referenced in the replacement string.

Trimming Without Regular Expressions

Although regular expressions are fast, it's worth considering the performance of trimming without their help. Here's one way to do so:

```
// trim 6
String.prototype.trim = function() {
    var start = 0,
        end = this.length - 1,
        ws = " \n\r\t\f\x0b\xa0\u1680\u180e\u2000\u2001\u2002\u2003
\u2004\u2005\u2006\u2007\u2008\u2009\u200a\u200b\u2028\u2029\u202f
\u205f\u3000\ufeff";

    while (ws.indexOf(this.charAt(start)) > -1) {
        start++;
    }
    while (end > start && ws.indexOf(this.charAt(end)) > -1) {
        end--;
    }

    return this.slice(start, end + 1);
}
```

The ws variable in this code includes all whitespace characters as defined by ECMA-Script 5. For efficiency reasons, copying any part of the string is avoided until the trimmed version's start and end positions are known.

It turns out that this smokes the regex competition when there is only a bit of whitespace on the ends of the string. The reason is that although regular expressions are well suited for removing whitespace from the beginning of a string, they're not as fast at trimming from the end of long strings. As noted in the section "When Not to Use Regular Expressions" on page 99, a regex cannot jump to the end of a string without considering characters along the way. However, this implementation does just that, with the second `while` loop working backward from the end of the string until it finds a nonwhitespace character.

Although this version is not affected by the overall length of the string, it has its own weakness: long leading and trailing whitespace. That's because looping over characters to check whether they are whitespace can't match the efficiency of a regex's optimized search code.

A Hybrid Solution

The final approach for this section is to combine a regex's universal efficiency at trimming leading whitespace with the nonregex method's speed at trimming trailing characters.

```
// trim 7
String.prototype.trim = function() {
    var str = this.replace(/^\s+/, ""),
        end = str.length - 1,
        ws = /\s/;

    while (ws.test(str.charAt(end))) {
        end--;
    }

    return str.slice(0, end + 1);
}
```

This hybrid method remains insanely fast when trimming only a bit of whitespace, and removes the performance risk of strings with long leading whitespace and whitespace-only strings (although it maintains the weakness for strings with long trailing whitespace). Note that this solution uses a regex in the loop to check whether characters at the end of the string are whitespace. Although using a regex for this adds a bit of performance overhead, it lets you defer the list of whitespace characters to the browser for the sake of brevity and compatibility.

The general trend for all `trim` methods described here is that overall string length has more impact than the number of characters to be trimmed in regex-based solutions, whereas nonregex solutions that work backward from the end of the string are unaffected by overall string length but more significantly affected by the amount of whitespace to trim. The simplicity of using two regex substitutions provides consistently respectable performance cross-browser with varying string contents and lengths, and therefore it's arguably the best all-around solution. The hybrid solution is exceptionally fast with long strings at the cost of slightly longer code and a weakness in some browsers for long, trailing whitespace. See Table 5-2 for all the gory details.

Table 5-2. Cross-browser performance of various trim implementations

Browser	Time (ms)[a]						
	Trim 1[b]	Trim 2	Trim 3	Trim 4	Trim 5[c]	Trim 6	Trim 7
IE 7	80/80	315/312	547/539	36/42	218/224	14/1015	18/409
IE 8	70/70	252/256	512/425	26/30	216/222	4/334	12/205
Firefox 3	136/147	164/174	650/600	1098/1525	1416/1488	21/151	20/144
Firefox 3.5	130/147	157/172	500/510	1004/1437	1344/1394	21/332	18/50
Safari 3.2.3	253/253	424/425	351/359	27/29	541/554	2/140	5/80
Safari 4	37/37	33/31	69/68	32/33	510/514	<0.5/29	4/18
Opera 9.64	494/517	731/748	9066/9601	901/955	1953/2016	<0.5/210	20/241
Opera 10	75/75	94/100	360/370	46/46	514/514	2/186	12/198
Chrome 2	78/78	66/68	100/101	59/59	140/142	1/37	24/55

[a] Reported times were generated by trimming a large string (40 KB) 100 times, first with 10 and then 1,000 spaces added to each end.

[b] Tested without the /\s\s*$/ optimization.

[c] Tested without the noncapturing group optimization.

Summary

Intensive string operations and incautiously crafted regexes can be major performance obstructions, but the advice in this chapter helps you avoid common pitfalls.

- When concatenating numerous or large strings, array joining is the only method with reasonable performance in IE7 and earlier.

- If you don't need to worry about IE7 and earlier, array joining is one of the slowest ways to concatenate strings. Use simple + and += operators instead, and avoid unnecessary intermediate strings.

- Backtracking is both a fundamental component of regex matching and a frequent source of regex inefficiency.

- Runaway backtracking can cause a regex that usually finds matches quickly to run slowly or even crash your browser when applied to partially matching strings. Techniques for avoiding this problem include making adjacent tokens mutually exclusive, avoiding nested quantifiers that allow matching the same part of a string more than one way, and eliminating needless backtracking by repurposing the atomic nature of lookahead.

- A variety of techniques exist for improving regex efficiency by helping regexes find matches faster and spend less time considering nonmatching positions (see "More Ways to Improve Regular Expression Efficiency" on page 96).

- Regexes are not always the best tool for the job, especially when you are merely searching for literal strings.

- Although there are many ways to trim a string, using two simple regexes (one to remove leading whitespace and another for trailing whitespace) offers a good mix of brevity and cross-browser efficiency with varying string contents and lengths. Looping from the end of the string in search of the first nonwhitespace characters, or combining this technique with regexes in a hybrid approach, offers a good alternative that is less affected by overall string length.

Responsive Interfaces

There's nothing more frustrating than clicking something on a web page and having nothing happen. This problem goes back to the origin of transactional web applications and resulted in the now-ubiquitous "please click only once" message that accompanies most form submissions. A user's natural inclination is to repeat any action that doesn't result in an obvious change, and so ensuring responsiveness in web applications is an important performance concern.

Chapter 1 introduced the browser UI thread concept. As a recap, most browsers have a single process that is shared between JavaScript execution and user interface updates. Only one of these operations can be performed at a time, meaning that the user interface cannot respond to input while JavaScript code is executed and vice versa. The user interface effectively becomes "locked" when JavaScript is executing; managing how long your JavaScript takes to execute is important to the perceived performance of a web application.

The Browser UI Thread

The process shared by JavaScript and user interface updates is frequently referred to as the browser UI thread (though the term "thread" is not necessarily accurate for all browsers). The UI thread works on a simple queuing system where tasks are kept until the process is idle. Once idle, the next task in the queue is retrieved and executed. These tasks are either JavaScript code to execute or UI updates to perform, which include redraws and reflows (discussed in Chapter 3). Perhaps the most interesting part of this process is that each input may result in one or more tasks being added to the queue.

Consider a simple interface where a button click results in a message being displayed on the screen:

```
<html>
<head>
    <title>Browser UI Thread Example</title>
</head>
<body>
```

```
<button onclick="handleClick()">Click Me</button>
<script type="text/javascript">

    function handleClick(){
        var div = document.createElement("div");
        div.innerHTML = "Clicked!";
        document.body.appendChild(div);
    }

</script>
</body>
</html>
```

When the button in this example is clicked, it triggers the UI thread to create and add two tasks to the queue. The first task is a UI update for the button, which needs to change appearance to indicate it was clicked, and the second is a JavaScript execution task containing the code for `handleClick()`, so that the only code being executed is this method and anything it calls. Assuming the UI thread is idle, the first task is retrieved and executed to update the button's appearance, and then the JavaScript task is retrieved and executed. During the course of execution, `handleClick()` creates a new `<div>` element and appends it to the `<body>` element, effectively making another UI change. That means that during the JavaScript execution, a new UI update task is added to the queue such that the UI is updated once JavaScript execution is complete. See Figure 6-1.

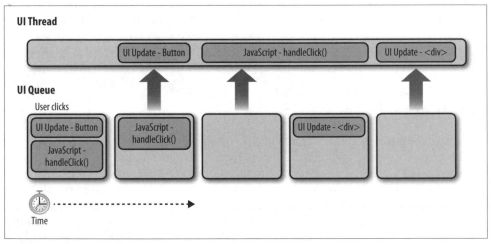

Figure 6-1. UI thread tasks get added as the user interacts with a page

When all UI thread tasks have been executed, the process becomes idle and waits for more tasks to be added to the queue. The idle state is ideal because all user actions then result in an immediate UI update. If the user tries to interact with the page while a task is being executed, not only will there not be an immediate UI update, but a new task for a UI update may not even be created and queued. In fact, most browsers stop queuing tasks for the UI thread while JavaScript is executing, which means that it is imperative to finish JavaScript tasks as quickly as possible so as not to adversely affect the user's experience.

Browser Limits

Browsers place limits on the amount of time that JavaScript take to execute. This is a necessary limitation to ensure that malicious coders can't lock up a user's browser or computer by performing intensive operations that will never end. There are two such limits: the *call stack size limit* (discussed in Chapter 4) and the *long-running script limit*. The long-running script limit is sometimes called the long-running script timer or the runaway script timer, but the basic idea is that the browser keeps track of how long a script has been running and will stop it once a certain limit is hit. When the limit is reached, a dialog is displayed to the user, such as the one in Figure 6-2.

Figure 6-2. Internet Explorer's long-running script warning dialog is displayed when more than 5 million statements have been executed

There are two ways of measuring how long a script is executing. The first is to keep track of how many statements have been executed since the script began. This approach means that the script may run for different periods of time on different machines, as the available memory and CPU speed can affect how long it takes to execute a single statement. The second approach is to track the total amount of time that the script has been executing. The amount of script that can be processed within a set amount of time also varies based on the user's machine capabilities, but the script is always stopped after a set amount of time. Not surprisingly, each browser has a slightly different approach to long-running script detection:

- Internet Explorer, as of version 4, sets a default limit of 5 million statements; this limit is stored in a Windows registry setting called *HKEY_CURRENT_USER\Software\Microsoft\InternetExplorer\Styles\MaxScriptStatements*.

- Firefox has a default limit of 10 seconds; this limit is stored in the browser's configuration settings (accessible by typing **about:config** in the address box) as the *dom.max_script_run_time* key.

- Safari has a default limit of 5 seconds; this setting cannot be altered, but you can disable the timer by enabling the *Develop* menu and selecting *Disable Runaway JavaScript Timer*.

- Chrome has no separate long-running script limit and instead relies on its generic crash detection system to handle such instances.

- Opera has no long-running script limit and will continue to execute JavaScript code until it has finished, though, due to Opera's architecture, this will not cause system instability while the execution is completed.

When the browser's long-running script limit is reached, a dialog is displayed to the user, regardless of any other error-handling code on the page. This is a major usability issue because most Internet users are not technically savvy and would therefore be confused about the meaning of the error message as well as which option (to stop the script or allow it to continue) is appropriate.

If your script triggers this dialog in any browser, it means the script is simply taking too long to complete its task. It also indicates that the user's browser has become unresponsive to input while the JavaScript code is continuing to execute. From a developer's point of view, there is no way to recover from a long-running script dialog's appearance; you can't detect it and therefore can't adjust to any issues that might arise as a result. Clearly, the best way to deal with long-running script limits is to avoid them in the first place.

How Long Is Too Long?

Just because the browser allows a script to continue executing up to a certain number of seconds doesn't mean you should allow it do so. In fact, the amount of time that your JavaScript code executes continuously should be much smaller than the browser-imposed limits in order to create a good user experience. Brendan Eich, creator of JavaScript, is quoted as having once said, "[JavaScript] that executes in whole seconds is probably doing something wrong...."

If whole seconds are too long for JavaScript to execute, what is an appropriate amount of time? As it turns out, even one second is too long for a script to execute. The total amount of time that a single JavaScript operation should take (at a maximum) is 100 milliseconds. This number comes from research conducted by Robert Miller in 1968.[*] Interestingly, usability expert Jakob Nielsen noted[†] in his book *Usability*

---

[*] Miller, R. B., "Response time in man-computer conversational transactions," *Proc. AFIPS Fall Joint Computer Conference*, Vol. 33 (1968), 267–277. Available at *http://portal.acm.org/citation.cfm?id=1476589.1476628*.

[†] Available online at *www.useit.com/papers/responsetime.html*.

Engineering (Morgan Kaufmann, 1994) that this number hasn't changed over time and, in fact, was reaffirmed in 1991 by research at Xerox-PARC.‡

Nielsen states that if the interface responds to user input within 100 milliseconds, the user feels that he is "directly manipulating the objects in the user interface." Any amount of time more than 100 milliseconds means the user feels disconnected from the interface. Since the UI cannot update while JavaScript is executing, the user cannot feel in control of the interface if that execution takes longer than 100 milliseconds.

A further complication is that some browsers won't even queue UI updates while Java-Script is executing. For example, if you click a button while some JavaScript code is executing, the browser may not queue up the UI update to redraw the button as pressed or any JavaScript initiated by the button. The result is an unresponsive UI that appears to "hang" or "freeze."

Each browser behaves in roughly the same way. When a script is executing, the UI does not update from user interaction. JavaScript tasks created as a result of user interaction during this time are queued and then executed, in order, when the original JavaScript task has been completed. UI updates caused by user interaction are automatically skipped over at this time because the priority is given to the dynamic aspects of the page. Thus, a button clicked while a script is executing will never look like it was clicked, even though its `onclick` handler will be executed.

 Internet Explorer throttles JavaScript tasks triggered by user interaction so that it recognizes only two repeated actions in a row. For example, clicking on a button four times while a script is executing results in the `onclick` event handler being called only twice.

Even though browsers try to do something logical in these cases, all of these behaviors lead to a disjointed user experience. The best approach, therefore, is to prevent such circumstances from occurring by limiting any JavaScript task to 100 milliseconds or less. This measurement should be taken on the slowest browser you must support (for tools that measure JavaScript performance, see Chapter 10).

Yielding with Timers

Despite your best efforts, there will be times when a JavaScript task cannot be completed in 100 milliseconds or less because of its complexity. In these cases, it's ideal to yield control of the UI thread so that UI updates may occur. Yielding control means stopping JavaScript execution and giving the UI a chance to update itself before continuing to execute the JavaScript. This is where JavaScript timers come into the picture.

‡ Card, S. K., G.G. Robertson, and J.D. Mackinlay, "The information visualizer: An information workspace," *Proc. ACM CHI'91 Conf.* (New Orleans: 28 April–2 May), 181–188. Available at *http://portal.acm.org/citation .cfm?id=108874*.

Timer Basics

Timers are created in JavaScript using either `setTimeout()` or `setInterval()`, and both accept the same arguments: a function to execute and the amount of time to wait (in milliseconds) before executing it. The `setTimeout()` function creates a timer that executes just once, whereas the `setInterval()` function creates a timer that repeats periodically.

The way that timers interact with the UI thread is helpful for breaking up long-running scripts into shorter segments. Calling `setTimeout()` or `setInterval()` tells the JavaScript engine to wait a certain amount of time and then add a JavaScript task to the UI queue. For example:

```
function greeting(){
    alert("Hello world!");
}

setTimeout(greeting, 250);
```

This code inserts a JavaScript task to execute the `greeting()` function into the UI queue after 250 milliseconds have passed. Prior to that point, all other UI updates and JavaScript tasks are executed. Keep in mind that the second argument indicates when the task should be added to the UI queue, which is not necessarily the time that it will be executed; the task must wait until all other tasks already in the queue are executed, just like any other task. Consider the following:

```
var button = document.getElementById("my-button");
button.onclick = function(){

    oneMethod();

    setTimeout(function(){
        document.getElementById("notice").style.color = "red";
    }, 250);
};
```

When the button in this example is clicked, it calls a method and then sets a timer. The code to change the `notice` element's color is contained in a timer set to be queued in 250 milliseconds. That 250 milliseconds starts from the time at which `setTimeout()` is called, not when the overall function has finished executing. So if `setTimeout()` is called at a point in time n, then the JavaScript task to execute the timer code is added to the UI queue at $n + 250$. Figure 6-3 shows this relationship when the button in this example is clicked.

Keep in mind that the timer code can never be executed until after the function in which it was created is completely executed. For example, if the previous code is changed such that the timer delay is smaller and there is another function call after the timer is created, it's possible that the timer code will be queued before the `onclick` event handler has finished executing:

```
var button = document.getElementById("my-button");
button.onclick = function(){

    oneMethod();

    setTimeout(function(){
        document.getElementById("notice").style.color = "red";
    }, 50);

    anotherMethod();
};
```

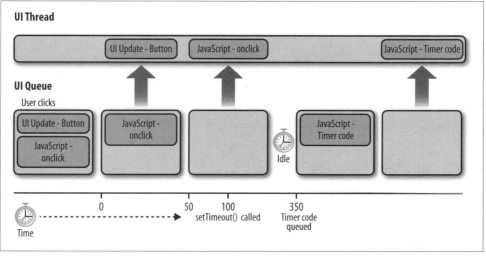

Figure 6-3. The second argument of setTimeout() indicates when the new JavaScript task should be inserted into the UI queue

If `anotherMethod()` takes longer than 50 milliseconds to execute, then the timer code is added to the queue before the `onclick` handler is finished. The effect is that the timer code executes almost immediately after the `onclick` handler has executed completely, without a noticeable delay. Figure 6-4 illustrates this situation.

In either case, creating a timer creates a pause in the UI thread as it switches from one task to the next. Consequently, timer code resets all of the relevant browser limits, including the long-running script timer. Further, the call stack is reset to zero inside of the timer code. These characteristics make timers the ideal cross-browser solution for long-running JavaScript code.

 The `setInterval()` function is almost the same as `setTimeout()`, except that the former repeatedly adds JavaScript tasks into the UI queue. The main difference is that it will not add a JavaScript task into the UI queue if a task created by the same `setInterval()` call is already present in the UI queue.

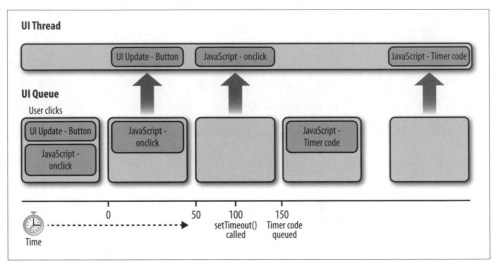

Figure 6-4. There may be no noticeable delay in timer code execution if the function in which setTimeout() is called takes longer to execute than the timer delay

Timer Precision

JavaScript timer delays are often imprecise, with slips of a few milliseconds in either direction. Just because you specify 250 milliseconds as the timer delay doesn't necessarily mean the task is queued exactly 250 milliseconds after `setTimeout()` is called. All browsers make an attempt to be as accurate as possible, but oftentimes a slip of a few milliseconds in either direction occurs. For this reason, timers are unreliable for measuring actual time passed.

Timer resolution on Windows systems is 15 milliseconds, meaning that it will interpret a timer delay of 15 as either 0 or 15, depending on when the system time was last updated. Setting timer delays of less than 15 can cause browser locking in Internet Explorer, so the smallest recommended delay is 25 milliseconds (which will end up as either 15 or 30) to ensure a delay of at least 15 milliseconds.

This minimum timer delay also helps to avoid timer resolution issues in other browsers and on other systems. Most browsers show some variance in timer delays when dealing with 10 milliseconds or smaller.

Array Processing with Timers

One common cause of long-running scripts is loops that take too long to execute. If you've already tried the loop optimization techniques presented in Chapter 4 but haven't been able to reduce the execution time enough, then timers are your next optimization step. The basic approach is to split up the loop's work into a series of timers.

Typical loops follow a simple pattern, such as:

```
for (var i=0, len=items.length; i < len; i++){
    process(items[i]);
}
```

Loops with this structure can take too long to execute due to the complexity of `process()`, the size of `items`, or both. In my book *Professional JavaScript for Web Developers*, Second Edition (Wrox 2009), I lay out the two determining factors for whether a loop can be done asynchronously using timers:

- Does the processing have to be done synchronously?
- Does the data have to be processed sequentially?

If the answer to both of these questions is "no," then the code is a good candidate for using timers to split up the work. A basic pattern for asynchronous code execution is:

```
var todo = items.concat();  //create a clone of the original

setTimeout(function(){

    //get next item in the array and process it
    process(todo.shift());

    //if there's more items to process, create another timer
    if(todo.length > 0){
        setTimeout(arguments.callee, 25);
    } else {
        callback(items);
    }

}, 25);
```

The basic idea of this pattern is to create a clone of the original array and use that as a queue of items to process. The first call to `setTimeout()` creates a timer to process the first item in the array. Calling `todo.shift()` returns the first item and also removes it from the array. This value is passed into `process()`. After processing the item, a check is made to determine whether there are more items to process. If there are still items in the `todo` array, there are more items to process and another timer is created. Because the next timer needs to run the same code as the original, `arguments.callee` is passed in as the first argument. This value points to the anonymous function in which the code is executing. If there are no further items to process, then a `callback()` function is called.

 The actual amount of time to delay each timer is largely dependent on your use case. Generally speaking, it's best to use at least 25 milliseconds because smaller delays leave too little time for most UI updates.

Because this pattern requires significantly more code that a regular loop, it's useful to encapsulate this functionality. For example:

```
function processArray(items, process, callback){
    var todo = items.concat();    //create a clone of the original

    setTimeout(function(){
        process(todo.shift());

        if (todo.length > 0){
            setTimeout(arguments.callee, 25);
        } else {
            callback(items);
        }

    }, 25);
}
```

The processArray() function implements the previous pattern in a reusable way and accepts three arguments: the array to process, the function to call on each item, and a callback function to execute when processing is complete. This function can be used as follows:

```
var items = [123, 789, 323, 778, 232, 654, 219, 543, 321, 160];

function outputValue(value){
    console.log(value);
}

processArray(items, outputValue, function(){
    console.log("Done!");
});
```

This code uses the processArray() method to output array values to the console and then prints a message when all processing is complete. By encapsulating the timer code inside of a function, it can be reused in multiple places without requiring multiple implementations.

 One side effect of using timers to process arrays is that the total time to process the array increases. This is because the UI thread is freed up after each item is processed and there is a delay before the next item is processed. Nevertheless, this is a necessary trade-off to avoid a poor user experience by locking up the browser.

Splitting Up Tasks

What we typically think of as one task can often be broken down into a series of subtasks. If a single function is taking too long to execute, check to see whether it can be broken down into a series of smaller functions that complete in smaller amounts of time. This is often as simple as considering a single line of code as an atomic task, even though multiple lines of code typically can be grouped together into a single task. Some functions are already easily broken down based on the other functions they call. For example:

```
function saveDocument(id){

    //save the document
    openDocument(id)
    writeText(id);
    closeDocument(id);

    //update the UI to indicate success
    updateUI(id);
}
```

If this function is taking too long, it can easily be split up into a series of smaller steps by breaking out the individual methods into separate timers. You can accomplish this by adding each function into an array and then using a pattern similar to the array-processing pattern from the previous section:

```
function saveDocument(id){

    var tasks = [openDocument, writeText, closeDocument, updateUI];

    setTimeout(function(){

        //execute the next task
        var task = tasks.shift();
        task(id);

        //determine if there's more
        if (tasks.length > 0){
            setTimeout(arguments.callee, 25);
        }
    }, 25);
}
```

This version of the function places each method into the **tasks** array and then executes only one method with each timer. Fundamentally, this now becomes an array-processing pattern, with the sole difference that processing an item involves executing the function contained in the item. As discussed in the previous section, this pattern can be encapsulated for reuse:

```
function multistep(steps, args, callback){

    var tasks = steps.concat();    //clone the array

    setTimeout(function(){

        //execute the next task
        var task = tasks.shift();
        task.apply(null, args || []);

        //determine if there's more
```

```
        if (tasks.length > 0){
            setTimeout(arguments.callee, 25);
        } else {
            callback();
        }
    }, 25);
}
```

The `multistep()` function accepts three arguments: an array of functions to execute, an array of arguments to pass into each function when it executes, and a callback function to call when the process is complete. This function can be used like the following:

```
function saveDocument(id){

    var tasks = [openDocument, writeText, closeDocument, updateUI];
    multistep(tasks, [id], function(){
        alert("Save completed!");
    });
}
```

Note that the second argument to `multistep()` must be an array, so one is created containing just `id`. As with array processing, this function is best used when the tasks can be processed asynchronously without affecting the user experience or causing errors in dependent code.

Timed Code

Sometimes executing just one task at a time is inefficient. Consider processing an array of 1,000 items for which processing a single item takes 1 millisecond. If one item is processed in each timer and there is a delay of 25 milliseconds in between, that means the total amount of time to process the array is $(25 + 1) \times 1,000 = 26,000$ milliseconds, or 26 seconds. What if you processed the items in batches of 50 with a 25-millisecond delay between them? The entire processing time then becomes $(1,000 / 50) \times 25 + 1,000 = 1,500$ milliseconds, or 1.5 seconds, and the user is still never blocked from the interface because the longest the script has executed continuously is 50 milliseconds. It's typically faster to process items in batches than one at a time.

If you keep 100 milliseconds in mind as the absolute maximum amount of time that JavaScript should be allowed to run continuously, then you can start optimizing the previous patterns. My recommendation is to cut that number in half and never let any JavaScript code execute for longer than 50 milliseconds continuously, just to make sure the code never gets close to affecting the user experience.

It's possible to track how long a piece of code has been running by using the native `Date` object. This is the way most JavaScript profiling works:

```
var start = +new Date(),
    stop;

someLongProcess();
```

```
stop = +new Date();

if(stop-start < 50){
    alert("Just about right.");
} else {
    alert("Taking too long.");
}
```

Since each new Date object is initialized with the current system time, you can time code by creating new Date objects periodically and comparing their values. The plus operator (+) converts the Date object into a numeric representation so that any further arithmetic doesn't involve conversions. This same basic technique can be used to optimize the previous timer patterns.

The processArray() method can be augmented to process multiple items per timer by adding in a time check:

```
function timedProcessArray(items, process, callback){
    var todo = items.concat();   //create a clone of the original

    setTimeout(function(){
        var start = +new Date();

        do {
            process(todo.shift());
        } while (todo.length > 0 && (+new Date() - start < 50));

        if (todo.length > 0){
            setTimeout(arguments.callee, 25);
        } else {
            callback(items);
        }

    }, 25);
}
```

The addition of a do-while loop in this function enables checking the time after each item is processed. The array will always contain at least one item when the timer function executes, so a post-test loop makes more sense than a pretest one. When run in Firefox 3, this function processes an array of 1,000 items, where process() is an empty function, in 38–43 milliseconds; the original processArray() function processes the same array in over 25,000 milliseconds. This is the power of timing tasks before breaking them up into smaller chunks.

Timers and Performance

Timers can make a huge difference in the overall performance of your JavaScript code, but overusing them can have a negative effect on performance. The code in this section has used sequenced timers such that only one timer exists at a time and new ones are created only when the last timer has finished. Using timers in this way will not result in performance issues.

Performance issues start to appear when multiple repeating timers are being created at the same time. Since there is only one UI thread, all of the timers compete for time to execute. Neil Thomas of Google Mobile researched this topic as a way of measuring performance on the mobile Gmail application for the iPhone and Android.§

Thomas found that low-frequency repeating timers—those occurring at intervals of one second or greater—had little effect on overall web application responsiveness. The timer delays in this case are too large to create a bottleneck on the UI thread and are therefore safe to use repeatedly. When multiple repeating timers are used with a much greater frequency (between 100 and 200 milliseconds), however, Thomas found that the mobile Gmail application became noticeably slower and less responsive.

The takeaway from Thomas's research is to limit the number of high-frequency repeating timers in your web application. Instead, Thomas suggests creating a single repeating timer that performs multiple operations with each execution.

Web Workers

Since JavaScript was introduced, there has been no way to execute code outside of the browser UI thread. The web workers API changes this by introducing an interface through which code can be executed without taking time on the browser UI thread. Originally part of HTML 5, the web workers API has been split out into its own specification (*http://www.w3.org/TR/workers/*); web workers have already been implemented natively in Firefox 3.5, Chrome 3, and Safari 4.

Web workers represent a potentially huge performance improvement for web applications because each new worker spawns its own thread in which to execute JavaScript. That means not only will code executing in a worker not affect the browser UI, but it also won't affect code executing in other workers.

Worker Environment

Since web workers aren't bound to the UI thread, it also means that they cannot access a lot of browser resources. Part of the reason that JavaScript and UI updates share the same process is because one can affect the other quite frequently, and so executing these tasks out of order results in a bad user experience. Web workers could introduce user interface errors by making changes to the DOM from an outside thread, but each web worker has its own global environment that has only a subset of JavaScript features available. The worker environment is made up of the following:

- A `navigator` object, which contains only four properties: `appName`, `appVersion`, `user Agent`, and `platform`

---

§ The full post is available online at *http://googlecode.blogspot.com/2009/07/gmail-for-mobile-html5-series -using.html*.

- A `location` object (same as on `window`, except all properties are read-only)
- A `self` object that points to the global worker object
- An `importScripts()` method that is used to load external JavaScript for use in the worker
- All ECMAScript objects, such as `Object`, `Array`, `Date`, etc.
- The `XMLHttpRequest` constructor
- The `setTimeout()` and `setInterval()` methods
- A `close()` method that stops the worker immediately

Because web workers have a different global environment, you can't create one from any JavaScript code. In fact, you'll need to create an entirely separate JavaScript file containing just the code for the worker to execute. To create a web worker, you must pass in the URL for the JavaScript file:

```
var worker = new Worker("code.js");
```

Once this is executed, a new thread with a new worker environment is created for the specified file. This file is downloaded asynchronously, and the worker will not begin until the file has been completely downloaded and executed.

Worker Communication

Communication between a worker and the web page code is established through an event interface. The web page code can pass data to the worker via the `postMessage()` method, which accepts a single argument indicating the data to pass into the worker. There is also an `onmessage` event handler that is used to receive information from the worker. For example:

```
var worker = new Worker("code.js");
worker.onmessage = function(event){
    alert(event.data);
};
worker.postMessage("Nicholas");
```

The worker receives this data through the firing of a `message` event. An `onmessage` event handler is defined, and the event object has a data property containing the data that was passed in. The worker can then pass information back to the web page by using its own `postMessage()` method:

```
//inside code.js
self.onmessage = function(event){
    self.postMessage("Hello, " + event.data + "!");
};
```

The final string ends up in the `onmessage` event handler for the worker. This messaging system is the only way in which the web page and the worker can communicate.

Only certain types of data can be passed using `postMessage()`. You can pass primitive values (strings, numbers, Booleans, `null`, and `undefined`) as well as instances of `Object` and `Array`; you cannot pass any other data types. Valid data is serialized, transmitted to or from the worker, and then deserialized. Even though it seems like the objects are being passed through directly, the instances are completely separate representations of the same data. Attempting to pass an unsupported data type results in a JavaScript error.

 Safari 4's implementation of workers only allows you to pass strings using `postMessage()`. The specification was updated after that point to allow serializable data to be passed through, which is how Firefox 3.5 implements workers.

Loading External Files

Loading extra JavaScript files into a worker is done via the `importScripts()` method, which accepts one or more URLs for JavaScript files to load. The call to `importScripts()` is blocking within the worker, so the script won't continue until all files have been loaded and executed. Since the worker is running outside of the UI thread, there is no concern about UI responsiveness when this blocking occurs. For example:

```
//inside code.js
importScripts("file1.js", "file2.js");

self.onmessage = function(event){
    self.postMessage("Hello, " + event.data + "!");
};
```

The first line in this code includes two JavaScript files so that they will be available in the context of the worker.

Practical Uses

Web workers are suitable for any long-running scripts that work on pure data and that have no ties to the browser UI. This may seem like a fairly small number of uses, but buried in web applications there are typically some data-handling approaches that would benefit from using a worker instead of timers.

Consider, for example, parsing a large JSON string (JSON parsing is discussed further in Chapter 7). Suppose that the data is large enough that parsing takes at least 500 milliseconds. That is clearly too long to allow JavaScript to run on the client, as it will interfere with the user experience. This particular task is difficult to break into small chunks with timers, so a worker is the ideal solution. The following code illustrates usage from a web page:

```
var worker = new Worker("jsonparser.js");

//when the data is available, this event handler is called
worker.onmessage = function(event){

    //the JSON structure is passed back
    var jsonData = event.data;

    //the JSON structure is used
    evaluateData(jsonData);
};

//pass in the large JSON string to parse
worker.postMessage(jsonText);
```

The code for the worker responsible for JSON parsing is as follows:

```
//inside of jsonparser.js

//this event handler is called when JSON data is available
self.onmessage = function(event){

    //the JSON string comes in as event.data
    var jsonText = event.data;

    //parse the structure
    var jsonData = JSON.parse(jsonText);

    //send back to the results
    self.postMessage(jsonData);
};
```

Note that even though `JSON.parse()` is likely to take 500 milliseconds or more, there is no need to write any additional code to split up the processing. This execution takes place on a separate thread, so you can let it run for as long as the parsing takes without interfering with the user experience.

The page passes a JSON string into the worker by using `postMessage()`. The worker receives the string as `event.data` in its `onmessage` event handler and then proceeds to parse it. When complete, the resulting JSON object is passed back to the page using the worker's `postMessage()` method. This object is then available as `event.data` in the page's `onmessage` event handler. Keep in mind that this presently works only in Firefox 3.5 and later, as Safari 4 and Chrome 3's implementations allow strings to be passed only between page and worker.

Parsing a large string is just one of many possible tasks that can benefit from web workers. Some other possibilities are:

- Encoding/decoding a large string
- Complex mathematical calculations (including image or video processing)
- Sorting a large array

Any time a process takes longer than 100 milliseconds to complete, you should consider whether a worker solution is more appropriate than a timer-based one. This, of course, is based on browser capabilities.

Summary

JavaScript and user interface updates operate within the same process, so only one can be done at a time. This means that the user interface cannot react to input while JavaScript code is executing and vice versa. Managing the UI thread effectively means ensuring that JavaScript isn't allowed to run so long that the user experience is affected. To that end, the following should be kept in mind:

- No JavaScript task should take longer than 100 milliseconds to execute. Longer execution times cause a noticeable delay in updates to the UI and negatively impact the overall user experience.
- Browsers behave differently in response to user interaction during JavaScript execution. Regardless of the behavior, the user experience becomes confusing and disjointed when JavaScript takes a long time to execute.
- Timers can be used to schedule code for later execution, which allows you to split up long-running scripts into a series of smaller tasks.
- Web workers are a feature in newer browsers that allow you to execute JavaScript code outside of the UI thread, thus preventing UI locking.

The more complex the web application, the more critical it is to manage the UI thread in a proactive manner. No JavaScript code is so important that it should adversely affect the user's experience.

Ajax

Ross Harmes

Ajax is a cornerstone of high-performance JavaScript. It can be used to make a page load faster by delaying the download of large resources. It can prevent page loads altogether by allowing for data to be transferred between the client and the server asynchronously. It can even be used to fetch all of a page's resources in one HTTP request. By choosing the correct transmission technique and the most efficient data format, you can significantly improve how your users interact with your site.

This chapter examines the fastest techniques for sending data to and receiving it from the server, as well as the most efficient formats for encoding data.

Data Transmission

Ajax, at its most basic level, is a way of communicating with a server without unloading the current page; data can be requested from the server or sent to it. There are several different ways of setting up this communication channel, each with its own advantages and restrictions. This section briefly examines the different approaches and discusses the performance implications of each.

Requesting Data

There are five general techniques for requesting data from a server:

- XMLHttpRequest (XHR)
- Dynamic script tag insertion
- iframes
- Comet
- Multipart XHR

The three that are used in modern high-performance JavaScript are XHR, dynamic script tag insertion, and multipart XHR. Use of Comet and iframes (as data transport techniques) tends to be extremely situational, and won't be covered here.

XMLHttpRequest

By far the most common technique used, XMLHttpRequest (XHR) allows you to asynchronously send and receive data. It is well supported across all modern browsers and allows for a fine degree of control over both the request sent and the data received. You can add arbitrary headers and parameters (both GET and POST) to the request, and read all of the headers returned from the server, as well as the response text itself. The following is an example of how it can be used:

```
var url = '/data.php';
var params = [
    'id=934875',
    'limit=20'
];

var req = new XMLHttpRequest();

req.onreadystatechange = function() {
    if (req.readyState === 4) {
        var responseHeaders = req.getAllResponseHeaders(); // Get the response
headers.
        var data = req.responseText; // Get the data.
        // Process the data here...
    }
}

req.open('GET', url + '?' + params.join('&'), true);
req.setRequestHeader('X-Requested-With', 'XMLHttpRequest'); // Set a request
header.
req.send(null); // Send the request.
```

This example shows how to request data from a URL, with parameters, and how to read the response text and headers. A readyState of 4 indicates that the entire response has been received and is available for manipulation.

It is possible to interact with the server response as it is still being transferred by listening for readyState 3. This is known as streaming, and it is a powerful tool for improving the performance of your data requests:

```
req.onreadystatechange = function() {

    if (req.readyState === 3) { // Some, but not all, data has been received.
        var dataSoFar = req.responseText;
        ...
    }
    else if (req.readyState === 4) { // All data has been received.
        var data = req.responseText;
        ...
```

```
        }
    }
```

Because of the high degree of control that XHR offers, browsers place some restrictions on it. You cannot use XHR to request data from a domain different from the one the code is currently running under, and older versions of IE do not give you access to `readyState` 3, which prevents streaming. Data that comes back from the request is treated as either a string or an XML object; this means large amounts of data will be quite slow to process.

Despite these drawbacks, XHR is the most commonly used technique for requesting data and is still the most powerful. It should be the one you look to first.

POST versus GET when using XHR. When using XHR to request data, you have a choice between using POST or GET. For requests that don't change the server state and only pull back data (this is called an *idempotent action*), use GET. GET requests are cached, which can improve performance if you're fetching the same data several times.

POST should be used to fetch data only when the length of the URL and the parameters are close to or exceed 2,048 characters. This is because Internet Explorer limits URLs to that length, and exceeding it will cause your request to be truncated.

Dynamic script tag insertion

This technique overcomes the biggest limitation of XHR: it can request data from a server on a different domain. It is a hack; instead of instantiating a purpose-built object, you use JavaScript to create a new script tag and set its source attribute to a URL in a different domain.

```
var scriptElement = document.createElement('script');
scriptElement.src = 'http://any-domain.com/javascript/lib.js';
document.getElementsByTagName('head')[0].appendChild(scriptElement);
```

But dynamic script tag insertion offers much less control than XHR. You can't send headers with the request. Parameters can only be passed using GET, not POST. You can't set timeouts or retry the request; in fact, you won't necessarily know if it fails. You must wait for all of the data to be returned before you can access any of it. You don't have access to the response headers or to the entire response as a string.

This last point is especially important. Because the response is being used as the source for a script tag, it *must* be executable JavaScript. You cannot use bare XML, or even bare JSON; any data, regardless of the format, must be enclosed in a callback function.

```
var scriptElement = document.createElement('script');
scriptElement.src = 'http://any-domain.com/javascript/lib.js';
document.getElementsByTagName('head')[0].appendChild(scriptElement);

function jsonCallback(jsonString) {
    var data = eval('(' + jsonString + ')');
    // Process the data here...
}
```

In this example, the *lib.js* file would enclose the data in the `jsonCallback` function:

```
jsonCallback({ "status": 1, "colors": [ "#fff", "#000", "#ff0000" ] });
```

Despite these limitations, this technique can be extremely fast. The response is executed as JavaScript; it is not treated as a string that must be further processed. Because of this, it has the potential to be the fastest way of getting data and parsing it into something you can access on the client side. We compare the performance of dynamic script tag insertion with the performance of XHR in the section on JSON, later in this chapter.

Beware of using this technique to request data from a server you don't directly control. JavaScript has no concept of permission or access control, so any code that you incorporate into your page using dynamic script tag insertion will have complete control over the page. This includes the ability to modify any content, redirect users to another site, or even track their actions on this page and send the data back to a third party. Use extreme caution when pulling in code from an external source.

Multipart XHR

The newest of the techniques mentioned here, multipart XHR (MXHR) allows you to pass multiple resources from the server side to the client side using only one HTTP request. This is done by packaging up the resources (whether they be CSS files, HTML fragments, JavaScript code, or base64 encoded images) on the server side and sending them to the client as a long string of characters, separated by some agreed-upon string. The JavaScript code processes this long string and parses each resource according to its mime-type and any other "header" passed with it.

Let's follow this process from start to finish. First, a request is made to the server for several image resources:

```
var req = new XMLHttpRequest();

req.open('GET', 'rollup_images.php', true);
req.onreadystatechange = function() {
    if (req.readyState == 4) {
        splitImages(req.responseText);
    }
};
req.send(null);
```

This is a very simple request. You are asking for data from `rollup_images.php`, and once you receive it, you send it to the function `splitImages`.

Next, on the server, the images are read and converted into strings:

```
// Read the images and convert them into base64 encoded strings.

$images = array('kitten.jpg', 'sunset.jpg', 'baby.jpg');
foreach ($images as $image) {

    $image_fh = fopen($image, 'r');
    $image_data = fread($image_fh, filesize($image));
```

```
        fclose($image_fh);
            $payloads[] = base64_encode($image_data);
        }
    }

    // Roll up those strings into one long string and output it.

    $newline = chr(1); // This character won't appear naturally in any base64 string.

    echo implode($newline, $payloads);
```

This piece of PHP code reads three images and converts them into long strings of base64 characters. They are concatenated using a single character, Unicode character 1, and output back to the client.

Once on the client side, the data is processed by the splitImages function:

```
function splitImages(imageString) {

    var imageData = imageString.split("\u0001");
    var imageElement;

    for (var i = 0, len = imageData.length; i < len; i++) {

        imageElement = document.createElement('img');
        imageElement.src = 'data:image/jpeg;base64,' + imageData[i];
        document.getElementById('container').appendChild(imageElement);
    }
}
```

This function takes the concatenated string and splits it up again into three pieces. Each piece is then used to create an image element, and that image element is inserted into the page. The image is *not* converted from a base64 string back to binary data; instead it is passed to the image element using a data: URL and the image/jpeg mime-type.

The end result is that three images have been passed to the browser as a single HTTP request. This could be done with 20 images or 100; the response would be larger, but it would still take only one HTTP request. It can also be expanded to other types of resources. JavaScript files, CSS files, HTML fragments, and images of many types can all be combined into one response. Any data type that can be handled as a string by JavaScript can be sent. Here are functions that will take strings for JavaScript code, CSS styles, and images and convert them into resources the browser can use:

```
function handleImageData(data, mimeType) {
    var img = document.createElement('img');
    img.src = 'data:' + mimeType + ';base64,' + data;
    return img;
}

function handleCss(data) {
    var style = document.createElement('style');
    style.type = 'text/css';

    var node = document.createTextNode(data);
```

```
        style.appendChild(node);
        document.getElementsByTagName('head')[0].appendChild(style);
    }

    function handleJavaScript(data) {
        eval(data);
    }
```

As MXHR responses grow larger, it becomes necessary to process each resource as it is received, rather than waiting for the entire response. This can be done by listening for readyState 3:

```
    var req = new XMLHttpRequest();
    var getLatestPacketInterval, lastLength = 0;

    req.open('GET', 'rollup_images.php', true);
    req.onreadystatechange = readyStateHandler;
    req.send(null);

    function readyStateHandler{
        if (req.readyState === 3 && getLatestPacketInterval === null) {

            // Start polling.

            getLatestPacketInterval = window.setInterval(function() {
                getLatestPacket();
              }, 15);
        }

        if (req.readyState === 4) {

            // Stop polling.

            clearInterval(getLatestPacketInterval);

            // Get the last packet.

            getLatestPacket();
        }
    }

    function getLatestPacket() {
        var length = req.responseText.length;
        var packet = req.responseText.substring(lastLength, length);

        processPacket(packet);
        lastLength = length;
    }
```

Once readyState 3 fires for the first time, a timer is started. Every 15 milliseconds, the response is checked for new data. Each piece of data is then collected until a delimiter character is found, and then everything is processed as a complete resource.

The code required to use MXHR in a robust manner is complex but worth further study. The complete library can be easily be found online at *http://techfoolery.com/mxhr/*.

There are some downsides to using this technique, the biggest being that none of the fetched resources are cached in the browser. If you fetch a particular CSS file using MXHR and then load it normally on the next page, it will not be in the cache. This is because the rolled-up resources are transmitted as a long string and then split up by the JavaScript code. Since there is no way to programmatically inject a file into the browser's cache, none of the resources fetched in this way will make it there.

Another downside is that older versions of Internet Explorer don't support readyState 3 or data: URLs. Internet Explorer 8 does support both of them, but workarounds must still be used for Internet Explorer 6 and 7.

Despite these downsides, there are still situations in which MXHR significantly improves overall page performance:

- Pages that contain a lot of resources that aren't used elsewhere on the site (and thus don't need to be cached), especially images
- Sites that already use a unique rolled-up JavaScript or CSS file on each page to reduce HTTP requests; because it is unique to each page, it's never read from cache unless that particular page is reloaded

Because HTTP requests are one of the most extreme bottlenecks in Ajax, reducing the number needed has a large effect on overall page performance. This is especially true when you are able to convert 100 image requests into a single multipart XHR request. Ad hoc testing with large numbers of images across modern browsers has shown this technique to be 4 to 10 times faster than making individual requests. Run these tests for yourself at *http://techfoolery.com/mxhr/*.

Sending Data

There are times when you don't care about retrieving data, and instead only want to send it to the server. You could be sending off nonpersonal information about a user to be analyzed later, or you could capture all script errors that occur and send the details about them to the server for logging and alerting. When data only needs to be sent to the server, there are two techniques that are widely used: XHR and beacons.

XMLHttpRequest

Though primarily used for requesting data from the server, XHR can also be used to send data back. Data can be sent back as GET or POST, as well as in any number of HTTP headers. This gives you an enormous amount of flexibility. XHR is especially useful when the amount of data you are sending back exceeds the maximum URL length in a browser. In that situation, you can send the data back as a POST:

```
var url = '/data.php';
var params = [
    'id=934875',
    'limit=20'
];
```

```
var req = new XMLHttpRequest();

req.onerror = function() {
    // Error.
};

req.onreadystatechange = function() {
    if (req.readyState == 4) {
        // Success.
    }
};

req.open('POST', url, true);
req.setRequestHeader('Content-Type', 'application/x-www-form-urlencoded');
req.setRequestHeader('Content-Length', params.length);
req.send(params.join('&'));
```

As you can see in this example, we do nothing if the post fails. This is usually fine when XHR is used to capture broad user statistics, but if it's crucial that the data makes it to the server, you can add code to retry on failure:

```
function xhrPost(url, params, callback) {

    var req = new XMLHttpRequest();

    req.onerror = function() {
        setTimeout(function() {
            xhrPost(url, params, callback);
        }, 1000);
    };

    req.onreadystatechange = function() {
        if (req.readyState == 4) {
            if (callback && typeof callback === 'function') {
                callback();
            }
        }
    };

    req.open('POST', url, true);
    req.setRequestHeader('Content-Type', 'application/x-www-form-urlencoded');
    req.setRequestHeader('Content-Length', params.length);
    req.send(params.join('&'));
}
```

When using XHR to send data back to the server, it is faster to use GET. This is because, for small amounts of data, a GET request is sent to the server in a single packet. A POST, on the other hand, is sent in a minimum of two packets, one for the headers and another for the POST body. A POST is better suited to sending large amounts of data to the server, both because the extra packet won't matter as much and because of Internet Explorer's URL length limit, which makes long GET requests impossible.

Beacons

This technique is very similar to dynamic script tag insertion. JavaScript is used to create a new `Image` object, with the `src` set to the URL of a script on your server. This URL contains the data we want to send back in the GET format of key-value pairs. Note that no `img` element has to be created or inserted into the DOM.

```
var url = '/status_tracker.php';
var params = [
    'step=2',
    'time=1248027314'
];

(new Image()).src = url + '?' + params.join('&');
```

The server takes this data and stores it; it doesn't have to send anything back to the client, since the image isn't actually displayed. This is the most efficient way to send information back to the server. There is very little overhead, and server-side errors don't affect the client side at all.

The simplicity of image beacons also means that you are restricted in what you can do. You can't send POST data, so you are limited to a fairly small number of characters before you reach the maximum allowed URL length. You *can* receive data back, but in very limited ways. It's possible to listen for the `Image` object's `load` event, which will tell you if the server successfully received the data. You can also check the width and height of the image that the server returned (if an image was returned) and use those numbers to inform you about the server's state. For instance, a width of 1 could be "success" and 2 could be "try again."

If you don't need to return data in your response, you should send a response code of `204 No Content` and no message body. This will prevent the client from waiting for a message body that will never come:

```
var url = '/status_tracker.php';
var params = [
    'step=2',
    'time=1248027314'
];

var beacon = new Image();
beacon.src = url + '?' + params.join('&');

beacon.onload = function() {
    if (this.width == 1) {
        // Success.
    }
    else if (this.width == 2) {
        // Failure; create another beacon and try again.
    }
};

beacon.onerror = function() {
```

```
    // Error; wait a bit, then create another beacon and try again.
};
```

Beacons are the fastest and most efficient way to send data back to the server. The server doesn't have to send back any response body at all, so you don't have to worry about downloading data to the client. The only downside is that it you are limited in the type of responses you can receive. If you need to pass large amounts of data back to the client, use XHR. If you only care about sending data to the server (with possibly a very simple response), use image beacons.

Data Formats

When considering data transmission techniques, you must take into account several factors: feature set, compatibility, performance, and direction (to or from the server). When considering data formats, the only scale you need for comparison is speed.

There isn't one data format that will always be better than the others. Depending on what data is being transferred and its intended use on the page, one might be faster to download, while another might be faster to parse. In this section, we create a widget for searching among users and implement it using each of the four major categories of data formats. This will require us to format a list of users on the server, pass it back to the browser, parse that list into a native JavaScript data structure, and search it for a given string. Each of the data formats will be compared based on the file size of the list, the speed of parsing it, and the ease with which it's formed on the server.

XML

When Ajax first became popular, XML was the data format of choice. It had many things going for it: extreme interoperability (with excellent support on both the server side and the client side), strict formatting, and easy validation. JSON hadn't been formalized yet as an interchange format, and almost every language used on servers had a library available for working with XML.

Here is an example of our list of users encoded as XML:

```
<?xml version="1.0" encoding='UTF-8'?>
<users total="4">
    <user id="1">
        <username>alice</username>
        <realname>Alice Smith</realname>
        <email>alice@alicesmith.com</email>
    </user>
    <user id="2">
        <username>bob</username>
        <realname>Bob Jones</realname>
        <email>bob@bobjones.com</email>
    </user>
    <user id="3">
        <username>carol</username>
```

```
        <realname>Carol Williams</realname>
        <email>carol@carolwilliams.com</email>
    </user>
    <user id="4">
        <username>dave</username>
        <realname>Dave Johnson</realname>
        <email>dave@davejohnson.com</email>
    </user>
</users>
```

Compared to other formats, XML is extremely verbose. Each discrete piece of data requires a lot of structure, and the ratio of data to structure is extremely low. XML also has a slightly ambiguous syntax. When encoding a data structure into XML, do you make object parameters into attributes of the object element or independent child elements? Do you make long, descriptive tag names, or short ones that are efficient but indecipherable? Parsing this syntax is equally ambiguous, and you must know the layout of an XML response ahead of time to be able to make sense of it.

In general, parsing XML requires a great deal of effort on the part of the JavaScript programmer. Aside from knowing the particulars of the structure ahead of time, you must also know exactly how to pull apart that structure and painstakingly reassemble it into a JavaScript object. This is far from an easy or automatic process, unlike the other three data formats.

Here is an example of how to parse this particular XML response into an object:

```
function parseXML(responseXML) {

    var users = [];
    var userNodes = responseXML.getElementsByTagName('users');
    var node, usernameNodes, usernameNode, username,
        realnameNodes, realnameNode, realname,
        emailNodes, emailNode, email;

    for (var i = 0, len = userNodes.length; i < len; i++) {

        node = userNodes[i];
        username = realname = email = '';

        usernameNodes = node.getElementsByTagName('username');
        if (usernameNodes && usernameNodes[0]) {
            usernameNode = usernameNodes[0];
            username = (usernameNodes.firstChild) ?
                usernameNodes.firstChild.nodeValue : '';
        }

        realnameNodes = node.getElementsByTagName('realname');
        if (realnameNodes && realnameNodes[0]) {
            realnameNode = realnameNodes[0];
            realname = (realnameNodes.firstChild) ?
                realnameNodes.firstChild.nodeValue : '';
        }

        emailNodes = node.getElementsByTagName('email');
```

```
        if (emailNodes && emailNodes[0]) {
            emailNode = emailNodes[0];
            email = (emailNodes.firstChild) ?
                emailNodes.firstChild.nodeValue : '';
        }

        users[i] = {
            id: node.getAttribute('id'),
            username: username,
            realname: realname,
            email: email
        };
    }

    return users;
}
```

As you can see, it requires checking each tag to ensure that it exists before reading its value. It is heavily dependent on the structure of the XML.

A more efficient approach would be to encode each of the values as an attribute of the <user> tag. This results in a smaller file size for the same amount of data. Here is an example of the user list with the values encoded as attributes:

```
<?xml version="1.0" encoding='UTF-8'?>
<users total="4">
    <user id="1-id001" username="alice" realname="Alice Smith"
        email="alice@alicesmith.com" />
    <user id="2-id001" username="bob" realname="Bob Jones"
        email="bob@bobjones.com" />
    <user id="3-id001" username="carol" realname="Carol Williams"
        email="carol@carolwilliams.com" />
    <user id="4-id001" username="dave" realname="Dave Johnson"
        email="dave@davejohnson.com" />
</users>
```

Parsing this simplified XML response is significantly easier:

```
function parseXML(responseXML) {

    var users = [];
    var userNodes = responseXML.getElementsByTagName('users');

    for (var i = 0, len = userNodes.length; i < len; i++) {
        users[i] = {
            id: userNodes[i].getAttribute('id'),
            username: userNodes[i].getAttribute('username'),
            realname: userNodes[i].getAttribute('realname'),
            email: userNodes[i].getAttribute('email')
        };
    }

    return users;
}
```

XPath

Though it is beyond the scope of this chapter, XPath can be much faster than `getElementsByTagName` when parsing an XML document. The caveat is that it is not universally supported, so you must also write fallback code using the older style of DOM traversal. At this time, DOM Level 3 XPath has been implemented by Firefox, Safari, Chrome, and Opera. Internet Explorer 8 has a similar but slightly less advanced interface.

Response sizes and parse times

Let's take a look at the performance numbers for XML in the following table.

Format	Size	Download time	Parse time	Total load time
Verbose XML	582,960 bytes	999.4 ms	343.1 ms	1342.5 ms
Simple XML	437,960 bytes	475.1 ms	83.1 ms	558.2 ms

 Each of the data types has been tested using user lists with lengths of 100, 500, 1,000, and 5,000. Each list was downloaded and parsed 10 times in the same browser, and averages were taken for download time, parse time, and file size. Full results for all data formats and transfer techniques, as well as tests you can run yourself, can be found at *http://techfoolery.com/formats/*.

As you can see, using favoring attributes over child tags leads to a smaller file size and a significantly faster parse time. This is mostly due to the fact that you don't have to walk the DOM on the XML structure as much, and can instead simply read attributes.

Should you consider using XML? Given its prevalence in public APIs, you often have no choice. If the data is only available in XML, you roll up your sleeves and write code to parse it. But if there is any other format available, prefer that instead. The performance numbers you see here for verbose XML are extremely slow compared to more advanced techniques. For browsers that support it, XPath would improve the parse time, but at the cost of writing and maintaining three separate code paths (one for browsers that support DOM Level 3 XPath, one for Internet Explorer 8, and one for all other browsers). The simple XML format compares more favorably, but is still an order of magnitude slower than the fastest format. XML has no place in high-performance Ajax.

JSON

Formalized and popularized by Douglas Crockford, JSON is a lightweight and easy-to-parse data format written using JavaScript object and array literal syntax. Here is an example of the user list written in JSON:

```
[
    { "id": 1, "username": "alice", "realname": "Alice Smith",
      "email": "alice@alicesmith.com" },
    { "id": 2, "username": "bob", "realname": "Bob Jones",
      "email": "bob@bobjones.com" },
    { "id": 3, "username": "carol", "realname": "Carol Williams",
      "email": "carol@carolwilliams.com" },
    { "id": 4, "username": "dave", "realname": "Dave Johnson",
      "email": "dave@davejohnson.com" }
]
```

The users are represented as objects, and the list of users is an array, just as any other array or object would be written out in JavaScript. This means that when evaled or wrapped in a callback function, JSON data is executable JavaScript code. Parsing a string of JSON in JavaScript is as easy as using eval():

```
function parseJSON(responseText) {
    return eval('(' + responseText + ')');
}
```

 A note about JSON and eval: using eval in your code is dangerous, especially when using it to evaluate third-party JSON data (which could possibly contain malicious or malformed code). Whenever possible, use the JSON.parse() method to parse the string natively. This method will catch syntax errors in the JSON and allow you to pass in a function that can be used to filter or transform the results. Currently this method is implemented in Firefox 3.5, Internet Explorer 8, and Safari 4. Most JavaScript libraries contain JSON parsing code that will call the native version, if present, or a slightly less robust nonnative version otherwise. A reference implementation of a nonnative version can be found at *http://json.org/json2.js*. For the sake of consistency, eval will be used in the code example.

Just as with XML, it is possible to distill this format into a simpler version. In this case, we can replace the attribute names with shortened (though less readable) versions:

```
[
    { "i": 1, "u": "alice", "r": "Alice Smith", "e": "alice@alicesmith.com" },
    { "i": 2, "u": "bob", "r": "Bob Jones", "e": "bob@bobjones.com" },
    { "i": 3, "u": "carol", "r": "Carol Williams",
      "e": "carol@carolwilliams.com" },
    { "i": 4, "u": "dave", "r": "Dave Johnson", "e": "dave@davejohnson.com" }
]
```

This gives us the same data with less structure and fewer bytes overall to transmit to the browser. We can even take it a step further and remove the attribute names completely. This format is even less readable than the other two and is much more brittle, but the file size is much smaller: almost half the size of the verbose JSON format.

```
[
    [ 1, "alice", "Alice Smith", "alice@alicesmith.com" ],
    [ 2, "bob", "Bob Jones", "bob@bobjones.com" ],
```

```
    [ 3, "carol", "Carol Williams", "carol@carolwilliams.com" ],
    [ 4, "dave", "Dave Johnson", "dave@davejohnson.com" ]
]
```

Successful parsing requires that the order of the data must be maintained. That being said, it is trivial to convert this format into one that maintains the same attribute names as the first JSON format:

```
function parseJSON(responseText) {

    var users = [];
    var usersArray = eval('(' + responseText + ')');

    for (var i = 0, len = usersArray.length; i < len; i++) {
        users[i] = {
            id: usersArray[i][0],
            username: usersArray[i][1],
            realname: usersArray[i][2],
            email: usersArray[i][3]
        };
    }

    return users;
}
```

In this example, we use eval() to convert the string into a native JavaScript array. That array of arrays is then converted into an array of objects. Essentially, you are trading a smaller file size and faster eval() time for a more complicated parse function. The following table lists the performance numbers for the three JSON formats, transferred using XHR.

Format	Size	Download time	Parse time	Total load time
Verbose JSON	487,895 bytes	527.7 ms	26.7 ms	554.4 ms
Simple JSON	392,895 bytes	498.7 ms	29.0 ms	527.7 ms
Array JSON	292,895 bytes	305.4 ms	18.6 ms	324.0 ms

JSON formed using arrays wins every category, with the smallest file size, the fastest average download time, and the fastest average parse time. Despite the fact that the parse function has to iterate through all 5,000 entries in the list, it is still more than 30% faster to parse.

JSON-P

The fact that JSON can be executed natively has several important performance implications. When XHR is used, JSON data is returned as a string. This string is then evaluated using eval() to convert it into a native object. However, when dynamic script tag insertion is used, JSON data is treated as just another JavaScript file and executed as native code. In order to accomplish this, the data must be wrapped in a callback function. This is known as "JSON with padding," or JSON-P. Here is our user list formatted as JSON-P:

```
parseJSON([
    { "id": 1, "username": "alice", "realname": "Alice Smith",
        "email": "alice@alicesmith.com" },
    { "id": 2, "username": "bob", "realname": "Bob Jones",
        "email": "bob@bobjones.com" },
    { "id": 3, "username": "carol", "realname": "Carol Williams",
        "email": "carol@carolwilliams.com" },
    { "id": 4, "username": "dave", "realname": "Dave Johnson",
        "email": "dave@davejohnson.com" }
]);
```

JSON-P adds a small amount to the file size with the callback wrapper, but such an increase is insignificant compared to the improved parse times. Since the data is treated as native JavaScript, it is parsed at native JavaScript speeds. Here are the same three JSON formats transmitted as JSON-P.

Format	Size	Download time	Parse time	Total load time
Verbose JSON-P	487,913 bytes	598.2 ms	0.0 ms	598.2 ms
Simple JSON-P	392,913 bytes	454.0 ms	3.1 ms	457.1 ms
Array JSON-P	292,912 bytes	316.0 ms	3.4 ms	319.4 ms

File sizes and download times are almost identical to the XHR tests, but parse times are almost 10 times faster. The parse time for verbose JSON-P is zero, since no parsing is needed; it is already in a native format. The same is true for simple JSON-P and array JSON-P, but each had to be iterated through to convert it to the format that verbose JSON-P gives you naturally.

The fastest JSON format is JSON-P formed using arrays. Although this is only slightly faster than JSON transmitted using XHR, that difference increases as the size of the list grows. If you are working on a project that requires a list with 10,000 or 100,000 elements in it, favor JSON-P over JSON.

There is one reason to avoid using JSON-P that has nothing to do with performance: since JSON-P must be executable JavaScript, it can be called by anyone and included in any website using dynamic script tag insertion. JSON, on the other hand, is not valid JavaScript until it is evaled, and can only be fetched as a string using XHR. Do not encode any sensitive data in JSON-P, because you cannot ensure that it will remain private, even with random URLs or cookies.

Should you use JSON?

JSON has several advantages when compared to XML. It is a much smaller format, with less of the overall response size being used as structure and more as data. This is especially true when the data contains arrays rather than objects. JSON is extremely interoperable, with encoding and decoding libraries available for most server-side languages. It is trivial to parse on the client side, allowing you to spend more time writing code to actually do something with the data. And, most importantly for web developers, it is one of the best performing formats, both because it is relatively small over the wire and because it can be parsed so quickly. JSON is a cornerstone of high-performance Ajax, especially when used with dynamic script tag insertion.

HTML

Often the data you are requesting will be turned into HTML for display on the page. Converting a large data structure into simple HTML can be done relatively quickly in JavaScript, but it can be done much faster on the server. One technique to consider is forming all of the HTML on the server and then passing it intact to the client; the JavaScript can then simply drop it in place with `innerHTML`. Here is an example of the user list encoded as HTML:

```html
<ul class="users">
    <li class="user" id="1-id002">
        <a href="http://www.site.com/alice/" class="username">alice</a>
        <span class="realname">Alice Smith</span>
        <a href="mailto:alice@alicesmith.com"
            class="email">alice@alicesmith.com</a>
    </li>
    <li class="user" id="2-id002">
        <a href="http://www.site.com/bob/" class="username">bob</a>
        <span class="realname">Bob Jones</span>
        <a href="mailto:bob@bobjones.com" class="email">bob@bobjones.com</a>
    </li>
    <li class="user" id="3-id002">
        <a href="http://www.site.com/carol/" class="username">carol</a>
        <span class="realname">Carol Williams</span>
        <a href="mailto:carol@carolwilliams.com"
            class="email">carol@carolwilliams.com</a>
    </li>
    <li class="user" id="4-id002">
        <a href="http://www.site.com/dave/" class="username">dave</a>
        <span class="realname">Dave Johnson</span>
        <a href="mailto:dave@davejohnson.com"
            class="email">dave@davejohnson.com</a>
    </li>
</ul>
```

The problem with this technique is that HTML is a verbose data format, more so even than XML. On top of the data itself, you could have nested HTML tags, each with IDs, classes, and other attributes. It's possible to have the HTML formatting take up more space than the actual data, though that can be mitigated by using as few tags and attributes as possible. Because of this, you should use this technique only when the client-side CPU is more limited than bandwidth.

On one extreme, you have a format that consists of the smallest amount of structure required to parse the data on the client side, such as JSON. This format is extremely quick to download to the client machine; however, it takes a lot of CPU time to convert this format into HTML to display on the page. A lot of string operations are required, which are one of the slowest things you can do in JavaScript.

On the other extreme, you have HTML created on the server. This format is much larger over the wire and takes longer to download, but once it's downloaded, displaying it on the page requires a single operation:

```
document.getElementById('data-container').innerHTML = req.responseText;
```

The following table shows the performance numbers for the user list encoded using HTML. Keep in mind the main different between this format and all others: "parsing" in this case refers to the action of inserting the HTML in the DOM. Also, HTML cannot be easily or quickly iterated through, unlike a native JavaScript array.

Format	Size	Download time	Parse time	Total load time
HTML	1,063,416 bytes	273.1 ms	121.4 ms	394.5 ms

As you can see, HTML is significantly larger over the wire, and also takes a long time to parse. This is because the single operation to insert the HTML into the DOM is deceptively simple; despite the fact that it is a single line of code, it still takes a significant amount of time to load that much data into a page. These performance numbers do deviate slightly from the others, in that the end result is not an array of data, but instead HTML elements displayed on a page. Regardless, they still illustrate the fact that HTML, as a data format, is slow and bloated.

Custom Formatting

The ideal data format is one that includes just enough structure to allow you to separate individual fields from each other. You can easily make such a format by simply concatenating your data with a separator character:

```
Jacob;Michael;Joshua;Matthew;Andrew;Christopher;Joseph;Daniel;Nicholas;
Ethan;William;Anthony;Ryan;David;Tyler;John
```

These separators essentially create an array of data, similar to a comma-separated list. Through the use of different separators, you can create multidimensional arrays. Here is our user list encoded as a character-delimited custom format:

```
1:alice:Alice Smith:alice@alicesmith.com;
2:bob:Bob Jones:bob@bobjones.com;
3:carol:Carol Williams:carol@carolwilliams.com;
4:dave:Dave Johnson:dave@davejohnson.com
```

This type of format is extremely terse and offers a very high data-to-structure ratio (significantly higher than any other format, excluding plain text). Custom formats are quick to download over the wire, and they are fast and easy to parse; you simply call split() on the string, using your separator as the argument. More complex custom formats with multiple separators require loops to split all the data (but keep in mind that these loops are extremely fast in JavaScript). `split()` is one of the fastest string operations, and can typically handle separator-delimited lists of 10,000+ elements in a matter of milliseconds. Here is an example of how to parse the preceding format:

```
function parseCustomFormat(responseText) {

    var users = [];
    var usersEncoded = responseText.split(';');
    var userArray;

    for (var i = 0, len = usersEncoded.length; i < len; i++) {

        userArray = usersEncoded[i].split(':');

        users[i] = {
            id: userArray[0],
            username: userArray[1],
            realname: userArray[2],
            email: userArray[3]
        };
    }

    return users;
}
```

When creating you own custom format, one of the most important decisions is what to use as the separators. Ideally, they should each be a single character, and they should not be found naturally in your data. Low-number ASCII characters work well and are easy to represent in most server-side languages. For example, here is how you would use ASCII characters in PHP:

```
function build_format_custom($users) {

    $row_delimiter = chr(1); // \u0001 in JavaScript.
    $field_delimiter = chr(2); // \u0002 in JavaScript.

    $output = array();
    foreach ($users as $user) {
        $fields = array($user['id'], $user['username'], $user['realname'],
$user['email']);
        $output[] = implode($field_delimiter, $fields);
    }

    return implode($row_delimiter, $output);
}
```

These control characters are represented in JavaScript using Unicode notation (e.g., \u0001). The `split()` function can take either a string or a regular expression as an argument. If you expect to have empty fields in your data, then use a string; if the delimiter is passed as a regular expression, `split()` in IE ignores the second delimiter when two are right next to each other. The two argument types are equivalent in other browsers.

```
// Regular expression delimiter.
var rows = req.responseText.split(/\u0001/);

// String delimiter (safer).
var rows = req.responseText.split("\u0001");
```

Here are the performance numbers for a character delimited custom format, using both XHR and dynamic script tag insertion:

Format	Size	Download time	Parse time	Total load time
Custom Format (XHR)	222,892 bytes	63.1 ms	14.5 ms	77.6 ms
Custom Format (script insertion)	222,912 bytes	66.3 ms	11.7 ms	78.0 ms

Either XHR or dynamic script tag insertion can be used with this format. Since the response is parsed as a string in both cases, there is no real difference in performance. For very large datasets, it's hands down the fastest format, beating out even natively executed JSON in parse speed and overall load time. This format makes it feasible to send huge amounts of data to the client side in a very short amount of time.

Data Format Conclusions

Favor lightweight formats in general; the best are JSON and a character-delimited custom format. If the data set is large and parse time becomes an issue, use one of these two techniques:

- JSON-P data, fetched using dynamic script tag insertion. This treats the data as executable JavaScript, not a string, and allows for extremely fast parsing. This can be used across domains, but shouldn't be used with sensitive data.
- A character-delimited custom format, fetched using either XHR or dynamic script tag insertion and parsed using split(). This technique parses extremely large datasets slightly faster than the JSON-P technique, and generally has a smaller file size.

The following table and Figure 7-1 show all of the performance numbers again (in order from slowest to fastest), so that you can compare each of the formats in one place. HTML is excluded, since it isn't directly comparable to the other formats.

Format	Size	Download time	Parse time	Total load time
Verbose XML	582,960 bytes	999.4 ms	343.1 ms	1342.5 ms
Verbose JSON-P	487,913 bytes	598.2 ms	0.0 ms	598.2 ms
Simple XML	437,960 bytes	475.1 ms	83.1 ms	558.2 ms
Verbose JSON	487,895 bytes	527.7 ms	26.7 ms	554.4 ms
Simple JSON	392,895 bytes	498.7 ms	29.0 ms	527.7 ms
Simple JSON-P	392,913 bytes	454.0 ms	3.1 ms	457.1 ms

Format	Size	Download time	Parse time	Total load time
Array JSON	292,895 bytes	305.4 ms	18.6 ms	324.0 ms
Array JSON-P	292,912 bytes	316.0 ms	3.4 ms	319.4 ms
Custom Format (script insertion)	222,912 bytes	66.3 ms	11.7 ms	78.0 ms
Custom Format (XHR)	222,892 bytes	63.1 ms	14.5 ms	77.6 ms

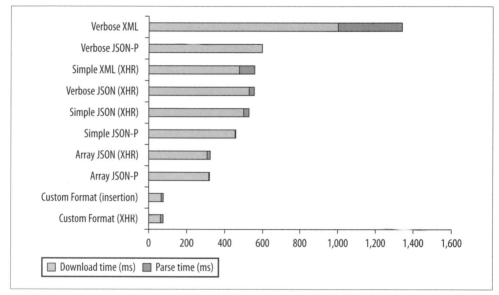

Figure 7-1. A comparison of data format download and parse times

Keep in mind that these numbers are from a single test run in a single browser. The results should be used as general indicators of performance, not as hard numbers. You can run these tests yourself at *http://techfoolery.com/formats/*.

Ajax Performance Guidelines

Once you have selected the most appropriate data transmission technique and data format, you can start to consider other optimization techniques. These can be highly situational, so be sure that your application fits the profile before considering them.

Cache Data

The fastest Ajax request is one that you don't have to make. There are two main ways of preventing an unnecessary request:

- On the server side, set HTTP headers that ensure your response will be cached in the browser.
- On the client side, store fetched data locally so that it doesn't have be requested again.

The first technique is the easiest to set up and maintain, whereas the second gives you the highest degree of control.

Setting HTTP headers

If you want your Ajax responses to be cached by the browser, you must use GET to make the request. But simply using GET isn't sufficient; you must also send the correct HTTP headers with the response. The `Expires` header tells the browser how long a response can be cached. The value is a date; after that date has passed, any requests for that URL will stop being delivered from cache and will instead be passed on to the server. Here is what an `Expires` header looks like:

```
Expires:    Mon, 28 Jul 2014 23:30:00 GMT
```

This particular `Expires` header tells the browser to cache this response until July 2014. This is called a *far future* `Expires` header, and it is useful for content that will never change, such as images or static data sets.

The date in an `Expires` header is a GMT date. It can be set in PHP using this code:

```
$lifetime = 7 * 24 * 60 * 60; // 7 days, in seconds.
header('Expires: ' . gmdate('D, d M Y H:i:s', time() + $lifetime) . ' GMT');
```

This will tell the browser to cache the file for 7 days. To set a far future `Expires` header, set the lifetime to something longer; this example tells the browser to cache the file for 10 years:

```
$lifetime = 10 * 365 * 24 * 60 * 60; // 10 years, in seconds.
header('Expires: ' . gmdate('D, d M Y H:i:s', time() + $lifetime) . ' GMT');
```

An `Expires` header is the easiest way to make sure your Ajax responses are cached on the browser. You don't have to change anything in your client-side code, and can continue to make Ajax requests normally, knowing that the browser will send the request on to the server only if the file isn't in cache. It's also easy to implement on the server side, as all languages allow you to set headers in one way or another. This is the simplest approach to ensuring your data is cached.

Storing data locally

Instead of relying on the browser to handle caching, you can also do it in a more manual fashion, by storing the responses you receive from the server. This can be done by putting the response text into an object, keyed by the URL used to fetch it. Here is an example of an XHR wrapper that first checks to see whether a URL has been fetched before:

```
    var localCache = {};

    function xhrRequest(url, callback) {

        // Check the local cache for this URL.

        if (localCache[url]) {
            callback.success(localCache[url]);
            return;
        }

        // If this URL wasn't found in the cache, make the request.

        var req = createXhrObject();
        req.onerror = function() {
            callback.error();
        };

        req.onreadystatechange = function() {
            if (req.readyState == 4) {

                if (req.responseText === '' || req.status == '404') {
                    callback.error();
                    return;
                }

                // Store the response on the local cache.

                localCache[url] = req.responseText;
                callback.success(req.responseText);
            }
        };

        req.open("GET", url, true);
        req.send(null);
    }
```

Overall, setting an Expires header is a better solution. It's easier to do and it caches responses across page loads and sessions. But a manual cache can be useful in situations where you want to be able to programmatically expire a cache and fetch fresh data. Imagine a situation where you would like to use cached data for every request, except when the user takes an action that causes one or more of the cached responses to become invalid. In this case, removing those responses from the cache is trivial:

```
delete localCache['/user/friendlist/'];
delete localCache['/user/contactlist/'];
```

A local cache also works well for users browsing on mobile devices. Most of the browsers on such devices have small or nonexistent caches, and a manual cache is the best option for preventing unnecessary requests.

Know the Limitations of Your Ajax Library

All JavaScript libraries give you access to an Ajax object, which normalizes the differences between browsers and gives you a consistent interface. Most of the time this is a very good thing, as it allows you to focus on your project rather than the details of how XHR works in some obscure browser. However, in giving you a unified interface, these libraries must also simplify the interface, because not every browser implements each feature. This prevents you from accessing the full power of XMLHttpRequest.

Some of the techniques we covered in this chapter can be implemented only by accessing the XHR object directly. Most notable of these is the streaming feature of multipart XHR. By listening for readyState 3, we can start to slice up a large response before it's completely received. This allows us to handle pieces of the response in real time, and it is one of the reasons that MXHR improves performance so much. Most JavaScript libraries, though, do not give you direct access to the readystatechange event. This means you must wait until the *entire* response is received (which may be a considerable amount of time) before you can start to use any part of it.

Using the XMLHttpRequest object directly is not as daunting as it seems. A few quirks aside, the most recent versions of all major browsers support the XMLHttpRequest object in the same way, and all offer access to the different readyStates. You can support older versions of IE with just a few more lines of code. Here is an example of a function that will return an XHR object, which you can then interact with directly (this is a modified version of what the YUI 2 Connection Manager uses):

```
function createXhrObject() {

    var msxml_progid = [
        'MSXML2.XMLHTTP.6.0',
        'MSXML3.XMLHTTP',
        'Microsoft.XMLHTTP',   // Doesn't support readyState 3.
        'MSXML2.XMLHTTP.3.0',  // Doesn't support readyState 3.
    ];

    var req;
    try {
        req = new XMLHttpRequest(); // Try the standard way first.
    }
    catch(e) {
        for (var i = 0, len = msxml_progid.length; i < len; ++i) {
            try {
                req = new ActiveXObject(msxml_progid[i]);
                break;
            }
            catch(e2) {  }
        }
    }
    finally {
        return req;
    }
}
```

This will first try the versions of `XMLHttp` that do support `readyState` 3, and then fall back to the ones that don't in case those versions aren't available.

Interacting directly with the XHR object also reduces the amount of function overhead, further improving performance. Just beware that by forgoing the use of an Ajax library, you may encounter some problems with older and more obscure browsers.

Summary

High-performance Ajax consists of knowing the specific requirements of your situation and selecting the correct data format and transmission technique to match.

As data formats, plain text and HTML are highly situational, but they can save CPU cycles on the client side. XML is widely available and supported almost everywhere, but it is extremely verbose and slow to parse. JSON is lightweight and quick to parse (when treated as native code and not a string), and almost as interoperable as XML. Character-delimited custom formats are extremely lightweight and the quickest to parse for large datasets, but may take additional programming effort to format on the server side and parse on the client side.

When requesting data, XHR gives you the most control and flexibility when pulling from the page's domain, though it treats all incoming data as a string, potentially slowing down the parse times. Dynamic script tag insertion, on the other hand, allows for cross-domain requests and native execution of JavaScript and JSON, though it offers a less robust interface and cannot read headers or response codes. Multipart XHR can be used to reduce the number of requests, and can handle different file types in a single response, though it does not cache the resources received. When sending data, image beacons are a simple and efficient approach. XHR can also be used to send large amounts of data in a POST.

In addition to these formats and transmission techniques, there are several guidelines that will help your Ajax appear to be faster:

- Reduce the number of requests you make, either by concatenating JavaScript and CSS files, or by using MXHR.
- Improve the perceived loading time of your page by using Ajax to fetch less important files after the rest of the page has loaded.
- Ensure your code fails gracefully and can handle problems on the server side.
- Know when to use a robust Ajax library and when to write your own low-level Ajax code.

Ajax offers one of the largest areas for potential performance improvements on your site, both because so many sites use asynchronous requests heavily and because it can offer solutions to problems that aren't even related to it, such as having too many resources to load. Creative use of XHR can be the difference between a sluggish, uninviting page and one that responds quickly and efficiently; it can be the difference between a site that users hate to interact with and one that they love.

Programming Practices

Every programming language has pain points and inefficient patterns that develop over time. The appearance of these traits occurs as people migrate to the language and start pushing its boundaries. Since 2005, when the term "Ajax" emerged, web developers have pushed JavaScript and the browser further than it was ever pushed before. As a result, some very specific patterns emerged, both as best practices and as suboptimal ones. These patterns arise because of the very nature of JavaScript on the Web.

Avoid Double Evaluation

JavaScript, like many scripting languages, allows you to take a string containing code and execute it from within running code. There are four standard ways to accomplish this: `eval()`, the `Function()` constructor, `setTimeout()`, and `setInterval()`. Each of these functions allows you to pass in a string of JavaScript code and have it executed. Some examples:

```
var num1 = 5,
    num2 = 6,

    //eval() evaluating a string of code
    result = eval("num1 + num2"),

    //Function() evaluating strings of code
    sum = new Function("arg1", "arg2", "return arg1 + arg2");

//setTimeout() evaluating a string of code
setTimeout("sum = num1 + num2", 100);

//setInterval() evaluating a string of code
setInterval("sum = num1 + num2", 100);
```

Whenever you're evaluating JavaScript code from within JavaScript code, you incur a double evaluation penalty. This code is first evaluated as normal, and then, while executing, another evaluation happens to execute the code contained in a string. Double evaluation is a costly operation and takes much longer than if the same code were included natively.

As a point of comparison, the time it takes to access an array item varies from browser to browser but varies far more dramatically when the array item is accessed using eval(). For example:

```
//faster
var item = array[0];

//slower
var item = eval("array[0]");
```

The difference across browsers becomes dramatic if 10,000 array items are read using eval() instead of native code. Table 8-1 shows the different times for this operation.

Table 8-1. Speed comparison of native code versus eval() for accessing 10,000 array items

Browser	Native code (ms)	eval() code (ms)
Firefox 3	10.57	822.62
Firefox 3.5	0.72	141.54
Chrome 1	5.7	106.41
Chrome 2	5.17	54.55
Internet Explorer 7	31.25	5086.13
Internet Explorer 8	40.06	420.55
Opera 9.64	2.01	402.82
Opera 10 Beta	10.52	315.16
Safari 3.2	30.37	360.6
Safari 4	22.16	54.47

This dramatic difference in array item access time is due to the creation of a new interpreter/compiler instance each time eval() is called. The same process occurs for Function(), setTimeout(), and setInterval(), automatically making code execution slower.

Most of the time, there is no need to use eval() or Function(), and it's best to avoid them whenever possible. For the other two functions, setTimeout() and setInterval(), it's recommended to pass in a function as the first argument instead of a string. For example:

```
setTimeout(function(){
    sum = num1 + num2;
}, 100);

setInterval(function(){
    sum = num1 + num2;
}, 100);
```

Avoiding double evaluation is key to achieving the most optimal JavaScript runtime performance possible.

 Optimizing JavaScript engines often cache the result of repeated code evaluations using `eval()`. If you are repeatedly evaluating the same code string, you will see greater performance improvements in Safari 4 and all versions of Chrome.

Use Object/Array Literals

There are multiple ways to create objects and arrays in JavaScript, but nothing is faster than creating object and array literals. Without using literals, typical object creation and assignment looks like this:

```
//create an object
var myObject = new Object();
myObject.name = "Nicholas";
myObject.count = 50;
myObject.flag = true;
myObject.pointer = null;

//create an array
var myArray = new Array();
myArray[0] = "Nicholas";
myArray[1] = 50;
myArray[2] = true;
myArray[3] = null;
```

Although there is technically nothing wrong with this approach, literals are evaluated faster. As an added bonus, literals take up less space in your code, so the overall file size is smaller. The previous code can be rewritten using literals in the following way:

```
//create an object
var myObject = {
    name: "Nicholas",
    count: 50,
    flag: true,
    pointer: null
};

//create an array
var myArray = ["Nicholas", 50, true, null];
```

The end result of this code is the same as the previous version, but it is executed faster in almost all browsers (Firefox 3.5 shows almost no difference). As the number of object properties and array items increases, so too does the benefit of using literals.

Don't Repeat Work

One of the primary performance optimization techniques in computer science overall is work avoidance. The concept of work avoidance really means two things: don't do work that isn't required, and don't repeat work that has already been completed. The first part is usually easy to identify as code is being refactored. The second part—not repeating work—is usually more difficult to identify because work may be repeated in any number of places and for any number of reasons.

Perhaps the most common type of repeated work is browser detection. A lot of code has forks based on the browser's capabilities. Consider event handler addition and removal as an example. Typical cross-browser code for this purpose looks like the following:

```
function addHandler(target, eventType, handler){
    if (target.addEventListener){  //DOM2 Events
        target.addEventListener(eventType, handler, false);
    } else {   //IE
        target.attachEvent("on" + eventType, handler);
    }
}

function removeHandler(target, eventType, handler){
    if (target.removeEventListener){  //DOM2 Events
        target.removeEventListener(eventType, handler, false);
    } else {   //IE
        target.detachEvent("on" + eventType, handler);
    }
}
```

The code checks for DOM Level 2 Events support by testing for addEventListener() and removeEventListener(), which is supported by all modern browsers except Internet Explorer. If these methods don't exist on the target, then IE is assumed and the IE-specific methods are used.

At first glance, these functions look fairly optimized for their purpose. The hidden performance issue is in the repeated work done each time either function is called. Each time, the same check is made to see whether a certain method is present. If you assume that the only values for target are actually DOM objects, and that the user doesn't magically change his browser while the page is loaded, then this evaluation is repetitive. If addEventListener() was present on the first call to addHandler() then it's going to be present for each subsequent call. Repeating the same work with every call to a function is wasteful, and there are a couple of ways to avoid it.

Lazy Loading

The first way to eliminate work repetition in functions is through *lazy loading*. Lazy loading means that no work is done until the information is necessary. In the case of the previous example, there is no need to determine which way to attach or detach event handlers until someone makes a call to the function. Lazy-loaded versions of the previous functions look like this:

```
function addHandler(target, eventType, handler){

    //overwrite the existing function
    if (target.addEventListener){    //DOM2 Events
        addHandler = function(target, eventType, handler){
            target.addEventListener(eventType, handler, false);
        };
    } else {    //IE
        addHandler = function(target, eventType, handler){
            target.attachEvent("on" + eventType, handler);
        };
    }

    //call the new function
    addHandler(target, eventType, handler);
}

function removeHandler(target, eventType, handler){

    //overwrite the existing function
    if (target.removeEventListener){    //DOM2 Events
        removeHandler = function(target, eventType, handler){
            target.addEventListener(eventType, handler, false);
        };
    } else {    //IE
        removeHandler = function(target, eventType, handler){
            target.detachEvent("on" + eventType, handler);
        };
    }

    //call the new function
    removeHandler(target, eventType, handler);
}
```

These two functions implement a lazy-loading pattern. The first time either method is called, a check is made to determine the appropriate way to attach or detach the event handler. Then, the original function is overwritten with a new function that contains just the appropriate course of action. The last step during that first function call is to execute the new function with the original arguments. Each subsequent call to addHandler() or removeHandler() avoids further detection because the detection code was overwritten by a new function.

Calling a lazy-loading function always takes longer the first time because it must run the detection and then make a call to another function to accomplish the task. Subsequent calls to the same function, however, are much faster since they have no detection logic. Lazy loading is best used when the function won't be used immediately on the page.

Conditional Advance Loading

An alternative to lazy-loading functions is *conditional advance loading*, which does the detection upfront, while the script is loading, instead of waiting for the function call. The detection is still done just once, but it comes earlier in the process. For example:

```
var addHandler = document.body.addEventListener ?
                 function(target, eventType, handler){
                     target.addEventListener(eventType, handler, false);
                 }:
                 function(target, eventType, handler){
                     target.attachEvent("on" + eventType, handler);
                 };

var removeHandler = document.body.removeEventListener ?
                 function(target, eventType, handler){
                     target.removeEventListener(eventType, handler, false);
                 }:
                 function(target, eventType, handler){
                     target.detachEvent("on" + eventType, handler);
                 };
```

This example checks to see whether `addEventListener()` and `removeEventListener()` are present and then uses that information to assign the most appropriate function. The ternary operator returns the DOM Level 2 function if these methods are present and otherwise returns the IE-specific function. The result is that all calls to `addHandler()` and `removeHandler()` are equally fast, as the detection cost occurs upfront.

Conditional advance loading ensures that all calls to the function take the same amount of time. The trade-off is that the detection occurs as the script is loading rather than later. Advance loading is best to use when a function is going to be used right away and then again frequently throughout the lifetime of the page.

Use the Fast Parts

Even though JavaScript is often blamed for being slow, there are parts of the language that are incredibly fast. This should come as no surprise, since JavaScript engines are built in lower-level languages and are therefore compiled. Though it's easy to blame the engine when JavaScript appears slow, the engine is typically the fastest part of the process; it's your code that is actually running slowly. There are parts of the engine that are much faster than others because they allow you to bypass the slow parts.

Bitwise Operators

Bitwise operators are one of the most frequently misunderstood aspects of JavaScript. General opinion is that developers don't understand how to use these operators and frequently mistake them for their Boolean equivalents. As a result, bitwise operators are used infrequently in JavaScript development, despite their advantages.

JavaScript numbers are all stored in IEEE-754 64-bit format. For bitwise operations, though, the number is converted into a signed 32-bit representation. Each operator then works directly on this 32-bit representation to achieve a result. Despite the conversion, this process is incredibly fast when compared to other mathematical and Boolean operations in JavaScript.

If you're unfamiliar with binary representation of numbers, JavaScript makes it easy to convert a number into a string containing its binary equivalent by using the `toString()` method and passing in the number 2. For example:

```
var num1 = 25,
    num2 = 3;

alert(num1.toString(2));    //"11001"
alert(num2.toString(2));    //   "11"
```

Note that this representation omits the leading zeros of a number.

There are four bitwise logic operators in JavaScript:

Bitwise AND
> Returns a number with a 1 in each bit where both numbers have a 1

Bitwise OR
> Returns a number with a 1 in each bit where either number has a 1

Bitwise XOR
> Returns a number with a 1 in each bit where exactly one number has a 1

Bitwise NOT
> Returns 1 in each position where the number has a 0 and vice versa

These operators are used as follows:

```
//bitwise AND
var result1 = 25 & 3;       //1
alert(result.toString(2));  //"1"

//bitwise OR
var result2 = 25 | 3;       //27
alert(resul2.toString(2));  //"11011"

//bitwise XOR
var result3 = 25 ^ 3;       //26
alert(resul3.toString(2));  //"11000"

//bitwise NOT
var result = ~25;           //-26
alert(resul2.toString(2));  //"-11010"
```

There are a couple of ways to use bitwise operators to speed up your JavaScript. The first is to use bitwise operations instead of pure mathematical operations. For example, it's common to alternate table row colors by calculating the modulus of 2 for a given number, such as:

```
for (var i=0, len=rows.length; i < len; i++){
    if (i % 2) {
        className = "even";
    } else {
        className = "odd";
    }

    //apply class
}
```

Calculating mod 2 requires the number to be divided by 2 to determine the remainder. If you were to look at the underlying 32-bit representation of numbers, a number is even if its first bit is 0 and is odd if its first bit is 1. This can easily be determined by using a bitwise AND operation on a given number and the number 1. When the number is even, the result of bitwise AND 1 is 0; when the number is odd, the result of bitwise AND 1 is 1. That means the previous code can be rewritten as follows:

```
for (var i=0, len=rows.length; i < len; i++){
    if (i & 1) {
        className = "odd";
    } else {
        className = "even";
    }

    //apply class
}
```

Although the code change is small, the bitwise AND version is up to 50% faster than the original (depending on the browser).

The second way to use bitwise operators is a technique known as a *bitmask*. Bitmasking is a popular technique in computer science when there are a number of Boolean options that may be present at the same time. The idea is to use each bit of a single number to indicate whether or not the option is present, effectively turning the number into an array of Boolean flags. Each option is given a value equivalent to a power of 2 so that the mask works. For example:

```
var OPTION_A = 1;
var OPTION_B = 2;
var OPTION_C = 4;
var OPTION_D = 8;
var OPTION_E = 16;
```

With the options defined, you can create a single number that contains multiple settings using the bitwise OR operator:

```
var options = OPTION_A | OPTION_C | OPTION_D;
```

You can then check whether a given option is available by using the bitwise AND operator. The operation returns 0 if the option isn't set and 1 if the option is set:

```
//is option A in the list?
if (options & OPTION_A){
    //do something
```

```
    }

    //is option B in the list?
    if (options & OPTION_B){
        //do something
    }
```

Bitmask operations such as this are quite fast because, as mentioned previously, the work is happening at a lower level of the system. If there are a number of options that are being saved together and checked frequently, bitmasks can help to speed up the overall approach.

 JavaScript also supports left shift (<<), right shift (>>), and signed right shift (>>>) bitwise operators.

Native Methods

No matter how optimal your JavaScript code is, it will never be faster than the native methods provided by the JavaScript engine. The reason for this is simple: the native parts of JavaScript—those already present in the browser before you write a line of code—are all written in a lower-level language such as C++. That means these methods are compiled down to machine code as part of the browser and therefore don't have the same limitations as your JavaScript code.

A common mistake of inexperienced JavaScript developers is to perform complex mathematical operations in code when there are better performing versions available on the built-in `Math` object. The `Math` object contains properties and methods designed to make mathematical operations easier. There are several mathematical constants available:

Constant	Meaning
`Math.E`	The value of E, the base of the natural logarithm
`Math.LN10`	The natural logarithm of 10
`Math.LN2`	The natural logarithm of 2
`Math.LOG2E`	The base-2 logarithm of E
`Math.LOG10E`	The base-10 logarithm of E
`Math.PI`	The value of π
`Math.SQRT1_2`	The square root of ½
`Math.SQRT2`	The square root of 2

Each of these values is precalculated, so there is no need for you to calculate them yourself. There are also methods to handle mathematical calculations:

Method	Meaning
`Math.abs(num)`	The absolute value of *num*
`Math.exp(num)`	$Math.E^{num}$
`Math.log(num)`	The logarithm of *num*
`Math.pow(num, power)`	num^{power}
`Math.sqrt(num)`	The square root of *num*
`Math.acos(x)`	The arc cosine of *x*
`Math.asin(x)`	The arc sine of *x*
`Math.atan(x)`	The arc tangent of *x*
`Math.atan2(y, x)`	The arc tangent of *y/x*
`Math.cos(x)`	The cosine of *x*
`Math.sin(x)`	The sine of *x*
`Math.tan(x)`	The tangent of *x*

Using these methods is faster than recreating the same functionality in JavaScript code. Whenever you need to perform complex mathematical calculations, look to the `Math` object first.

Another example is the Selectors API, which allows querying of a DOM document using CSS selectors. CSS queries were implemented natively in JavaScript and truly popularized by the jQuery JavaScript library. The jQuery engine is widely considered the fastest engine for CSS querying, but it is still much slower than the native methods. The native `querySelector()` and `querySelectorAll()` methods complete their tasks, on average, in 10% of the time it takes for JavaScript-based CSS querying.[*] Most JavaScript libraries have now moved to use the native functionality when available to speed up their overall performance.

Always use native methods when available, especially for mathematical calculations and DOM operations. The more work that is done with compiled code, the faster your code becomes.

Chrome actually implements a fair amount of its native JavaScript functionality in JavaScript. Because Chrome uses a just-in-time JavaScript compiler for both native functionality and your code, there is sometimes little performance difference between the two.

---

[*] According to the SlickSpeed test suite at *http://www2.webkit.org/perf/slickspeed/*.

Summary

JavaScript presents some unique performance challenges related to the way you organize your code. As web applications have become more advanced, containing more and more lines of JavaScript to function, some patterns and antipatterns have emerged. Some programming practices to keep in mind:

- Avoid the double evaluation penalty by avoiding the use of `eval()` and the `Function()` constructor. Also, pass functions into `setTimeout()` and `setInterval()` instead of strings.

- Use object and array literals when creating new objects and arrays. They are created and initialized faster than nonliteral forms.

- Avoid doing the same work repeatedly. Use lazy loading or conditional advance loading when browser-detection logic is necessary.

- When performing mathematical operations, consider using bitwise operators that work directly on the underlying representation of the number.

- Native methods are always faster than anything you can write in JavaScript. Use native methods whenever available.

As with many of the techniques and approaches covered in this book, you will see the greatest performance gains when these optimizations are applied to code that is run frequently.

Building and Deploying High-Performance JavaScript Applications

Julien Lecomte

According to a 2007 study by Yahoo!'s Exceptional Performance team, 40%–60% of Yahoo!'s users have an empty cache experience, and about 20% of all page views are done with an empty cache (*http://yuiblog.com/blog/2007/01/04/performance-research -part-2/*). In addition, another more recent study by the Yahoo! Search team, which was independently confirmed by Steve Souders of Google, indicates that roughly 15% of the content delivered by large websites in the United States is served uncompressed.

These facts emphasize the need to make sure that JavaScript-based web applications are delivered as efficiently as possible. While part of that work is done during the design and development cycles, the build and deployment phase is also essential and often overlooked. If care is not taken during this crucial phase, the performance of your application will suffer, no matter how much effort you've put into making it faster.

The purpose of this chapter is to give you the necessary knowledge to efficiently assemble and deploy a JavaScript-based web application. A number of concepts are illustrated using Apache Ant, a Java-based build tool that has quickly become an industry standard for building applications for the Web. Toward the end of the chapter, a custom agile build tool written in PHP5 is presented as an example.

Apache Ant

Apache Ant (*http://ant.apache.org/*) is a tool for automating software build processes. It is similar to make, but is implemented in Java and uses XML to describe the build process, whereas make uses its own Makefile format. Ant is a project of the Apache Software Foundation (*http://www.apache.org/licenses/*).

The main benefit of Ant over `make` and other tools is its portability. Ant itself is available on many different platforms, and the format of Ant's build files is platform-independent.

An Ant build file is written in XML and named *build.xml* by default. Each build file contains exactly one project and at least one target. An Ant target can depend on other targets.

Targets contain task elements: actions that are executed atomically. Ant comes with a great number of built-in tasks, and optional tasks can be added if needed. Also, custom tasks can be developed in Java for use in an Ant build file.

A project can have a set of properties, or variables. A property has a name and a value. It can be set from within the build file using the **property** task, or might be set outside of Ant. A property can be evaluated by placing its name between ${and }.

The following is an example build file. Running the default target (`dist`) compiles the Java code contained in the source directory and packages it as a JAR archive.

```
<?xml version="1.0" encoding="UTF-8"?>
<project name="MyProject" default="dist" basedir=".">

  <!-- set global properties for this build -->
  <property name="src"    location="src"/>
  <property name="build" location="build"/>
  <property name="dist"  location="dist"/>

  <target name="init">
    <!-- Create the time stamp -->
    <tstamp/>
    <!-- Create the build directory structure used by compile -->
    <mkdir dir="${build}"/>
  </target>

  <target name="compile" depends="init" description="compile the source">
    <!-- Compile the java code from ${src} into ${build} -->
    <javac srcdir="${src}" destdir="${build}"/>
  </target>

  <target name="dist" depends="compile" description="generate the distribution">
    <!-- Create the distribution directory -->
    <mkdir dir="${dist}/lib"/>
    <!-- Put everything in ${build} into the MyProject-${DSTAMP}.jar file -->
    <jar jarfile="${dist}/lib/MyProject-${DSTAMP}.jar" basedir="${build}"/>
  </target>

  <target name="clean" description="clean up">
    <!-- Delete the ${build} and ${dist} directory trees -->
    <delete dir="${build}"/>
    <delete dir="${dist}"/>
  </target>

</project>
```

Although Apache Ant is used to illustrate the core concepts of this chapter, many other tools are available to build web applications. Among them, it is worth noting that Rake (*http://rake.rubyforge.org/*) has been gaining popularity in recent years. Rake is a Ruby-based build program with capabilities similar to `make`. Most notably, Rakefiles (Rake's version of Makefiles) are written using standard Ruby syntax, and are therefore platform-independent.

Combining JavaScript Files

According to Yahoo!'s Exceptional Performance team, the first and probably most important guideline for speeding up your website, especially for first-time visitors, is to reduce the number of HTTP requests required to render the page (*http://yuiblog.com/blog/2006/11/28/performance-research-part-1/*). This is where you should start looking for optimizations because combining assets usually requires a fairly small amount of work and has the greatest potential benefit for your users.

Most modern websites use several JavaScript files: usually a small library, which contains a set of utilities and controls to simplify the development of richly interactive web applications across multiple browsers, and some site-specific code, split into several logical units to keep the developers sane. CNN (*http://www.cnn.com/*), for example, uses the Prototype and Script.aculo.us libraries. Their front page displays a total of 12 external scripts and more than 20 inline script blocks. One simple optimization would be to group some, if not all, of this code into one external JavaScript file, thereby dramatically cutting down the number of HTTP requests necessary to render the page.

Apache Ant provides the ability to combine several files via the `concat` task. It is important, however, to remember that JavaScript files usually need to be concatenated in a specific order to respect dependencies. Once these dependencies have been established, using a `filelist` or a combination of `fileset` elements allows the order of the files to be preserved. Here is what the Ant target looks like:

```
<target name="js.concatenate">
    <concat destfile="${build.dir}/concatenated.js">
        <filelist dir="${src.dir}"
            files="a.js, b.js"/>
        <fileset dir="${src.dir}"
            includes="*.js"
            excludes="a.js, b.js"/>
    </concat>
</target>
```

This target creates the file *concatenated.js* under the build directory, as a result of the concatenation of *a.js*, followed by *b.js*, followed by all the other files under the source directory in alphabetical order.

Note that if any of the source files (except possibly the last one) does not end with either a semicolon or a line terminator, the resulting concatenated file may not contain valid

JavaScript code. This can be fixed by instructing Ant to check whether each concatenated source file is terminated by a newline, using the `fixlastline` attribute:

```
<concat destfile="${build.dir}/concatenated.js" fixlastline="yes">
    ...
</concat>
```

Preprocessing JavaScript Files

In computer science, a preprocessor is a program that processes its input data to produce output that is used as input to another program. The output is said to be a preprocessed form of the input data, which is often used by some subsequent programs like compilers. The amount and kind of processing done depends on the nature of the preprocessor; some preprocessors are only capable of performing relatively simple textual substitutions and macro expansions, while others have the power of fully fledged programming languages.

—http://en.wikipedia.org/wiki/Preprocessor

Preprocessing your JavaScript source files will not make your application faster by itself, but it will allow you to, among other things, conditionally instrument your code in order to measure how your application is performing.

Since no preprocessor is specifically designed to work with JavaScript, it is necessary to use a lexical preprocessor that is flexible enough that its lexical analysis rules can be customized, or else use one that was designed to work with a language for which the lexical grammar is close enough to JavaScript's own lexical grammar. Since the C programming language syntax is close to JavaScript, the C preprocessor (`cpp`) is a good choice. Here is what the Ant target looks like:

```
<target name="js.preprocess" depends="js.concatenate">
    <apply executable="cpp" dest="${build.dir}">
        <fileset dir="${build.dir}"
            includes="concatenated.js"/>
        <arg line="-P -C -DDEBUG"/>
        <srcfile/>
        <targetfile/>
        <mapper type="glob"
            from="concatenated.js"
            to="preprocessed.js"/>
    </apply>
</target>
```

This target, which depends on the `js.concatenate` target, creates the file *preprocessed.js* under the build directory as a result of running `cpp` on the previously concatenated file. Note that `cpp` is run using the standard `-P` (inhibit generation of line markers) and `-C` (do not discard comments) options. In this example, the `DEBUG` macro is also defined.

With this target, you can now use the macro definition (`#define`, `#undef`) and the conditional compilation (`#if`, `#ifdef`, `#ifndef`, `#else`, `#elif`, `#endif`) directives directly inside your JavaScript files, allowing you, for example, to conditionally embed (or remove) profiling code:

```
#ifdef DEBUG

(new YAHOO.util.YUILoader({
    require: ['profiler'],
    onSuccess: function(o) {
        YAHOO.tool.Profiler.registerFunction('foo', window);
    }
})).insert();

#endif
```

If you plan to use multiline macros, make sure you use the Unix end-of-line character (LF). You may use the fixcrlf Ant task to automatically fix that for you.

Another example, not strictly related to performance but demonstrating how powerful JavaScript preprocessing can be, is the use of "variadic macros" (macros accepting a variable number of arguments) and file inclusion to implement JavaScript assertions. Consider the following file named *include.js*:

```
#ifndef _INCLUDE_JS_
#define _INCLUDE_JS_

#ifdef DEBUG
function assert(condition, message) {
    // Handle the assertion by displaying an alert message
    // possibly containing a stack trace for example.
}
#define ASSERT(x, ...) assert(x, ## __VA_ARGS__)
#else
#define ASSERT(x, ...)
#endif /* DEBUG */

#endif /* _INCLUDE_JS_ */
```

You can now write JavaScript code that looks like the following:

```
#include "include.js"

function myFunction(arg) {
    ASSERT(YAHOO.lang.isString(argvar), "arg should be a string");
    ...
#ifdef DEBUG
    YAHOO.log("Log this in debug mode only");
#endif
    ...
}
```

The assertion and the extra logging code appear only when the DEBUG macro is set during development. These statements disappear in the final production build.

JavaScript Minification

JavaScript minification is the process by which a JavaScript file is stripped of everything that does not contribute to its execution. This includes comments and unnecessary whitespace. The process typically reduces the file size by half, resulting in faster downloads, and encourages programmers to write better, more extensive inline documentation.

JSMin (*http://www.crockford.com/javascript/jsmin.html*), developed by Douglas Crockford, remained the standard in JavaScript minification for a long time. However, as web applications kept growing in size and complexity, many felt it was time to push Java-Script minification a step further. This is the main reason behind the development of the YUI Compressor (*http://developer.yahoo.com/yui/compressor/*), a tool that performs all kinds of smart operations in order to offer a higher level of compaction than other tools in a completely safe way. In addition to stripping comments and unnecessary whitespace, the YUI Compressor offers the following features:

- Replacement of local variable names with shorter (one-, two-, or three-character) variable names, picked to optimize gzip compression downstream
- Replacement of bracket notation with dot notation whenever possible (e.g., `foo["bar"]` becomes `foo.bar`)
- Replacement of quoted literal property names whenever possible (e.g., `{"foo":"bar"}` becomes `{foo:"bar"}`)
- Replacement of escaped quotes in strings (e.g., `'aaa\'bbb'` becomes `"aaa'bbb"`)
- Constant folding (e.g., `"foo"+"bar"` becomes `"foobar"`)

Running your JavaScript code through the YUI Compressor results in tremendous savings compared to JSMin without any further action. Consider the following numbers on the core files of the YUI library (version 2.7.0, available at *http://developer.yahoo .com/yui/*):

Raw `yahoo.js`, `dom.js` and `event.js`	192,164 bytes
`yahoo.js`, `dom.js` and `event.js` + JSMin	47,316 bytes
`yahoo.js`, `dom.js` and `event.js` + YUI Compressor	**35,896 bytes**

In this example, the YUI Compressor offers 24% savings out of the box compared to JSMin. However, there are things you can do to increase the byte savings even further. Storing local references to objects/values, wrapping code in a closure, using constants for repeated values, and avoiding `eval` (and its relatives, the `Function` constructor, `setTimeout`, and `setInterval` when used with a string literal as the first argument), the `with` keyword, and JScript conditional comments all contribute to making the minified file smaller. Consider the following function, designed to toggle the `selected` class on the specified DOM element (220 bytes):

```
function toggle (element) {
    if (YAHOO.util.Dom.hasClass(element, "selected")){
        YAHOO.util.Dom.removeClass(element, "selected");
    } else {
        YAHOO.util.Dom.addClass(element, "selected");
    }
}
```

The YUI Compressor will transform this code into the following (147 bytes):

```
function toggle(a){if(YAHOO.util.Dom.hasClass(a,"selected")){
YAHOO.util.Dom.removeClass(a,"selected")}else{YAHOO.util.Dom.
addClass(a,"selected")}};
```

If you refactor the original version by storing a local reference to YAHOO.util.Dom and using a constant for the "selected" value, the code becomes (232 bytes):

```
function toggle (element) {
    var YUD = YAHOO.util.Dom, className = "selected";
    if (YUD.hasClass(element, className)){
        YUD.removeClass(element, className);
    } else {
        YUD.addClass(element, className);
    }
}
```

This version shows even greater savings after minification using the YUI Compressor (115 bytes):

```
function toggle(a){var c=YAHOO.util.Dom,b="selected";if(c.hasClass(a,b)){
c.removeClass(a,b)}else{c.addClass(a,b)}};
```

The compaction ratio went from 33% to 48%, which is a staggering result given the small amount of work needed. However, it is important to note that gzip compression, happening downstream, may yield conflicting results; in other words, the smallest minified file may not always give the smallest gzipped file. That strange result is a direct consequence of lowering the amount of redundancy in the original file. In addition, this kind of microoptimization incurs a small runtime cost because variables are now used in place of literal values, thus requiring additional lookups. Therefore, I usually recommend not abusing these techniques, although it may still be worth considering them when serving content to user agents that don't support (or advertise their support for) gzip compression.

In November 2009, Google released an even more advanced minification tool called the Closure Compiler (*http://code.google.com/closure/compiler/*). This new tool goes further than the YUI Compressor when using its advanced optimizations option. In this mode, the Closure Compiler is extremely aggressive in the ways that it transforms code and renames symbols. Although it yields incredible savings, it requires the developer to be very careful and to ensure that the output code works the same way as the input code. It also makes debugging more difficult because almost all of the symbols are renamed. The Closure library does come with a Firebug extension, named the Closure Inspector (*http://code.google.com/closure/compiler/docs/inspector.html*), that provides a mapping between the obfuscated symbols and the original symbols. Nevertheless, this extension is not available on browsers other than Firefox, which may be a problem when debugging browser-specific code paths, and debugging still remains harder than with other, less aggressive minification tools.

Buildtime Versus Runtime Build Processes

Concatenation, preprocessing, and minification are steps that can take place either at buildtime or at runtime. Runtime build processes are very useful during development, but generally are not recommended in a production environment for scalability reasons. As a general rule for building high-performance applications, everything that can be done at buildtime should not be done at runtime.

Whereas Apache Ant is definitely an offline build program, the agile build tool presented toward the end of this chapter represents a middle ground whereby the same tool can be used during development and to create the final assets that will be used in a production environment.

JavaScript Compression

When a web browser requests a resource, it usually sends an `Accept-Encoding` HTTP header (starting with HTTP/1.1) to let the web server know what kinds of encoding transformations it supports. This information is primarily used to allow a document to be compressed, enabling faster downloads and therefore a better user experience. Possible values for the `Accept-Encoding` value tokens include: `gzip`, `compress`, `deflate`, and `identity` (these values are registered by the Internet Assigned Numbers Authority, or IANA).

If the web server sees this header in the request, it will choose the most appropriate encoding method and notify the web browser of its decision via the `Content-Encoding` HTTP header.

`gzip` is by far the most popular encoding. It generally reduces the size of the payload by 70%, making it a weapon of choice for improving the performance of a web application. Note that gzip compression should be used primarily on text responses, including JavaScript files. Other file types, such as images or PDF files, should not be gzipped, because they are already compressed and trying to compress them again is a waste of server resources.

If you use the Apache web server (by far the most popular), enabling gzip compression requires installing and configuring either the `mod_gzip` module (for Apache 1.3 and available at *http://www.schroepl.net/projekte/mod_gzip/*) or the `mod_deflate` module (for Apache 2).

Recent studies done independently by Yahoo! Search and Google have shown that roughly 15% of the content delivered by large websites in the United States is served uncompressed. This is mostly due to a missing `Accept-Encoding` HTTP header in the request, stripped by some corporate proxies, firewalls, or even PC security software. Although gzip compression is an amazing tool for web developers, one must be mindful of this fact and strive to write code as concisely as possible. Another technique is to serve alternate JavaScript content to users who are not going to benefit from gzip compression but could benefit from a lighter experience (although users should be given the choice to switch back to the full version).

To that effect, it is worth mentioning Packer (*http://dean.edwards.name/packer/*), a JavaScript minifier developed by Dean Edwards. Packer is able to shrink JavaScript files beyond what the YUI Compressor can do. Consider the following results on the jQuery library (version 1.3.2, available at *http://www.jquery.com/*):

jQuery	120,180 bytes
jQuery + YUI Compressor	56,814 bytes
jQuery + Packer	**39,351 bytes**
Raw jQuery + gzip	34,987 bytes
jQuery + YUI Compressor + gzip	**19,457 bytes**
jQuery + Packer + gzip	*19,228 bytes*

After gzipping, running the jQuery library through Packer or the YUI Compressor yields very similar results. However, files compressed using Packer incur a fixed runtime cost (about 200 to 300 milliseconds on my modern laptop). Therefore, using the YUI Compressor in combination with gzipping always gives the best results. However, Packer can be used with some success for users on slow lines that don't support gzip compression, for whom the cost of unpacking is negligible compared to the cost of downloading large amounts of code. The only downside to serving different JavaScript content to different users is increased QA costs.

Caching JavaScript Files

Making HTTP components cacheable will greatly improve the experience of repeat visitors to your website. As a concrete example, loading the Yahoo! home page (*http://www.yahoo.com/*) with a full cache requires 90% fewer HTTP requests and 83% fewer bytes to download than with an empty cache. The round-trip time (the elapsed time between the moment a page is requested and the firing of the `onload` event) goes from 2.4 seconds to 0.9 seconds (*http://yuiblog.com/blog/2007/01/04/performance-research-part-2/*). Although caching is most often used on images, it should be used on all static components, including JavaScript files.

Web servers use the `Expires` HTTP response header to let clients know how long a resource can be cached. The format is an absolute timestamp in RFC 1123 format. An example of its use is: `Expires: Thu, 01 Dec 1994 16:00:00 GMT`. To mark a response as "never expires," a web server sends an `Expires` date approximately one year in the future from the time at which the response is sent. Web servers should never send `Expires` dates more than one year in the future according to the HTTP 1.1 RFC (RFC 2616, section 14.21).

If you use the Apache web server, the `ExpiresDefault` directive allows you to set an expiration date relative to the current date. The following example applies this directive to images, JavaScript files, and CSS stylesheets:

```
<FilesMatch "\.(jpg|jpeg|png|gif|js|css|htm|html)$">
    ExpiresActive on
    ExpiresDefault "access plus 1 year"
</FilesMatch>
```

Some web browsers, especially when running on mobile devices, may have limited caching capabilities. For example, the Safari web browser on the iPhone does not cache a component if its size is greater than 25KB uncompressed (see *http://yuiblog.com/blog/2008/02/06/iphone-cacheability/*) or 15KB for the iPhone 3.0 OS. In those cases, it is relevant to consider a trade-off between the number of HTTP components and their cacheability by splitting them into smaller chunks.

You can also consider using client-side storage mechanisms if they are available, in which case the JavaScript code must itself handle the expiration.

Finally, another technique is the use of the HTML 5 offline application cache, implemented in Firefox 3.5, Safari 4.0, and on the iPhone beginning with iPhone OS 2.1. This technology relies on a manifest file listing the resources to be cached. The manifest file is declared by adding a `manifest` attribute to the `<html>` tag (note the use of the HTML 5 DOCTYPE):

```
<!DOCTYPE html>
<html manifest="demo.manifest">
```

The manifest file uses a special syntax to list offline resources and must be served using the `text/cache-manifest` mime type. More information on offline web application caching can be found on the W3C website at *http://www.w3.org/TR/html5/offline.html*.

Working Around Caching Issues

Adequate cache control can really enhance the user experience, but it has a downside: when revving up your application, you want to make sure your users get the latest version of the static content. This is accomplished by renaming static resources whenever they change.

Most often, developers add a version or a build number to filenames. Others like to append a checksum. Personally, I like to use a timestamp. This task can be automated using Ant. The following target takes care of renaming JavaScript files by appending a timestamp in the form of `yyyyMMddhhmm`:

```
<target name="js.copy">
    <!-- Create the time stamp -->
    <tstamp/>
    <!-- Rename JavaScript files by appending a time stamp -->
    <copy todir="${build.dir}">
        <fileset dir="${src.dir}" includes="*.js"/>
        <globmapper from="*.js" to="*-${DSTAMP}${TSTAMP}.js"/>
    </copy>
</target>
```

Using a Content Delivery Network

A content delivery network (CDN) is a network of computers distributed geographically across the Internet that is responsible for delivering content to end users. The primary reasons for using a CDN are reliability, scalability, and above all, performance. In fact, by serving content from the location closest to the user, CDNs are able to dramatically decrease network latency.

Some large companies maintain their own CDN, but it is generally cost effective to use a third-party CDN provider such as Akamai Technologies (*http://www.akamai.com/*) or Limelight Networks (*http://www.limelightnetworks.com/*).

Switching to a CDN is usually a fairly simple code change and has the potential to dramatically improve end-user response times.

It is worth noting that the most popular JavaScript libraries are all accessible via a CDN. For example, the YUI library is served directly from the Yahoo! network (server name is *yui.yahooapis.com*, details available at *http://developer.yahoo.com/yui/articles/hosting/*), and jQuery, Dojo, Prototype, Script.aculo.us, MooTools, YUI, and other libraries are all available directly via Google's CDN (server name is *ajax.googleapis.com*, details available at *http://code.google.com/apis/ajaxlibs/*).

Deploying JavaScript Resources

The deployment of JavaScript resources usually amounts to copying files to one or several remote hosts, and also sometimes to running a set of shell commands on those hosts, especially when using a CDN, to distribute the newly added files across the delivery network.

Apache Ant gives you several options to copy files to remote servers. You could use the copy task to copy files to a locally mounted filesystem, or you could use the optional FTP or SCP tasks. My personal preference is to go directly to using the scp utility, which is available on all major platforms. Here is a very simple example demonstrating this:

```
<apply executable="scp" failonerror="true" parallel="true">
    <fileset dir="${build.dir}" includes="*.js"/>
    <srcfile/>
    <arg line="${live.server}:/var/www/html/"/>
</apply>
```

Finally, in order to execute shell commands on a remote host running the SSH daemon, you can use the optional SSHEXEC task or simply invoke the ssh utility directly, as demonstrated in the following example, to restart the Apache web server on a Unix host:

```
<exec executable="ssh" failonerror="true">
    <arg line="${live.server}"/>
    <arg line="sudo service httpd restart"/>
</exec>
```

Agile JavaScript Build Process

Traditional build tools are great, but most web developers find them very cumbersome because it is necessary to manually compile the solution after every single code change. Instead, it's preferable to just have to refresh the browser window and skip the compilation step altogether. As a consequence, few web developers use the techniques outlined in this chapter, resulting in applications or websites that perform poorly. Thankfully, it is fairly simple to write a tool that combines all these advanced techniques, allowing web developers to work efficiently while still getting the most performance out of their application.

smasher is a PHP5 application based on an internal tool used by Yahoo! Search. It combines multiple JavaScript files, preprocesses them, and optionally minifies their content. It can be run from the command line, or during development to handle web requests and automatically combine resources on the fly. The source code can be found at *http://github.com/jlecomte/smasher*, and contains the following files:

smasher.php
> Core file

smasher.xml
> Configuration file

smasher
> Command-line wrapper

smasher_web.php
> Web server entry point

smasher requires an XML configuration file containing the definition of the groups of files it will combine, as well as some miscellaneous information about the system. Here is an example of what this file looks like:

```
<?xml version="1.0" encoding="utf-8"?>
<smasher>
    <temp_dir>/tmp/</temp_dir>
    <root_dir>/home/jlecomte/smasher/files/</root_dir>
    <java_bin>/usr/bin/java</java_bin>
    <yuicompressor>/home/jlecomte/smasher/yuicompressor-2-4-2.jar</yuicompressor>

    <group id="yui-core">
        <file type="css" src="reset.css" />
```

```
        <file type="css" src="fonts.css" />
        <file type="js" src="yahoo.js" />
        <file type="js" src="dom.js" />
        <file type="js" src="event.js" />
    </group>

    <group id="another-group">
        <file type="js" src="foo.js" />
        <file type="js" src="bar.js" />
        <macro name="DEBUG" value="1" />
    </group>

    ...

</smasher>
```

Each group element contains a set of JavaScript and/or CSS files. The root_dir top-level element contains the path to the directory where these files can be found. Optionally, group elements can also contain a list of preprocessing macro definitions.

Once this configuration file has been saved, you can run smasher from the command line. If you run it without any of the required parameters, it will display some usage information before exiting. The following example shows how to combine, preprocess, and minify the core YUI JavaScript files:

```
$ ./smasher -c smasher.xml -g yui-core -t js
```

If all goes well, the output file can be found in the working directory, and is named after the group name (yui-core in this example) followed by a timestamp and the appropriate file extension (e.g., *yui-core-200907191539.js*).

Similarly, you can use smasher to handle web requests during development by placing the file *smasher_web.php* somewhere under your web server document root and by using a URL similar to this one:

```
http://<host>/smasher_web.php?conf=smasher.xml&group=yui-core&type=css&nominify
```

By using different URLs for your JavaScript and CSS assets during development and in production, it is now possible to work efficiently while still getting the most performance out of the build process.

Summary

The build and deployment process can have a tremendous impact on the performance of a JavaScript-based application. The most important steps in this process are:

- Combining JavaScript files to reduce the number of HTTP requests
- Minifying JavaScript files using the YUI Compressor
- Serving JavaScript files compressed (gzip encoding)

- Making JavaScript files cacheable by setting the appropriate HTTP response headers and work around caching issues by appending a timestamp to filenames
- Using a Content Delivery Network to serve JavaScript files; not only will a CDN improve performance, it should also manage compression and caching for you

All these steps should be automated using publicly available build tools such as Apache Ant or using a custom build tool tailored to your specific needs. If you make the build process work for you, you will be able to greatly improve the performance of web applications or websites that require large amounts of JavaScript code.

Tools

Matt Sweeney

Having the right software is essential for identifying bottlenecks in both the loading and running of scripts. A number of browser vendors and large-scale websites have shared techniques and tools to help make the Web faster and more efficient. This chapter focuses on some of the free tools available for:

Profiling
> Timing various functions and operations during script execution to identify areas for optimization

Network analysis
> Examining the loading of images, stylesheets, and scripts and their effect on overall page load and rendering

When a particular script or application is performing less than optimally, a profiler can help prioritize areas for optimization. This can get tricky because of the range of supported browsers, but many vendors now provide a profiler along with their debugging tools. In some cases, performance issues may be specific to a particular browser; other times, the symptoms may occur across multiple browsers. Keep in mind that the optimizations applied to one browser *might* benefit other browsers, but they might have the opposite effect as well. Rather than assuming which functions or operations are slow, profilers ensure that optimization time is spent on the slowest areas of the system that affect the most browsers.

While the bulk of this chapter focuses on profiling tools, network analyzers can be highly effective in helping to ensure that scripts and pages are loading and running as quickly as possible. Before diving into tweaking code, you should be sure that all scripts and other assets are being loaded optimally. Image and stylesheet loading can affect the loading of scripts, depending on how many concurrent requests the browser allows and how many assets are being loaded.

Some of these tools provide tips on how to improve the performance of web pages. Keep in mind that the best way to interpret the information these tools provide is to learn more about the rationale behind the rules. As with most rules, there are exceptions, and a deeper understanding of the rules allows you to know when to break them.

JavaScript Profiling

The tool that comes with all JavaScript implementations is the language itself. Using the Date object, a measurement can be taken at any given point in a script. Before other tools existed, this was a common way to time script execution, and it is still occasionally useful. By default the Date object returns the current time, and subtracting one Date instance from another gives the elapsed time in milliseconds. Consider the following example, which compares creating elements from scratch with cloning from an existing element (see Chapter 3, *DOM Scripting*):

```
var start = new Date(),
    count = 10000,
    i, element, time;

 for (i = 0; i < count; i++) {
    element = document.createElement('div');
}

time = new Date() - start;
alert('created ' + count + ' in ' + time + 'ms');

start = new Date();
for (i = 0, i < count; i++) {
    element = element.cloneNode(false);
}

time = new Date() - start;
alert('created ' + count + ' in ' + time + 'ms');
```

This type of profiling is cumbersome to implement, as it requires manually instrumenting your own timing code. A Timer object that handles the time calculations and stores the data would be a good next step.

```
Var Timer = {
    _data: {},

    start: function(key) {
        Timer._data[key] = new Date();
    },

    stop: function(key) {
        var time = Timer._data[key];
        if (time) {
            Timer._data[key] = new Date() - time;
        }
    },

    getTime: function(key) {
        return Timer._data[key];
```

```
    }
};

Timer.start('createElement');
for (i = 0; i < count; i++) {
    element = document.createElement('div');
}

Timer.stop('createElement');
alert('created ' + count + ' in ' + Timer.getTime('createElement');
```

As you can see, this still requires manual instrumentation, but provides a pattern for building a pure JavaScript profiler. By extending the `Timer` object concept, a profiler can be constructed that registers functions and instruments them with timing code.

YUI Profiler

The YUI Profiler (*http://developer.yahoo.com/yui/profiler/*), contributed by Nicholas Zakas, is a JavaScript profiler written in JavaScript. In addition to timer functionality, it provides interfaces for profiling functions, objects, and constructors, as well as detailed reports of the profile data. It enables profiling across various browsers and data exporting for more robust reporting and analysis.

The YUI Profiler provides a generic timer that collects performance data. `Profiler` provides static methods for starting and stopping named timings and retrieving profile data.

```
var count = 10000, i, element;
    Y.Profiler.start('createElement');

    for (i = 0; i < count; i++) {
        element = document.createElement('div');
    }

    Y.Profiler.stop('createElement');

    alert('created ' + count + ' in  ' +
            Y.Profiler.getAverage('createElement') + 'ms');
```

This clearly improves upon the inline `Date` and `Timer` approach and provides additional profile data regarding the number of times called, as well as the average, minimum, and maximum times. This data is collected and can be analyzed alongside other profile results.

Functions can be registered for profiling as well. The registered function is instrumented with code that collects performance data. For example, to profile the global `initUI` method from Chapter 2, all that is required is the name:

```
Y.Profiler.registerFunction("initUI");
```

Many functions are bound to objects in order to prevent pollution of the global namespace. Object methods can be registered by passing the object in as the second argument to registerFunction. For example, assume an object called uiTest that implements two initUI approaches as uiTest.test1 and uiTest.test2. Each can be registered individually:

```
Y.Profiler.registerFunction("test1", uiTest);
Y.Profiler.registerFunction("test2", uiTest);
```

This works well enough, but doesn't really scale for profiling many functions or an entire application. The registerObject method automatically registers every method bound to the object:

```
Y.Profiler.registerObject("uiTest", uiTest);
```

The first argument is the name of the object (for reporting purposes), and the second is the object itself. This will instrument profiling for all of the uiTest methods.

Objects that rely on prototype inheritance need special handling. YUI's profiler allows the registration of a constructor function that will instrument all methods on all instances of the object:

```
Y.Profiler.registerConstructor("MyWidget", myNameSpace);
```

Now every function on each instance of myNameSpace.MyWidget will be measured and reported on. An individual report can be retrieved as an object:

```
var initUIReport = Y.Profiler.getReport("initUI");
```

This provides an object containing the profile data, including an array of *points*, which are the timings for each call, in the order they were called. These points can be plotted and analyzed in other interesting ways to examine the variations in time. This object has the following fields:

```
{
    min: 100,
    max: 250,
    calls: 5,
    avg: 120,
    points: [100, 200, 250, 110, 100]
};
```

Sometimes you may want only the value of a particular field. Static Profiler methods provide discrete data per function or method:

```
var uiTest1Report = {
    calls: Y.Profiler.getCalls("uiTest.test1"),
    avg: Y.Profiler.getAvg("uiTest.test1")
};
```

A view that highlights the slowest areas of the code is really what is needed in order to properly analyze a script's performance. A report of all registered functions called on the object or constructor is also available:

```
var uiTestReport = Y.Profiler.getReport("uiTest");
```

This returns an object with the following data:

```
{
    test1: {
        min: 100,
        max: 250,
        calls: 10,
        avg: 120
    },
    test2:
        min: 80,
        max: 210,
        calls: 10,
        avg: 90
    }
};
```

This provides the opportunity to sort and view the data in more meaningful ways, allowing the slower areas of the code to be scrutinized more closely. A full report of all of the current profile data can also be generated. This, however, may contain useless information, such as functions that were called zero times or that are already meeting performance expectations. In order to minimize this type of noise, an optional function can be passed in to filter the data:

```
var fullReport = Y.Profiler.getFullReport(function(data) {
    return (data.calls > 0 && data.avg > 5);
};
```

The Boolean value returned will indicate whether the function should be included in the report, allowing the less interesting data to be suppressed.

When finished profiling, functions, objects, and constructors can be unregistered individually, clearing the profile data:

```
Y.Profiler.unregisterFunction("initUI");
Y.Profiler.unregisterObject("uiTests");
Y.Profiler.unregisterConstructor("MyWidget");
```

The `clear()` method keeps the current profile registry but clears the associated data. This function can be called individually per function or timing:

```
Y.Profiler.clear("initUI");
```

Or all data may be cleared at once by omitting the name argument:

```
Y.Profiler.clear();
```

Because it is in JSON format, the profile report data can be viewed in any number of ways. The simplest way to view it is on a web page by outputting as HTML. It can also be sent to a server, where it can be stored in a database for more robust reporting. This is especially useful when comparing various optimization techniques across browsers.

It is worth noting that anonymous functions are especially troublesome for this type of profiler because there is no name to report with. The YUI Profiler provides a mechanism for instrumenting anonymous functions, allowing them to be profiled. Registering an anonymous function returns a wrapper function that can be called instead of the anonymous function:

```
var instrumentedFunction =
    Y.Profiler.instrument("anonymous1", function(num1, num2){
        return num1 + num2;
    });
instrumentedFunction(3, 5);
```

This adds the data for the anonymous function to the Profiler's result set, allowing it to be retrieved in the same manner as other profile data:

```
var report = Y.Profiler.getReport("anonymous1");
```

Anonymous Functions

Depending on the profiler, some data can be obscured by the use of anonymous functions or function assignments. As this is a common pattern in JavaScript, many of the functions being profiled may be anonymous, making it difficult or impossible to measure and analyze. The best way to enable profiling of anonymous functions is to name them. Using pointers to object methods rather than closures will allow the broadest possible profile coverage.

Compare using an inline function:

```
myNode.onclick = function() {
    myApp.loadData();
};
```

with a method call:

```
myApp._onClick = function() {
    myApp.loadData();
};
myNode.onclick = myApp._onClick;
```

Using the method call allows any of the reviewed profilers to automatically instrument the onclick handler. This is not always practical, as it may require significant refactoring in order to enable profiling.

For profilers that automatically instrument anonymous functions, adding an inline name makes the reports more readable:

```
myNode.onclick = function myNodeClickHandler() {
    myApp.loadData();
};
```

This also works with functions declared as variables, which some profilers have trouble gleaning a name from:

```
var onClick = function myNodeClickHandler() {
    myApp.loadData();
};
```

The anonymous function is now *named*, providing most profilers with something meaningful to display along with the profile results. These names require little effort to implement, and can even be inserted automatically as part of a debug build process.

 Always use uncompressed versions of your scripts for debugging and profiling. This will ensure that your functions are easily identifiable.

Firebug

Firefox is a popular browser with developers, partially due to the Firebug addon (available at *http://www.getfirebug.com/*), which was developed initially by Joe Hewitt and is now maintained by the Mozilla Foundation. This tool has increased the productivity of web developers worldwide by providing insights into code that were never before possible.

Firebug provides a console for logging output, a traversable DOM tree of the current page, style information, the ability to introspect DOM and JavaScript objects, and more. It also includes a profiler and network analyzer, which will be the focus of this section. Firebug is also highly extensible, enabling custom panels to be easily added.

Console Panel Profiler

The Firebug Profiler is available as part of the Console panel (see Figure 10-1). It measures and reports on the execution of JavaScript on the page. The report details each function that is called while the profiler is running, providing highly accurate performance data and valuable insights into what may be causing scripts to run slowly.

| | | Console ▾ | HTML | CSS | Script | DOM | Net | Q | | Off |

Clear   Profile

>>>

Figure 10-1. FireBug Console panel

One way to run a profile is by clicking the Profile button, triggering the script, and clicking the Profile button again to stop profiling. Figure 10-2 shows a typical report of the profile data. This includes *Calls*, the number of times the function was called; *Own Time*, the time spent in the function itself; and *Time*, the overall time spent in a function and any function it may have called. The profiling is instrumented at the browser chrome level, so there is minimal overhead when profiling from the Console panel.

Function	Calls	Percent	Own Time	Time	Avg	Min	Max	File
a2()	1	8.66%	39.106ms	43.89ms	43.89ms	43.89ms	43.89ms	combo?me...0.1.32.js (line 8)
h()	150	7.31%	33.015ms	34.767ms	0.232ms	0.009ms	30.766ms	arcade_0.1.98.js (line 4)
h()	3337	5.66%	25.588ms	25.588ms	0.008ms	0.001ms	0.308ms	arcade-s..._0.1.0.js (line 2)
h()	143	3.72%	16.783ms	30.005ms	0.21ms	0.089ms	0.58ms	arcade_0.1.98.js (line 4)
ad_embedObj	1	3.62%	16.331ms	19.708ms	19.708ms	19.708ms	19.708ms	ad_eo_1.1.js (line 5)
h()	67	3.04%	13.748ms	33.157ms	0.495ms	0.036ms	3.716ms	arcade-s..._0.1.0.js (line 2)
h()	1092	2.88%	13.026ms	27.557ms	0.025ms	0.015ms	0.524ms	arcade_0.1.98.js (line 4)
h()	1104	2.67%	12.076ms	12.076ms	0.011ms	0.006ms	0.35ms	arcade_0.1.98.js (line 4)
h()	5290	2.54%	11.469ms	11.469ms	0.002ms	0.001ms	0.085ms	arcade_0.1.98.js (line 4)
h()	286	2.47%	11.153ms	35.975ms	0.126ms	0.04ms	0.322ms	arcade_0.1.98.js (line 4)
f	734	2.16%	9.748ms	10.715ms	0.015ms	0ms	0.313ms	arcade-s..._0.1.0.js (line 2)
h()	2354	1.79%	8.084ms	27.905ms	0.012ms	0.007ms	0.153ms	arcade_0.1.98.js (line 4)
h()	207	1.75%	7.903ms	115.32ms	0.557ms	0.023ms	14.992ms	arcade_0.1.98.js (line 4)
h()	73	1.57%	7.084ms	71.896ms	0.985ms	0.199ms	4.774ms	arcade_0.1.98.js (line 4)
h()	257	1.55%	6.000ms	6.000ms	0.07ms	0.001ms	0.425ms	arcade_0.1.98.js (line 4)

Figure 10-2. Firebug Profile panel

Console API

Firebug also provides a JavaScript interface to start and stop the profiler. This allows more precise control over which parts of the code are being measured. This also provides the option to name the report, which is valuable when comparing various optimization techniques.

```
console.profile("regexTest");
regexTest('foobar', 'foo');
console.profileEnd();
console.profile("indexOfTest");
indexOfTest('foobar', 'foo');
console.profileEnd();
```

Starting and stopping the profiler at the more interesting moments minimizes side effects and clutter from other scripts that may be running. One thing to keep in mind when invoking the profiler in this manner is that it does add overhead to the script. This is primarily due to the time required to generate the report after calling profileEnd(), which blocks subsequent execution until the report has been generated. Larger reports will take longer to generate, and may benefit from wrapping the call to profileEnd() in a setTimeout, making the report generation asynchronous and unblocking script execution.

 The JavaScript interface is available via the Firebug Console command line as well.

After ending the profile, a new report is generated, showing how long each function took, the number of times called, the percent of the total overhead, and other interesting data. This will provide insight as to where time should be spent optimizing function speeds and minimizing calls.

Like the YUI Profiler, Firebug's `console.time()` function can help measure loops and other operations that the profiler does not monitor. For example, the following times a small section of code containing a loop:

```
console.time("cache node");
for (var box = document.getElementById("box"),
        i = 0;
     i < 100; i++) {
    value = parseFloat(box.style.left) + 10;
    box.style.left = value + "px";
}
console.timeEnd("cache node");
```

After ending the timer, the time is output to the Console. This can be useful when comparing various optimization approaches. Additional timings can be captured and logged to the Console, making it easy to analyze results side by side. For example, to compare caching the node reference with caching a reference to the node's style, all that is needed is to write the implementation and drop in the timing code:

```
console.time("cache style");
for (var style = document.getElementById("box").style,
        i = 0;
     i < 100; i++) {
    value = parseFloat(style.left) + 10;
    style.left = value + "px";
}
console.timeEnd("cache style");
```

The Console API gives programmers the flexibility to instrument profiling code at various layers, and consolidates the results into reports that can be analyzed in many interesting ways.

 Clicking on a function displays it in the source file context. This is especially helpful for anonymous or obscurely named functions.

Net Panel

Often when encountering performance issues, it is good to step back from your code and take a look at the larger picture. Firebug provides a view of network assets in the Net panel (Figure 10-3). This panel provides a visualization of the pauses between scripts and other assets, providing deeper insight into the effect the script is having on the loading of other files and on the page in general.

The colored bars next to each asset break the loading life cycle into component phases (DNS lookup, waiting for response, etc.). The first vertical line (which displays as blue)

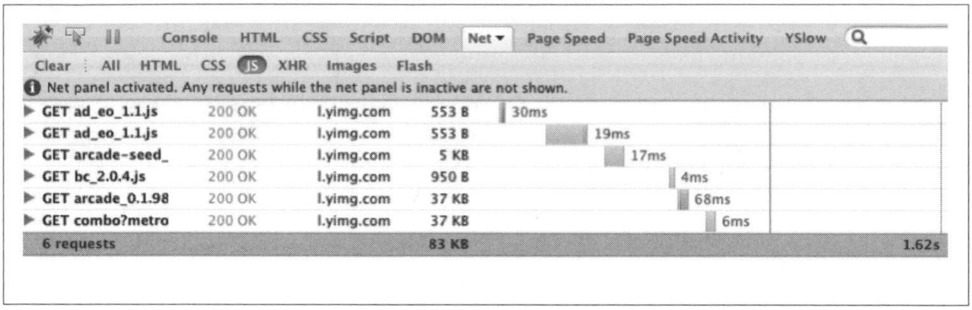

Figure 10-3. Firebug Net panel

indicates when the page's `DOMContentLoaded` event has fired. This event signals that the page's DOM tree is parsed and ready. The second vertical line (red) indicates when the window's `load` event has fired, which means that the DOM is ready and all external assets have completed loading. This gives a sense as to how much time is spent parsing and executing versus page rendering.

As you can see in the figure, there are a number of scripts being downloaded. Based on the timeline, each script appears to be waiting for the previous script prior to starting the next request. The simplest optimization to improve loading performance is to reduce the number of requests, especially script and stylesheet requests, which can block other assets and page rendering. When possible, combine all scripts into a single file in order to minimize the total number of requests. This applies to stylesheets and images as well.

Internet Explorer Developer Tools

As of version 8, Internet Explorer provides a development toolkit that includes a profiler. This toolkit is built into IE 8, so no additional download or installation is required. Like Firebug, the IE profiler includes function profiling and provides a detailed report that includes the number of calls, time spent, and other data points. It adds the ability to view the report as a call tree, profile native functions, and export the profile data. Although it lacks a network analyzer, the profiler can be supplemented with a generic tool such as Fiddler, which is outlined later in this chapter. See *http://msdn.microsoft.com/en-us/library/dd565628(VS.85).aspx* for more details.

IE 8's Profiler can be found with the Developer Tools (Tools → Developer Tools). After pressing the Start Profiling button, all subsequent JavaScript activity is monitored and profiled. Clicking Stop Profiling (same button, new label) stops the profiler and generates a new report. By default, F5 starts the profiler and Shift-F5 ends it.

The report provides both a flat function view of the time and duration of each call and a tree view showing the function call stack. The tree view allows you to walk through the call stack and identify slow code paths (see Figure 10-4). The IE profiler will use the variable name when no name is available for the function.

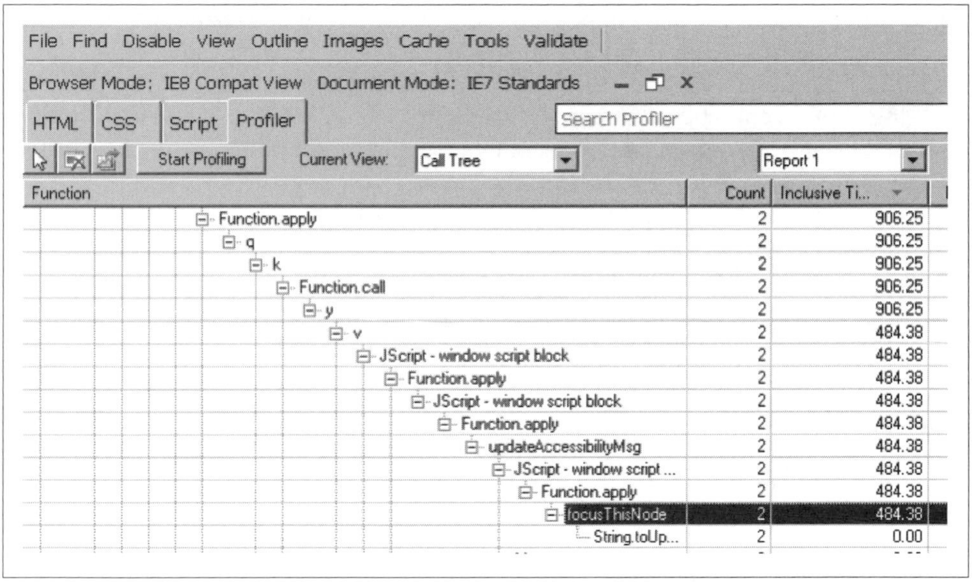

Function	Count	Inclusive Ti... ▾	
⊟ Function.apply	2	906.25	
⊟ q	2	906.25	
⊟ k	2	906.25	
⊟ Function.call	2	906.25	
⊟ y	2	906.25	
⊟ v	2	484.38	
⊟ JScript - window script block	2	484.38	
⊟ Function.apply	2	484.38	
⊟ JScript - window script block	2	484.38	
⊟ Function.apply	2	484.38	
⊟ updateAccessibilityMsg	2	484.38	
⊟ JScript - window script ...	2	484.38	
⊟ Function.apply	2	484.38	
⊟ focusThisNode	2	484.38	
└ String.toUp...	2	0.00	

Figure 10-4. IE 8 Profiler call tree

Right-click the profile result table to add and remove columns.

The IE Profiler also provides insight into native JavaScript object methods. This allows you to profile native objects in addition to implementation code, and makes it possible to do things such as compare `String::indexOf` with `RegExp::test` for determining whether an HTML element's `className` property begins with a certain value:

```
var count = 10000,
    element = document.createElement('div'),
    result, i, time;

element.className  = 'foobar';

for (i = 0; i < count; i++) {
    result = /^foo/.test(element.className);
}

for (i = 0; i < count; i++) {
    result = element.className.search(/^foo/);
}

for (i = 0; i < count; i++) {
    result = (element.className.indexOf('foo') === 0);
}
```

As seen in Figure 10-5, there appears to be a wide variation in time between these various approaches. Keep in mind that the average time of each call is zero. Native methods are generally the last place to look for optimizations, but this can be an interesting experiment when comparing approaches. Also keep in mind that with numbers this small, the results can be inconclusive due to rounding errors and system memory fluctuations.

Figure 10-5. Profile results for native methods

Although the IE Profiler does not currently offer a JavaScript API, it does have a console API with logging capabilities. This can be leveraged to port the `console.time()` and `console.timeEnd()` functions over from Firebug, allowing the same tests to run in IE.

```
if (console && !console.time) {
    console._timers = {};
    console.time = function(name) {
        console._timers[name] = new Date();
    };
    console.timeEnd = function(name) {
        var time = new Date() - console._timers[name];
        console.info(name + ': ' + time + 'ms');
    };
}
```

IE 8 profile results can be exported in *.csv* format using the Export Data button.

Safari Web Inspector

Safari, as of version 4, provides a profiler in addition to other tools, including a network analyzer, as part of its bundled Web Inspector. Like the Internet Explorer Developer Tools, the Web Inspector profiles native functions and provides an expandable call tree. It also includes a Firebug-like console API with profiling functionality, and a Resource panel for network analysis.

To access the Web Inspector, first make sure that the Develop menu is available. The Develop menu can be enabled by opening Preferences → Advanced and checking the "Show Develop menu in menu bar" box. The Web Inspector is then available under Develop → Show Web Inspector (or the keyboard shortcut Option-Command-I).

Profiles Panel

Clicking the Profile button brings up the Profile panel (Figure 10-6). Click the Enable Profiling button to enable the Profiles panel. To start profiling, click the Start Profiling button (the dark circle in the lower right). Click Stop Profiling (same button, now red) to stop the profile and show the report.

 You can also type Option-Shift-Command-P to start/stop profiling.

Self ▼	Total	Average	Calls	Function	
6.39s	7.38s	6.39s	1	(program)	
59.176ms	59.338ms	19.725ms	3	▼ f_set_cookie	
56.304ms	56.424ms	28.152ms	2	▼ (anonymous function)	combo:5
56.304ms	56.424ms	28.152ms	2	▼ M	combo:7
56.304ms	56.424ms	28.152ms	2	▼ (anonymous function)	combo:151
56.304ms	56.424ms	28.152ms	2	(program)	
2.872ms	2.914ms	2.872ms	1	▶ (anonymous function)	combo:4
58.071ms	60.393ms	1.815ms	32	▼ getBuddyInfo	
58.071ms	60.393ms	1.815ms	32	▼ f	combo:20
58.071ms	60.393ms	1.815ms	32	▼ (anonymous function)	combo:70
58.071ms	60.393ms	1.815ms	32	▼ a	combo:33
58.071ms	60.393ms	1.815ms	32	▼ c	combo:33
58.071ms	60.393ms	1.815ms	32	▼ (anonymous functi…	combo:39
58.071ms	60.393ms	1.815ms	32	▼ (anonymous fu…	combo:49
58.071ms	60.393ms	1.815ms	32	▼ (anonymous…	combo:72
58.071ms	60.393ms	1.815ms	32	▼ v	combo:20
58.071ms	60.393ms	1.815ms	32	▼ (program)	
58.071ms	60.393ms	1.815ms	32	(program)	
52.771ms	52.771ms	0.292ms	181	▶ evaluate	
31.203ms	31.362ms	15.601ms	2	▶ sendSubscribe	
29.163ms	29.163ms	0.435ms	67	▶ appendChild	

Figure 10-6. Safari Web Inspector Profile panel

Safari has emulated Firebug's JavaScript API (`console.profile()`, `console.time()`, etc.) in order to start and stop profiling programmatically. The functionality is the same as Firebug's, allowing you to name reports and timings for better profile management.

A name can also be passed to `console.profileEnd()`. This stops a specific profile in case multiple profiles are being run.

Safari provides both a Heavy (bottom-up) view of the profiled functions and a Tree (top-down) view of the call stack. The default Heavy view sorts the slowest functions first and allows traversal up the call stack, whereas the Tree view allows drilling from the top down into the execution path of the code from the outermost caller. Analyzing the call tree can help uncover more subtle performance issues related to how one function might be calling another.

Safari has also added support for a property called `displayName` for profiling purposes. This provides a way to add names to anonymous functions that will be used in the report output. Consider the following function assigned to the variable `foo`:

```
var foo = function() {
    return 'foo!';
};

console.profile('Anonymous Function');
foo();
console.profileEnd();
```

As shown in Figure 10-7, the resulting profile report is difficult to understand because of the lack of function names. Clicking on the URL to the right of the function shows the function in the context of the source code.

	Self ▼	Total	Average	Calls	Function	
Anonymous Function	1.42%	1.42%	1.42%	1	(anonymous function)	anon.html:8

Figure 10-7. Web Inspector Profile panel showing anonymous function

Adding a `displayName` will make the report readable. This also allows for more descriptive names that are not limited to valid function names.

```
var foo = function() {
    return 'foo!';
};
foo.displayName = 'I am foo';
```

As shown in Figure 10-8, the `displayName` now replaces the anonymous function. However, this property is available only in Webkit-based browsers. It also requires refactoring of truly anonymous functions, which is not advised. As discussed earlier, adding the name inline is the simplest way to name anonymous functions, and this approach works with other profilers:

```
var foo = function foo() {
    return 'foo!';
};
```

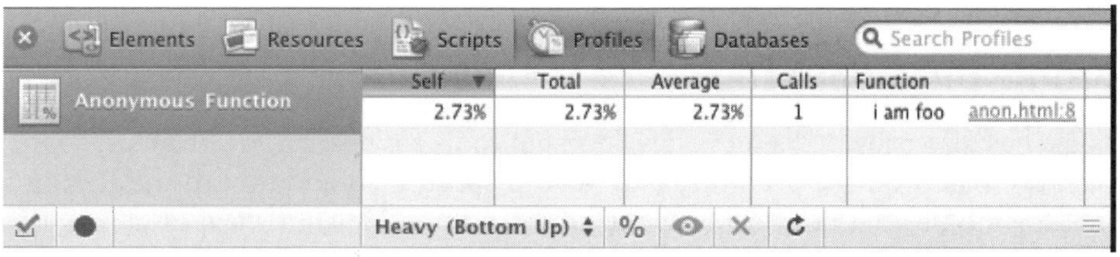

Figure 10-8. Web Inspector Profile panel showing displayName

Resources Panel

The Resources panel helps you better understand how Safari is loading and parsing scripts and other external assets. Like Firebug's Net panel, it provides a view of the resources, showing when a request was initiated and how long it took. Assets are conveniently color-coded to enhance readability. Web Inspector's Resources panel separates the size charting from time, minimizing the visual noise (see Figure 10-9).

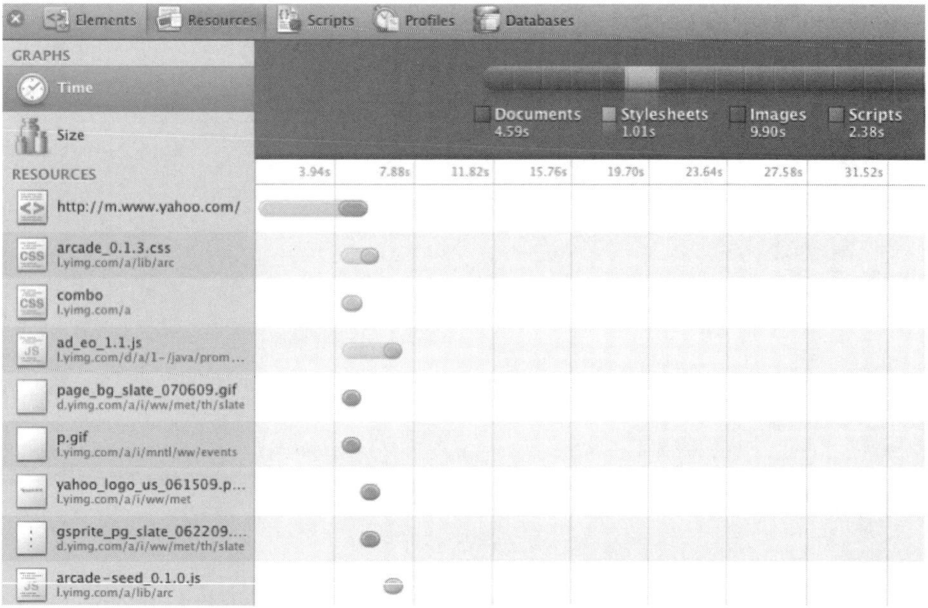

Figure 10-9. Safari Resources panel

Notice that unlike some browsers, Safari 4 is loading scripts in parallel and not blocking. Safari gets around the blocking requirement by ensuring that the scripts execute in the proper order. Keep in mind that this only applies to scripts initially embedded in HTML at load; dynamically added scripts block neither loading nor execution (see Chapter 1).

Chrome Developer Tools

Google has also provided a set of development tools for its Chrome browser, some of which are based on the WebKit/Safari Web Inspector. In addition to the Resources panel for monitoring network traffic, Chrome adds a Timeline view of all page and network events. Chrome includes the Web Inspector Profiles panel, and adds the ability to take "heap" snapshots of the current memory. As with Safari, Chrome profiles native functions and implements the Firebug Console API, including `console.profile` and `console.time`.

As shown in Figure 10-10, the Timeline panel provides an overview of all activities, categorized as either "Loading", "Scripting," or "Rendering". This enables developers to quickly focus on the slowest aspects of the system. Some events contain a subtree of other event rows, which can be expanded or hidden for more or less detail in the Records view.

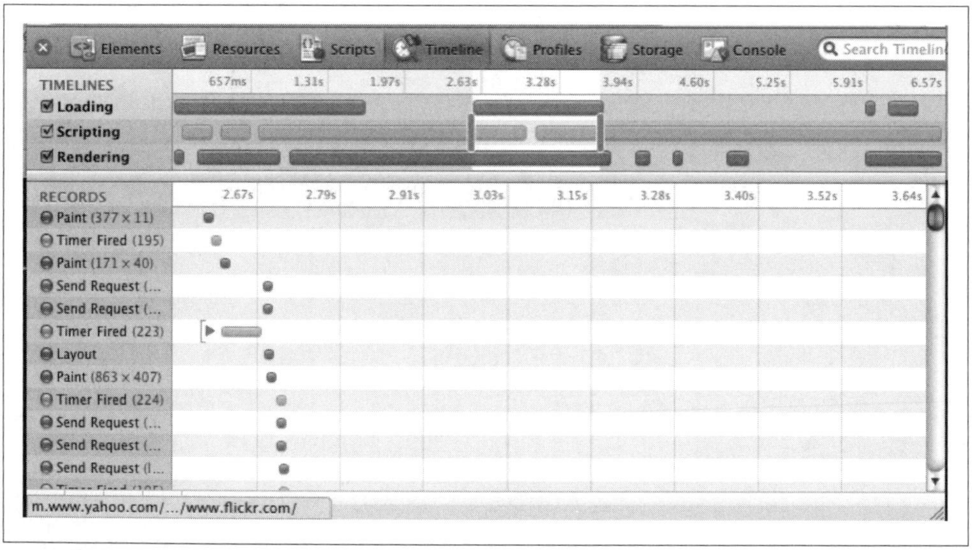

Figure 10-10. Chrome Developer Tools Timeline panel

Clicking the eye icon on Chrome's Profiles panel takes a snapshot of the current Java-Script memory heap (Figure 10-11). The results are grouped by constructor, and can be expanded to show each instance. Snapshots can be compared using the "Compared to Snapshot" option at the bottom of the Profiles panel. The +/- Count and Size columns show the differences between snapshots.

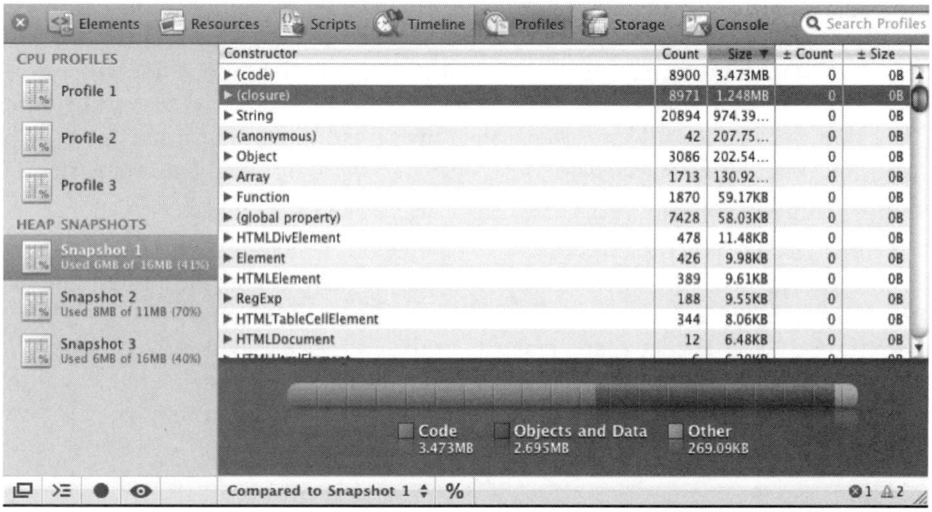

Figure 10-11. Chrome Developer Tools JavaScript heap snapshot

Script Blocking

Traditionally, browsers limit script requests to one at a time. This is done to manage dependencies between files. As long as a file that depends on another comes later in the source, it will be guaranteed to have its dependencies ready prior to execution. The gaps between scripts may indicate script blocking. Newer browsers such as Safari 4, IE 8, Firefox 3.5, and Chrome have addressed this by allowing parallel downloading of scripts but blocking execution, to ensure dependencies are ready. Although this allows the assets to download more quickly, page rendering is still blocked until all scripts have executed.

Script blocking may be compounded by slow initialization in one or more files, which could be worthy of some profiling, and potentially optimizing or refactoring. The loading of scripts can slow or stop the rendering of the page, leaving the user waiting. Network analysis tools can help identify and optimize gaps in the loading of assets. Visualizing these gaps in the delivery of scripts gives an idea as to which scripts are slower to execute. Such scripts may be worth deferring until after the page has rendered, or possibly optimizing or refactoring to reduce the execution time.

Page Speed

Page Speed is a tool initially developed for internal use at Google and later released as a Firebug addon that, like Firebug's Net panel, provides information about the resources being loaded on a web page. However, in addition to load time and HTTP status, it shows the amount of time spent parsing and executing JavaScript, identifies deferrable scripts, and reports on functions that aren't being used. This is valuable information that can help identify areas for further investigation, optimization, and possible refactoring. Visit *http://code.google.com/speed/page-speed/* for installation instructions and other product details.

The Profile Deferrable JavaScript option, available on the Page Speed panel, identifies files that can be deferred or broken up in order to deliver a smaller initial payload. Often, very little of the script running on a page is required to render the initial view. In Figure 10-12 you can see that a majority of the code being loaded is not used prior to the window's `load` event firing. Deferring code that isn't being used right away allows the initial page to load much faster. Scripts and other assets can then be selectively loaded later as needed.

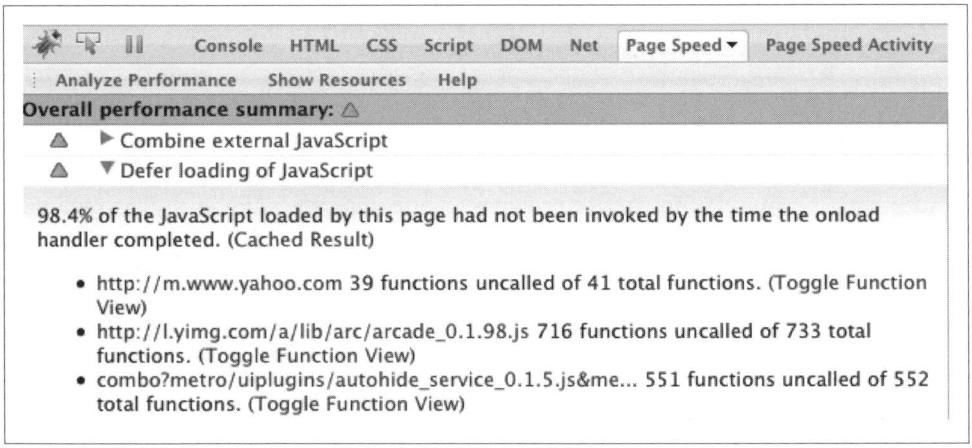

Figure 10-12. Page Speed deferrable JavaScript summary

Page Speed also adds a Page Speed Activity panel to Firebug. This panel is similar to Firebug's own Net panel, except that it provides more granular data about each request. This includes a breakdown of each script's life cycle, including parse and execution phases, giving a detailed account of the gaps between scripts. This can help identify areas where profiling and possible refactoring of the files are needed. As seen in the legend, Figure 10-13 shows the amount of time spent parsing the script in red and the time executing in blue. A long execution time may be worth looking into more closely with a profiler.

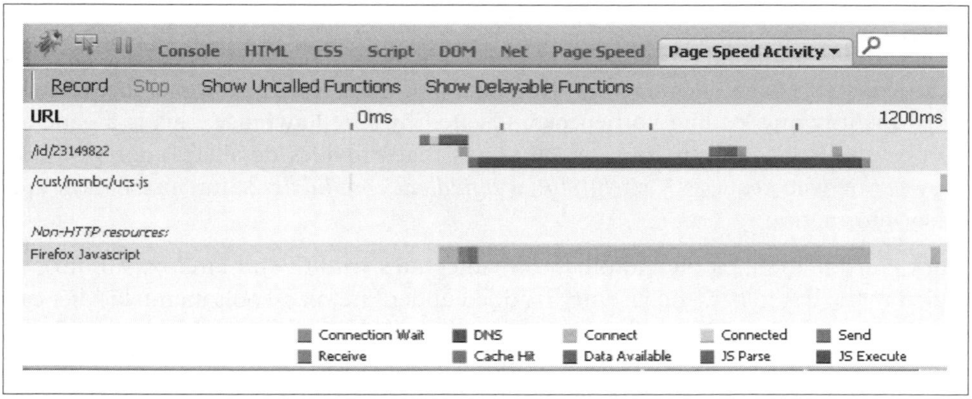

Figure 10-13. Page Speed parse and execution times

There may be significant time spent parsing and initializing scripts that are not being used until after the page has rendered. The Page Speed Activity panel can also provide a report on which functions were not called at all and which functions may be delayable, based on the time they were parsed versus the time they were first called (Figure 10-14).

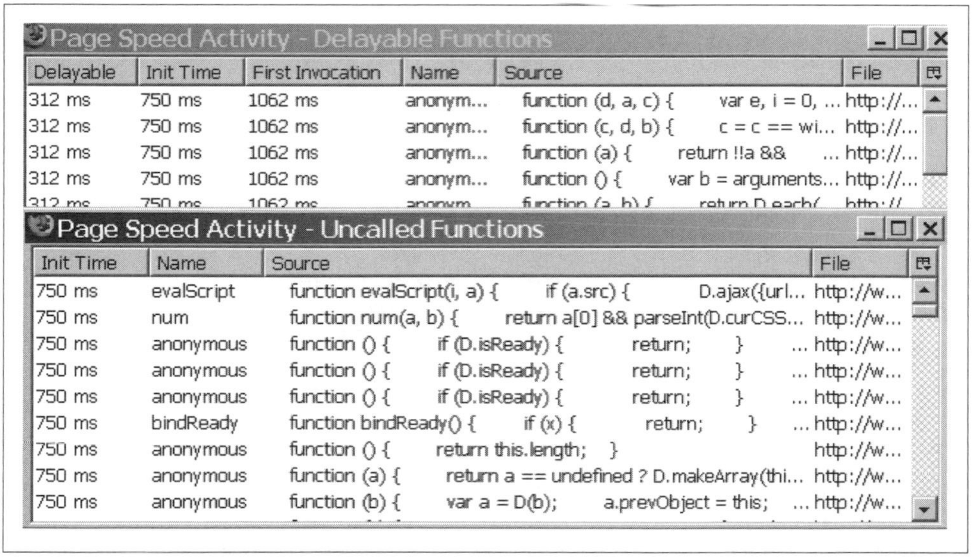

Figure 10-14. Reports for delayable and uncalled functions

These reports show the amount of time spent initializing the function that are either never called or that could be called later. Consider refactoring code to remove uncalled functions and to defer code that isn't needed during the initial render and setup phase.

Fiddler

Fiddler is an HTTP debugging proxy that examines the assets coming over the wire and helps identify any loading bottlenecks. Created by Eric Lawrence, this is a general-purpose network analysis tool for Windows that provides detailed reports on any browser or web request. Visit *http://www.fiddler2.com/fiddler2/* for installation and other information.

During installation, Fiddler automatically integrates with IE and Firefox. A button is added to the IE toolbar, and an entry is added under Firefox's Tools menu. Fiddler can also be started manually. Any browser or application that makes web requests can be analyzed. While running, all WinINET traffic is routed through Fiddler, allowing it to monitor and analyze the performance of downloaded assets. Some browsers (e.g., Opera and Safari) do not use WinINET, but they will detect the Fiddler proxy automatically, provided that it is running prior to launching the browser. Any program that allows for proxy settings can be manually run through Fiddler by pointing it at the Fiddler proxy (127.0.0.1, port: 8888).

Like Firebug, Web Inspector, and Page Speed, Fiddler provides a waterfall diagram that provides insights as to which assets are taking longer to load and which assets might be affecting the loading of other assets (Figure 10-15).

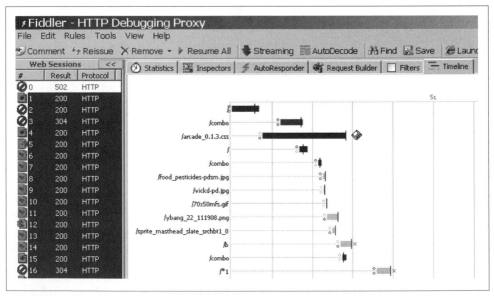

Figure 10-15. Fiddler waterfall diagram

Selecting one or more resources from the panel on the left shows them in the main view. Click the Timeline tab to visualize the assets over the wire. This view provides the timing of each asset relative to other assets, which allows you to study the effects of different loading strategies and makes it more obvious when something is blocking.

The Statistics tab shows a detailed view of the actual performance of all selected assets—giving insight into DNS Lookup and TCP/IP Connect times—as well as a breakout of the size of and type of the various assets being requested (Figure 10-16).

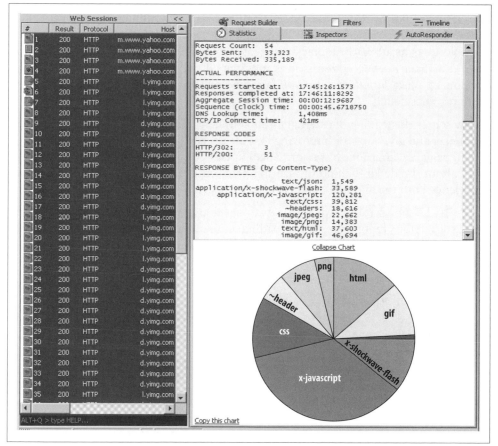

Figure 10-16. Fiddler Statistics tab

This data helps you decide which areas should be investigated further. For example, long DNS Lookup and TCP/IP Connect times may indicate a problem with the network. The resource chart makes it obvious which types of assets comprise the bulk of the page load, identifying possible candidates for deferred loading or profiling (in the case of scripts).

As Fiddler is available on Windows only, it is worth mentioning a shareware product called Charles Proxy that works on both Windows and Mac. Visit *http://www.charlesproxy.com/* for a free trial and detailed documentation.

YSlow

The YSlow tool provides performance insights into the overall loading and execution of the initial page view. This tool was originally developed internally at Yahoo! by Steve Souders as a Firefox addon (via GreaseMonkey). It has been made available to the public as a Firebug addon, and is maintained and updated regularly by Yahoo! developers. Visit *http://developer.yahoo.com/yslow/* for installation instructions and other product details.

YSlow scores the loading of external assets to the page, provides a report on page performance, and gives tips for improving loading speed. The scoring it provides is based on extensive research done by performance experts. Applying this feedback and reading more about the details behind the scoring helps ensure the fastest possible page load experience with the minimal number of resources.

Figure 10-17 shows YSlow's default view of a web page that has been analyzed. It will make suggestions for optimizing the loading and rendering speed of the page. Each of the scores includes a detailed view with additional information and an explanation of the rule's rationale.

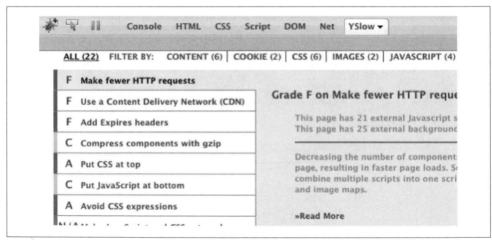

Figure 10-17. YSlow: All results

In general, improving the overall score will result in faster loading and execution of scripts. Figure 10-18 shows the results filtered by the JAVASCRIPT option, with some advice about how to optimize script delivery and execution.

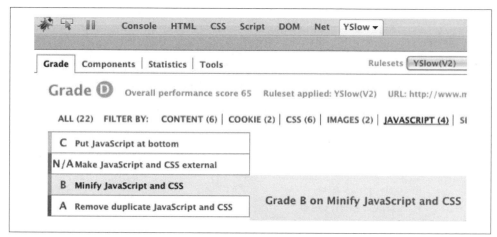

Figure 10-18. YSlow: JavaScript results

When interpreting the results, keep in mind that there may be exceptions to consider. These might include deciding when to make multiple requests for scripts versus combining into a single request, and which scripts or functions to defer until after the page renders.

dynaTrace Ajax Edition

The developers of dynaTrace, a robust Java/.NET performance diagnostic tool, have released an "Ajax Edition" that measures Internet Explorer performance (a Firefox version is coming soon). This free tool provides an end-to-end performance analysis, from network and page rendering to runtime scripts and CPU usage. The reports display all aspects together, so you can easily find where any bottlenecks may be occurring. The results can be exported for further dissection and analysis. To download, visit *http://ajax.dynatrace.com/pages/*.

The Summary report shown in Figure 10-19 provides a visual overview that allows you to quickly determine which area or areas need more attention. From here you can drill down into the various narrower reports for more granular detail regarding that particular aspect of performance.

The Network view, shown in Figure 10-20, provides a highly detailed report that breaks out time spent in each aspect of the network life cycle, including DNS lookup, connection, and server response times. This guides you to the specific areas of the network that might require some tuning. The panels below the report show the request and response headers (on the left) and the actual request response (on the right).

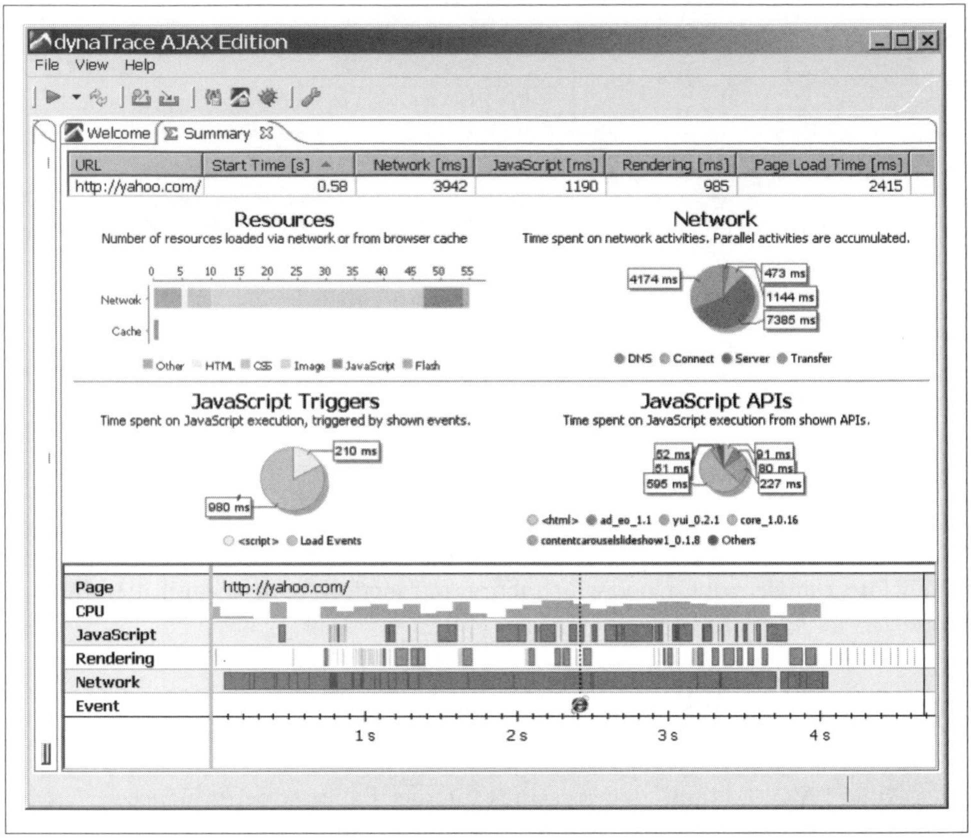

Figure 10-19. dynaTrace Ajax Edition: Summary report

Selecting the JavaScript Triggers view brings up a detailed report on each event that fired during the trace (see Figure 10-21). From here you can drill into specific events ("load", "click", "mouseover", etc.) to find the root cause of runtime performance issues.

This view includes any dynamic (Ajax) requests that a event may be triggering and any script "callback" that may be executed as a result of the request. This allows you to better understand the overall performance perceived by your users, which, because of the asynchronous nature of Ajax, might not be obvious in a script profile report.

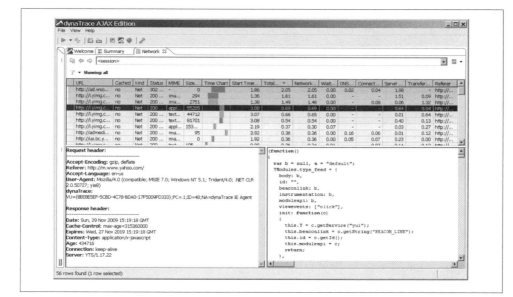

Figure 10-20. dynaTrace Ajax Edition: Network report

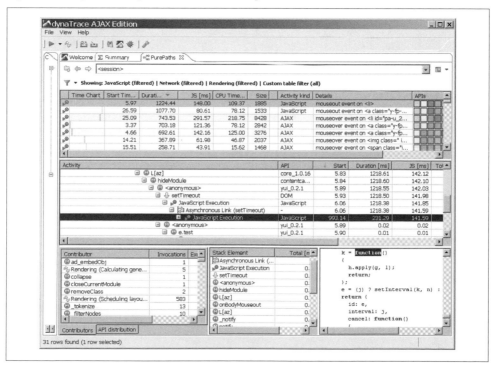

Figure 10-21. dynaTrace Ajax Edition PurePaths panel

Summary

When web pages or applications begin to feel slow, analyzing assets as they come over the wire and profiling scripts while they are running allows you to focus your optimization efforts where they are needed most.

- Use a network analyzer to identify bottlenecks in the loading of scripts and other page assets; this helps determine where script deferral or profiling may be needed.
- Although conventional wisdom says to minimize the number of HTTP requests, deferring scripts whenever possible allows the page to render more quickly, providing users with a better overall experience.
- Use a profiler to identify slow areas in script execution, examining the time spent in each function, the number of times a function is called, and the callstack itself provides a number of clues as to where optimization efforts should be focused.
- Although time spent and number of calls are usually the most valuable bits of data, looking more closely at how functions are being called might yield other optimization candidates.

These tools help to demystify the generally hostile programming environments that modern code must run in. Using them prior to beginning optimization will ensure that development time is spent focusing on the right problems.

Index

We'd like to hear your suggestions for improving our indexes. Send email to *index@oreilly.com*.

About the Author

Nicholas C. Zakas is a web software engineer who specializes in user interface design and implementation for web applications using JavaScript, Dynamic HTML, CSS, XML, and XSLT. He is currently principal front-end engineer for the Yahoo! home page and is a contributor to the Yahoo! User Interface (YUI) library, having written the Cookie Utility, Profiler, and YUI Test.

Nicholas is the author of *Professional JavaScript for Web Developers* and a co-author of *Professional Ajax* (both Wrox), and has contributed to other books. He has also written several online articles for WebReference, Sitepoint, and the YUI Blog.

Nicholas regularly gives talks about web development, JavaScript, and best practices. He has given talks at companies such as Yahoo!, LinkedIn, Google, and NASA, and at conferences such as the Ajax Experience, the Rich Web Experience, and Velocity.

Through his writing and speaking, Nicholas seeks to teach others the valuable lessons he's learned while working on some of the most popular and demanding web applications in the world.

For more information on Nicholas, see *http://www.nczonline.net/about/*.

Colophon

The animal on the cover of *High Performance JavaScript* is a short-eared owl (*Asio flammeus*). As its name suggests, the bird's signature ear tufts are small and appear simply as ridges on the top of its large head. These tufts become more visible, however, when the owl feels threatened and enters a defensive pose. A medium-sized owl, the bird has yellow eyes, mottled brown plumage with a pale, streaked chest, and dark bars on its broad wings.

One of the world's most widespread avian species, this is a migratory bird that can be found on every continent except Australia and Antarctica. The short-eared owl lives in open country, such as prairies, marshland, or tundra. It catches small mammals like voles (and the occasional bird) either by flying low to the ground or by perching on a short tree, then diving on its prey. The owls are most active at dawn, late afternoon, and dusk.

The flight of the short-eared owl is frequently compared to that of a moth or bat, as it moves back and forth with slow, irregular wing beats. During breeding season, males exhibit spectacular aerial courtship displays in which they clap their wings together, rise in circles to great heights, and dive rapidly toward the ground. The short-eared owl is also somewhat of a thespian in the animal world—it will play dead to avoid detection, or feign a crippled wing to lure predators away from its nest.

The cover image is from *Cassell's Natural History*. The cover font is Adobe ITC Garamond. The text font is Linotype Birka; the heading font is Adobe Myriad Condensed; and the code font is LucasFont's TheSansMonoCondensed.

Related Titles from O'Reilly

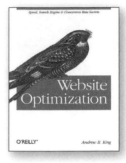

Web Programming

ActionScript 3.0 Cookbook

ActionScript 3.0 Design Patterns

ActionScript for Flash MX: The Definitive Guide,
 2nd Edition

Adobe AIR 1.5 Cookbook

Adobe AIR for JavaScript Developer's Pocket Guide

Advanced Rails

Ajax Design Patterns

Ajax Hacks

Ajax on Rails

Ajax: The Definitive Guide

Apache 2 Pocket Reference

Apache Cookbook, *2nd Edition*

Building Scalable Web Sites

Designing Web Navigation

Dojo: The Definitive Guide

Dynamic HTML: The Definitive Reference, *3rd Edition*

Essential ActionScript 3.0

Essential PHP Security

Ferret

Flash CS4: The Missing Manual

Flash Hacks

Head First HTML with CSS & XHTML

Head First JavaScript

Head First PHP & MySQL

High Performance Web Sites

HTTP: The Definitive Guide

JavaScript & DHTML Cookbook, *2nd Edition*

JavaScript Pocket Reference, *2nd Edition*

JavaScript: The Definitive Guide, *5th Edition*

JavaScript: The Good Parts

JavaScript: The Missing Manual

Learning ActionScript 3.0

Learning PHP and MySQL, *2nd Edition*

PHP Cookbook, *2nd Edition*

PHP Hacks

PHP in a Nutshell

PHP Pocket Reference, *2nd Edition*

Programming ColdFusion MX, *2nd Edition*

Programming Flex 2

Programming PHP, *2nd Edition*

Programming Amazon Web Services

Rails Cookbook

The ActionScript 3.0 Quick Reference Guide

Twitter API: Up and Running

Universal Design for Web Applications

Upgrading to PHP 5

Web Database Applications with PHP and MySQL,
 2nd Edition

Website Optimization

Web Site Cookbook

Webmaster in a Nutshell, *3rd Edition*

Get even more for your money.

Join the O'Reilly Community, and register the O'Reilly books you own.It's free, and you'll get:

- 40% upgrade offer on O'Reilly books
- Membership discounts on books and events
- Free lifetime updates to electronic formats of books
- Multiple ebook formats, DRM FREE
- Participation in the O'Reilly community
- Newsletters
- Account management
- 100% Satisfaction Guarantee

Signing up is easy:

1. **Go to: oreilly.com/go/register**
2. **Create an O'Reilly login.**
3. **Provide your address.**
4. **Register your books.**

Note: English-language books only

To order books online:

oreilly.com/order_new

For questions about products or an order:

orders@oreilly.com

To sign up to get topic-specific email announcements and/or news about upcoming books, conferences, special offers, and new technologies:

elists@oreilly.com

For technical questions about book content:

booktech@oreilly.com

To submit new book proposals to our editors:

proposals@oreilly.com

Many O'Reilly books are available in PDF and several ebook formats. For more information:

oreilly.com/ebooks

Spreading the knowledge of innovators   www.oreilly.com

Buy this book and get access to the online edition for 45 days—for free!

High Performance JavaScript

By Nicholas C. Zakas
March 2010, $34.99
ISBN 9780596802790

With Safari Books Online, you can:

Access the contents of thousands of technology and business books

- Quickly search over 7000 books and certification guides
- Download whole books or chapters in PDF format, at no extra cost, to print or read on the go
- Copy and paste code
- Save up to 35% on O'Reilly print books
- **New!** Access mobile-friendly books directly from cell phones and mobile devices

Stay up-to-date on emerging topics before the books are published

- Get on-demand access to evolving manuscripts.
- Interact directly with authors of upcoming books

Explore thousands of hours of video on technology and design topics

- Learn from expert video tutorials
- Watch and replay recorded conference sessions

To try out Safari and the online edition of this book FREE for 45 days,
go to *www.oreilly.com/go/safarienabled* and enter the coupon code TQTJZAA.
To see the complete Safari Library, visit safari.oreilly.com.

Spreading the knowledge of innovators   safari.oreilly.com

©2009 O'Reilly Media, Inc. O'Reilly logo is a registered trademark of O'Reilly Media, Inc. 00000